Risk-based Management in the World of Threats and Opportunities:
A Project Controls Perspective

Hi Ana,
Wishing you the best in the
future). I hope this book

RUFRAN C. FRAGO

P. Eng., PMP®, CCP, PMI-RMP®

gives you some of the information
you need managing your work.
All the best!

Risk-based Management in the

World of Threats and Opportunities

A Project Controls Perspective

Text copyright © 2015 Rufran C. Frago

For general information on our other products and services, please contact the Author/Publisher using e-mail address rcfrago@gmail.com.

For information about licensing the book brand or for related products or services, contact rcfrago@gmail.com.

ISBN-13: 978-1508758952 (Create Space assigned)
ISBN-10: 1508758956 (Create Space assigned)

ISBN 978-0-9947608-0-7 (Canada)

DEDICATION

To my dearest wife Ann who gave me the love, the strength, the energy, the time, the inspiration, and that continuing supply of delicious coffee to pursue my first book; thank you for all your patience and understanding. The happy confidence I feel each time you encourage me to carry on no matter what, is an undeniable testimony that you and I can do any good thing we set our minds on. I love you very much.

To my children, Maria Rasbel, Maria Zenka, and Jorrell who provided me the motivation to pursue many of my life's noble objectives, may you all live happily, healthy, and safely. May you continue to love, grow, and prosper in a world full of trickeries, challenges, and risks by finding hope, courage, and opportunities within.

To the beautiful Eva and Mia, our grandchildren, who I treasure so much, may both of you develop into intelligent and spiritually strong women. May you know and understand that it is wiser to use the learning experience of others rather than learning everything from your own. The art of living is to learn from the mistakes of others than making them yourselves. May God's Grace be your angel, and guide. No matter what your interests are in the future, always respect your parents and elders for a long, happy, and prosperous life. Take risk but be smart about it.

To my departed father, Sulpicio F. Frago, who taught me the philosophies of life, molding me to what I am now, and my mother, Belen C. Frago, who nurtured me so I develop confidence in my abilities to think freely, I offer my deepest gratitude and appreciation.

To my parents-in-law, Iluminada, and Eligio D. Elefante, I humbly honor and thank you for all the support you so unselfishly gave through the years of my married life. Who can forget the learning wisdom you shared, the vote of confidence during trying times, the spiritual guidance you inculcate, and your patience to listen?

Rufran C. Frago

CONTENTS

List of Figures

Preface

What is risk-based management (RBM) to you? Do you have a good understanding of this concept, and how it is applied? If you do, do you think it is the best and only approach? Do you think it is one of the best? How do you apply it in project management?

RBM is serious approach and philosophy that consider risk while managing any project endeavor throughout its lifecycle. Management by objectives is still present, but with more focus on risk management. Risk-based management increases the probability of success.

Projects do not fail – people do (Smith J. , 2012). We attribute the high failure rate of projects to a combination of factors, namely a lack of support from business leadership, incompetent project managers, and a firms' unwillingness to treat a project as they would a start-up business.

Of course, it is very clear that a project cancelled before it is fully completed is a failure. The degree of failure depends on how much stakeholder money and other resources have already been used and wasted. We must also consider the cascade effects of such failure to any company's bottom line. Crossing the bottom line can result to layoffs, across the board budget cuts, low dividend returns for stockholders, loss of reputation, and decreased stock price to name a few.

Risk-based management describes the available choices and options considered against their associated risks. Actions become possible when we are sure that we adequately comprehend the risks before us. Looking at how other types of management work makes the risk-based concept ideal, since it is a simple perspective that can easily integrate other concepts.

Decisions evolve from a situation where one has to make a choice. The option can be to do or not to do something. It can also be to select one option from a range of options. The most important objectives drive final decision. It is constrained by any, or combination of social, technical, business, safety, and environmental factors. Successful decision-making requires an understanding of each of these factors and objectives (RiskTec, 2013).

There are professionals who have difficulty accepting the term "risk-based." It simply means that risk should be the main contemplation, while keeping an eye to achieving business objectives. It is therefore a foundational concern in the pursuit of a goal. Pursuing a goal naturally results in risk management. This is how we end up with risk management. Under this paradigm, the concern revolves around the decisions we need to make, i.e. whether to avoid or mitigate in the case of a threat, and whether to enhance or exploit in the case of an opportunity.

Risk is not only a factor or featured element of management; it is the central concept at play. It should be the focus of management, second only (if not equal) to the main objectives. An excellent risk manager will see clearly that the objectives and end deliverables are part of the risk. They are the grand consequences of the positive risks (opportunities) identified, and the very reason why the project was initiated.

Risk-based management is as important as the objectives. Failing to mitigate the risk means failure to meet the objectives. When that happens, the risk is on equal footing and of the same importance as the objectives. I trust that you will find this book helpful as you proceed addressing the challenges of your own risk universe.

Rufran C. Frago, P. Eng., PMP®, CCP, PMI-RMP®

Calgary, Alberta, Canada

Icons Used in This Book

TIP: This icon underlines some helpful information.

REMINDER: This icon reminds readers of key points to remember.

CAUTION: This icon alerts reader to consider negative consequence.

Acknowledgments

Next to God, I am fortunate to have Ann, my dear wife and better half, who provided the greatest inspiration, coaching, and the extra push I needed leading up to the completion of this book. I was able to consolidate all my relevant previous works through her encouragement. She gave me the energy to formulate, and create new contents. Definitely, this book would not exist without her valuable blessing and loving direction.

Good friends, colleagues, and peers have contributed directly and indirectly to the contents of this book. Through the resurgence of various professional social networking portals such as LinkedIn, Slideshare, PMI Community of Practice, Oracle Community of Practice, AACE Forums, and several others, many fruitful collaborative discussions on the subject of risk-based management have incited me to think beyond the usual pattern of thought. Various discussions have ignited my imagination in such ways as to result in new ideas, concepts, and understandings of the subject that I now would like to share. Thanks to you all.

A big thank-you to Deogracias Fermin, and Marlon Ordonez, who both mentored me while I worked as the Planning Head and Safety Manager of JG Summit Petrochemical Corporation respectively back from 1998 to 2001.

Special thanks to Daniel Savard and John Gimenez. Daniel gave the opportunity to start fresh in Canada in 2002. He was a great lead and coach while we were working together with Halliburton-Kellogg, Brown, and Root (HKBR) in the Syncrude UE-1 Project. John Gimenez helped find the solution to some technical and work-related problems I encountered during my first year in North America.

I would like to recognize my former leader Heinz Dahn, who believed in me and brought me to Project Control Governance, giving me the chance to appreciate and spread my wings in the area of project risk management. A nod of gratitude to Larry Sondrol, PC Director-Suncor, my current leader, for listening to me, and giving me the opportunities to grow, develop, and continue my passion of educating myself.

Thanks to my colleagues and peers in the industry: Randall Daniels, CMRP, MMP, Nadeem Khawaja, RMP, Project Controls Specialist-Suncor, Azhar Syed, PMP, P. Eng., MBA, Jose Gonzalez Sardi, Planning Lead-Suncor, Kaleem Syed, B. Eng. Mechanical, EIT, CST, CCT, PCIT-Suncor Energy, for spending their valuable time to review and proofread the materials. Your valuable inputs help make this book possible. My sincere appreciation to my young Editor Aaron Swanbergson for his help.

The need to express risk-based management in a simpler and more personal view, derived from work specialization and day-to-day experience is a big motivation to write this book. I am happy to share ideas, methodology, principles, and approaches about risk that people need in any profession or individual endeavor because it works. Reading and understanding the contents will provide a high school graduate, a University student, a post graduate individual, an intermediate project controls specialist, up to any level of management professional with a good idea of what risk-based management is about.

Rufran C. Frago, P. Eng., PMP®, CCP, PMI-RMP®

Calgary, Alberta, Canada

Chapter 1

Risk Concepts and Philosophies

1.1.   Introduction to Risk

The challenge in writing this book is attempting to cover enough grounds on the topic of risk and risk-based management. The world we live in is full of risk. It is for this reason that I titled this book "Risk-based Management in the World of Threats and Opportunities." It seems too big to embrace and comprehend at first but later, actually not. Anyone who sets his mind to knowledge can earn it. Why would it not be? Huge information does not limit learning.

It is the willingness of man that dictates his mental faculty to expand or not to expand. Giving up the quest for knowledge stunts if not completely prevents great possibilities. If you are new to risk, I urge you to forge ahead!

We are all living and breathing risk daily. We are in the midst of it. This is proof that we already have some knowledge about it because we have the experience.

This book serves the needs of anyone fresh from high school. It caters to new managers, up to professional risk practitioners and experts. Young readers with no knowledge of risk-based management will find comfort digesting risk in simple terms. The journey of learning risk is most rewarding to the curious thinker. Curiosity generates interest. Interest produces efforts that result in good education.

The 2009 PMI Global Practice Standard for Project Risk Management, Chapter 2, Section 2.2 (page 9) defines risk as an uncertain future event or condition that could have a positive or negative effect on objectives if it occurs. In a project environment, the definition goes like this: project risk is an uncertain future event or condition that, if it occurs, could have a positive or negative effect on project objectives.

The same line of thinking will be true when one talks about a specific risk category such as financial risk, safety risk, business risk, operation risk, or others.

Two key components of risk are probability, and impact. They describe probability of achieving objectives and effect on objectives respectively. Possible future events must be evaluated and analysis done using the two measures. The probability dimension describes the uncertainty or certainty of a schedule or budget. Impact on the other hand describes the consequence of the risk just in case it does happen (PMI, Project Risk Management, 2013).

Risk is not equal to just any of its own singular attribute. The very existence of risk depends on the function of uncertainty, consequence, and time. How can risk be mistaken to be just a part of its wholeness?

The set theory makes us aware about the concept of uncertainty as a big system where risk resides. The reason why I asked the question emanates from the measure of uncertainty. Given a risk that revolves around a given objective, uncertainty as a system is impossible to measure.

The present accepted measure of uncertainty is probability. We can calculate the probability of an identified and specific risk because we can appreciate the uncertainty boundary (or field) where it lies. Understanding and awareness become a blur when one attempts to go outside this boundary. I refer to it as the uncertainty boundary of understanding.

The finite boundary or a piece of the whole uncertainty system is the only useful element in appreciating risk. It is a piece of the uncertainty concept that has practical use.

The idea of risk and its attributes appears simple enough, yet it can be bigger and more complex than it appears. Human comprehension is infinitely varied, limited only by an individual's imagination, and this will shape their understanding of the concept of risk. It is not surprising that, out of the many recent great exchanges, we have relatively new governing laws on Risk Management.

Have you ever stopped doing what you were doing, sat down, and asked yourself, "What is the purpose of life? What is it that people do every day? What is it that matters most to a person regardless of demographic?"

TIP There are various perspectives; however, it all comes down to one central element, and that is to manage risk. Yes, the purpose of life is managing risk.

Even in our sleep, and in our dreams, we administer risks. In our beliefs, in our religion, in our pursuit to be a good person, we manage risks. People have to manage daily the risk of sin, e.g. of temptation, of jealousy, gluttony, revenge, and greed. One needs to control his vice, his expenses, his career, and many others.

Why I did not think of that concept before is a mystery. It is in front of all of us and in the very fabric of our daily life. Risk management is the only thing we do for a living.

This intriguing concept drives the reason we go to work every day. We all have one main, central purpose yet we all go about it almost unconsciously.

This is how we choose our home. This is why we want to learn, why we think, and why we survive. It is something we all do in common. We may not recognize our close relationship to risk, but it exists nevertheless.

Read on and I will show you how to appreciate the nature of risk and the concept of risk management in the simplest terms.

1.2.   Risk Relativity

For a thief, a good security system is a threat. To a security guard, that same system is an opportunity to lessen the risk of robbery and to increase the chance of catching the thieves.

A person's perspective depends on which side of the fence they are sitting on. With that in mind, a risk can be a threat or an opportunity. Your business sees a threat and your competitor sees an opportunity. It is as simple as that.

Each individual player within the risk universe will see things a bit differently compared to the next person, with some people interpreting things in exactly the opposite fashion. In each case, the person can see only one attribute.

The simplistic objective point of view is that risk is either a threat or an opportunity, depending on the observer's orientation to the goal. If one sits on his most important goal and look at the potential risk, the resultant or prevailing consequence describes whether it is a threat or an opportunity.

Anyone who contemplate risk should consider that threats also bring with it opportunities and opportunities also brings threats.

These are underlining characteristics that all risk practitioners have to remind themselves always. Have you ever heard the saying, "every cloud has a silver lining"?

We can readily conclude that this tested adage found to be true for many centuries is actually a risk-based management concept.

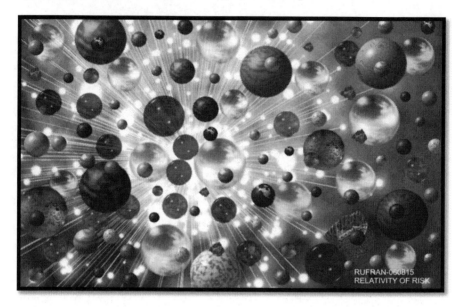

Figure 1 - Risk Universe

Now, if we could take an even more macroscopic view of the risk universe as an independent observer, we would be able to see risk from more than one perspective and gain a level of understanding that most of us never thought possible before - that risk is both a threat and an opportunity.

We can see both possibilities existing simultaneously. When we have no stake in the game, we can relate to both parties' positions.

 Risk is not absolute, but relative.

If one thinks about it a little deeper, the concept of risk becomes more evident. The risks of threat and opportunity are two sides of the same event. Obviously, events and objectives go hand in hand, as your objectives will depend on how you interpret events.

Using the set theory and imagining risk using a Venn diagram, one might imagine the concept of uncertainty as a big system where risk resides.

Given a singular risk that revolves around a given objective, considering a vast system called uncertainty, the probability of that risk is impossible to

4

measure.

We can calculate the probability of an identified and specific risk because we can appreciate the uncertainty boundary (or field) where the risk lies.

The finite boundary (a small piece of the whole uncertainty system) relevant to the objective is the only useful element in appreciating that risk, a piece of mathematical uncertainty that has practical use.

It is the kind of uncertainty with more reliable probabilistic basis.

We've all heard that beauty is in the eye of the beholder, meaning that the perception of beauty is subjective. Similarly, perception of risk is subjective because it is relative. It depends on how one interprets a situation. Duality in this sense points to two kinds of perceptions rather than two intrinsic attributes in one.

Many writers in the last few centuries have touched on the concepts of relativity and subjectivity when talking about how a person sees their surroundings.

Below, are some phrases about this, but it is up to you to make the comparison between these poetic relationships and people's perceptions of risk. I thought it would be fun to inject risk's syllogism and indirect association within some memorable quotes.

> In 1588, the English dramatist John Lyly, in his Euphues and His England, wrote: "...as neere is Fancie to Beautie [RISK], as the pricke to the Rose, as the stalke to the rynde, as the earth to the roote."
>
> Shakespeare expressed a similar sentiment in Love's Labours Lost, 1598. "Good Lord Boyet, my beauty [RISK], though but mean, / Needs not the painted flourish of your praise: / Beauty [RISK] is bought by judgment of the eye, / Not utter'd by base sale of chapmen's tongues."
>
> Benjamin Franklin, in Poor Richard's Almanack, 1741, wrote, "Beauty [RISK], like supreme dominion is but supported by opinion."

David Hume's Essays, Moral and Political, 1742, includes the statement that "Beauty [RISK] in things exists merely in the mind which contemplates them."

The person who is widely credited with coining the saying in its current form is Margaret Wolfe Hungerford (née Hamilton), who wrote many books, often under the pseudonym of 'The Duchess'.

In Molly Bawn (1878), readers will find the following line: "Beauty [RISK] is in the eye of the beholder (The Phrase Finder, 2015)."

TIP   Oftentimes, the discussion on subjects such as risk has a tendency to turn into something more esoteric. When that happens, as a Risk Manager, we should appreciate the brilliance of some people's individual premises, suppositions, commentaries, and conclusions, for they can add value and substance to what we already know.

There is an old tale about the three blind men who encountered an elephant for the first time and attempt to learn about it by touch alone. Somehow, I am now tempted to change the story to the three blind project managers who encountered risk for the first time and attempted to learn about it.

The story about the three project managers and a project is like the story of Jain's parable of The Blind Men and the Elephant. The parable is quite relevant to what we are discussing here.

> "One man felt a leg and said the elephant is like a pillar. The one who got hold of the tail said the elephant is like a rope. The one who felt the trunk said the elephant is like a tree branch; the one who feels the ear says the elephant is like a hand fan; the one who feels the belly says the elephant is like a wall; and the one who feels the tusk says the elephant is like a solid pipe."

The understanding of each man is distinctive because each traces a different part of the elephant. This very old story teaches us something important about how we go about our business. It is an excellent illustration of the relativity of risk.

The range of understanding runs a distance between true and false but never in absolute term. In effect, what each one of us experience might be a subjective truth and not the objective truth. This creates limitation to the accuracy of one's decision.

Although we may feel that we have known this all along, it is still quite revealing. Each of us must listen actively to understand others' perspectives. Don't hold onto our opinion just because it's our opinion.

Revise your previous programming, and don't presume that everything you see is true." This is the right avenue toward continuous education by identifying, recognizing, and appreciating the differences in ideas through reflexive thought processes.

TIP   The best way to understand the details is to zoom out. In order to understand the whole, one has to zoom in.

Figure 2 - Three Project Managers and the Elephant

It seems paradoxical, but zooming out permits us to see how everything interconnects and relates. Such a move is especially true to those who are at the front end, people who deals with the details so much that they lose appreciation of the whole.

They think that everything revolves around the work they do. They are lost in their own little world.

To increase awareness and appreciation, the only way is to zoom out! Zooming in is recommended to those who belongs to middle and higher management who do not deal with the details. If you are one of them, and would like to understand better, then it is time to focus in up a certain comfortable level.

Government technocrats have to understand the plight of the poor and underprivileged by visiting where they are. Generals can better appreciate the battle by going to the battlefield. Each lower level of detail provides new insights of the whole.

The experience will generate better decisions and action plans.

It is the zooming in and the zooming out of each risk manager that leads to the differences in how we individually explain the same elephant (subject).

It also proves that nobody is definitely wrong in his/her understanding, but most likely only limited.

Figure 3 - Zoom out and Zoom in

Only someone endowed with full awarenesscan fully appreciate the totality of this risk universe. I will have to say that if one zooms in, he/she will perceive risk as either "Threat OR Opportunity" and if one zooms out, he/she will see both "Threat AND Opportunity."

1.3.   Duality of Risk

What we should glean right away from the study of risk, is that, risk has a dual nature. The same risk you see as a threat could be an opportunity to another. How one perceives it will depend on an individual's or project's objective. It will also depend on the relationship the Risk Manager has to those objectives. In additions to impact, consequence, and time, one has to understand that business risk is dual. Keep that in the back of your mind.

During risk identification and assessment, considering the priority of driving objectives is critical. This is when one has to take what I call in risk-based management, the "objective point of view." An objective point of view is standing on the footing of each driving objectives and making the assessment.

Review the concept risk relativity (Section 1.2) to reflect on. I have not come across any such theory statement, or if something similar to it exists elsewhere. All that matter: it is one good way of explaining the fundamental concept of risk.

It is true that managers from different industries and educational backgrounds do not have the same concept of risk. Several refuse to accept that risk can be both an opportunity and a threat.

Business risk to them is not dual. It is just pure risk. It is either zero or a threat. Gains are never part of the equation. Welcome to the world of insurance.

Nobody has presented any authoritative research identifying the source of the dual character of risk. It is not evident when risk management theorists started to extend the notion of risk to include positive risk. Related to this, there were rigorous and immersing discussions in the ISO 31000 Standard Group about the origin of the word risk.

> One particular thread said that it is an Arabic word "Rizk" which means "good or bad, positive or negative," and has very old roots. Other people assert that the word came from Latin or Greek by citing examples of Dutch and Portuguese sailors using the word "risky" on their maps to designate closed or undiscovered areas. This is not necessarily consistent with the meaning of risk today. The word they refer to is "risicum" which means cliff or rocky area. When

they used the word "risky", they meant "unknown, undiscovered areas." These sailors use "risky" to describe cases where they just did not know what was there. The word "risky" is almost the same as "rizqy" meaning places of possibility where new objectives to be found, objectives being both type good and evil (Skjong, 2005).

According to the Online Etymology Dictionary, the word risk (n.) started as early as the 1660, risque, from French risque (16c.), from Italian risco, riscio (modern rischio), from riscare "run into danger," of uncertain origin. The anglicized spelling first recorded 1728. Spanish riesgo and German Risiko are Italian loan words. Risk aversion is recorded from 1942; risk factor from 1906; risk management from 1963; and risk taker from 1892. From 1680, the word risk (n.) is used. It was from the French word risquer, and from Italian riscare, or rischaire.

From these historical footnotes, it appears that there was no dual meaning to risk since its first formally recorded usage in the 1660s. The evolution of the word is quite easy to appreciate.

There is effort here to re-brand management as risk management. Management has always managed risks, but the degree of sophistication has changed. Some say that nobody needs to know risk management, that all we need is a uniform concept of risk. This is not true.

This is like saying that all you need is the tennis ball, not the rackets, not another player, and not the rules. Looking at all types of management as managing risks has its own merits, and can be one key to making the concept of management simpler.

Risk's duality makes sense through and through. PMBOK conveyed this character of risk better than any other similar organization. It successfully explained the notion of positive risks in full with simplicity.

Risk-based management has to be practical or fit-for-purpose to be effective, and should have an approved framework. This yardstick does not have to be rigid to work properly.

One great example of risk offered by a university student is when one buys a stock. It can go up, go down, or stay the same. The way risk professionals looked at risk has changed over the years such that we are now looking at risk as dual, with two opposite facets: threat and opportunity.

1.4. Risks and Objectives

I was fortunate enough to have the opportunity to exchange ideas with some amazing think tanks on the subject of risk. Their inspiring dissertations were brilliant and thought provoking.

The experience served as driver to inspect the things I know, question them, and identify what I still need to know. I hope that you will have the same experience reading this book.

One day, strolling down the street towards Calgary c-train station, I asked myself: Is there risk without an objective? Is there an objective without risk? Did not think much of it until I accidentally found the answer in a rather interesting story titled "The Mouse Trap."

The story seems to point to an unseen, sensitive dependency of succeeding events on an initial non-related situation (commonly called the Butterfly Effect). In the story, this initial situation is the presence of a mousetrap.

The Butterfly Effect (Chaos Theory) describes a situation where a small change in one state in a deterministic nonlinear system can result in large differences to a later state (Lorenz, Butterfly Effect, 1972). Some of you might appreciate this, but some of you might just scoff at the suggested relevance to the subject we are trying to understand.

A safety perspective will point to the mousetrap as definitely related to the chain of events that occurred. A simple root cause analysis can identify the possible causes of the final event or even intermediate event.

The sequence of events assessment based on domino theory first proposed by H. W. Heinrich is a good tool as well.

He theorized that the chain of accidents factors consisted of origin, social environment, personal mistake, unsafe act, hazard, accident itself, and the resulting injury or death (Elliott, Risk Assessment and Treatment, 2012).

Risks revolve around objective or objectives so you have to be careful who provides the inputs during risk assessment. Whose interest you represent provides the framework of understanding. Ensure clarity on what you are asking or what you are after.

I want you to reflect on the logic of another story below. The situation calls for more understanding than meets the eye. Once you digest the message, you will appreciate that risk in fact, is relative.

Aesop was a slave and storyteller who lived around 620 to 560 BC in Ancient Greece. Aesop's Fables are a collection of short stories personifying various animals (Wikipedia\Aesops, 2015).

One of his fables, The Wasp and the Snake, is one of my favorites. It is a fitting story related to decision-making where readers can reflect on the moral and ethical questions affecting risk-based management.

A WASP seated himself upon the head of a Snake and, striking him unceasingly with his stings, wounded him to death. The Snake, being in great torment and not knowing how to rid himself of his enemy, saw a wagon heavily laden with wood, and went and purposely placed his head under the wheels, saying, "At least my enemy and I shall perish together."

What do you think of the fable?

What lesson in risk-based management did you derive from it?

How would you compare it with how you deal with a serious problem, an almost insurmountable challenge?

You did notice that the problem is the wasp and it drove the snake to act knowing fully well the fatal consequence.

It is an emotional decision driven by frustration and anger, isn't it?

Sometimes, corporations and individuals follow the same track of thinking. We often hear a familiar warning from those who have experienced it, "…be careful, it's a jungle out there."

This line of thoughts brought by the pain of competition, leads to such decisions. It touches one's decisions affecting the interest of others versus the objective point of view, which is a perspective relating to self-interest.

It touches the modern core of business competition, of maintaining the competitive edge, and destroying anything that stands on the way

Some risk practitioners say that risk is neutral.

This will occur only if the observer has no stake or objective related to the identified risk. The consequence has no value to him. The probability of it occurring does not matter as far as he is concerned.

One can also argue that a risk is neutral if the total quantitative values associated with its attributes of threat and opportunity cancel out. It is a matter of perspective and to some national leaders, can be a morbid one.

If the President says, let's kill a thousand so that a thousand may live, or fifty of the most important people may live. Will the value of the two consequences cancelling out, a good representation of risk being neutral? Of course not! But then again, it's my take, not him, not you, and not his adviser. It's his!

It only means that such a statement is not useful as a principle or rule. Never the less, it is not impossible for some people to see it that way. That is how paradigm works. A risk paradigm with such definition makes a person executes decision in a simplistic way to the detriment of other stakeholders.

Figure 4 - Chaos and Domino Theory

1.5. Risks and the Fable

Here is a story of a mouse that saw the risk to its objectives. The whole situation demonstrates why risk is relative. It successfully underlines the fact that failure to identify risks can actually undermine some of our unstated or undefined objectives.

Read this short fable and you will see that risks and objectives are in a system and one continuum (SmilePls.com, 2013. Story of a Mouse and a Mousetrap)

> "There was a mouse merrily living with a chicken, a pig, and a cow in a farmyard. One day while the mouse was looking through the wall

crack, he saw the farmer and his wife open a package. "What food might this contain?" the mouse wondered. He was devastated to discover it was a mousetrap!

The mouse realized that he was in big trouble. He retreated to the farmyard and proclaimed this warning: "There is a mousetrap in the house! There is a mousetrap in the house!"

The chicken clucked and scratched, raised her head and said, "Mr. Mouse, I can tell this is a grave concern to you, but it is of no consequence to me. THAT IS NOT MY PROBLEM! I cannot be bothered by it."

The mouse turned to the pig and told him, "There is a mousetrap in the house! There is a mousetrap in the house!"

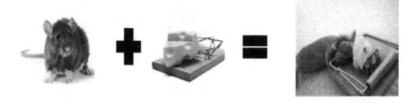

GRAND PLAN & OBJECTIVE

Figure 5 - Risk & Objectives: The Mouse and the Mousetrap

The pig sympathized, but said, "I am so very sorry, Mr. Mouse, but there is nothing I can do about it but pray. Be assured you are in my prayers."

The mouse turned to the cow and said, "There is a mousetrap in the house! There is a mousetrap in the house!"

The cow said, "Wow, Mr. Mouse. I'm sorry for you, but it's no skin off my nose."
Mr. Mouse returned to the house, head down and dejected, to face the farmer's mousetrap all alone…

That very night, a sound was heard, the sound of a mousetrap catching its prey. The farmer's wife rushed to see what it was. In the darkness, she did not see it. It was a venomous snake with its tail caught in the trap. Unfortunately, the snake bit the farmer's wife.

The farmer rushed her to the hospital. She still has a fever when she returned home. Everyone knows you treat a fever with fresh chicken soup. The farmer took his hatchet to the farmyard for the soup's main ingredient – the chicken!
Despite the soup, his wife's sickness continued. Friends and neighbors came to sit with her around the clock. To feed them, the farmer butchered the pig!

Alas, the farmer's wife did not get well. She eventually died.
Large number of people came for her funeral and the farmer had to slaughter the cow to provide enough meat for all of them for the funeral luncheon.

And the mouse looked upon it all from his crack in the wall with great sadness."

The farmer's objective was to kill the mouse. The outcome was that his wife died. This is an excellent example of the unexpected consequence. The consequence came as a surprise to the farmer and brought an unforeseen major effect.

The probability was not determined nor calculated. Nobody has foreseen it. It is a black swan event.

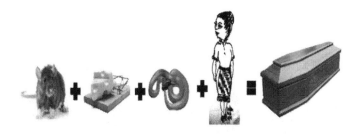

GRAND PLAN THWARTED BY UNIDENTIFIED RISK

Figure 6 - Effect of Unknown Risk

1.6.   Risk as a Function of Time

I have just delivered a short presentation in a University project management course under sponsorship of a local oil and gas company when a student followed me out to ask about risk as a function of time. It is amazing that many talks about risks without delving or even mentioning the time element. To underscore its role is almost like trying desperately to instill a modern concept in the skull of a cave man.

As you can imagine, I was quite happy to oblige. Time is one of the essential risk attributes often missed that I feel anyone who shows interest on the subject, is a friend. Learning starts with interest. He was quite interested how I explained in class the risk concepts surrounding impact and consequence. However, he was doubly interested on how time plays a major part to risk-based management and how to visualize risk against a timeline.

It is worth the time for any risk practitioner to reflect on risk and time. To underline the importance of time is a huge consideration in making decision. It is a vital component to touch on when explaining action plan to stakeholders.

TIP   Time is an important, mandatory consideration in risk and risk-based management (Figure 76). As the time element increases into the future, the probabilities of achieving the deliverables change. The probability can go up or down depending on the objective, and nature or measure of the projected consequence.

Police will say, for example, "…the probability of finding a missing child alive decreases as the days pass by" for obvious reasons we are all aware of. If a walk-a-ton has no time limit, the probability of each participant completing the race increases. It is not a hundred percent that all will finish considering a time constraint. One can expect a hundred percent probability of completion if one is to finish the race next month or month after, or within a year. The risk taken against the background of time makes it more revealing. It makes us appreciate risk more!

Another example is home fires. It starts small and spread quickly. There is relatively very little time before it burns one to the ground. In fact, in less than 30 seconds a small flame can get completely out of control and turn into a serious fire. History will show that it only takes minutes for thick black smoke to fill a house and then consumed in flames. How does one mitigate the consequence of fire? What is the probability of dying if caught up inside the house in 60 seconds from when the fire starts? What is the probability of surviving a conflagration within 15 seconds from when the fire started? As you

16

can clearly imagine, the longer the time you stay inside the house from when the fire started, the lesser the probability of you surviving the ordeal.

The transport Manager operating the Red Arrow fleet of busses travelling from Calgary to Edmonton asked, "What is the probability of snowing?" This question casually asked, seems to be perfectly fine. A closer look however, makes it fundamentally flawed and incomplete. This is a risk question that is not properly answerable because it is without the time dimension of risk. The answer will come out without much thought and that makes the feedback less useful to a good risk manager. A risk professional knows that the answer based on personal assumptions introduces bias. It can be anything and wide ranging and nobody intelligent enough has the capacity to normalize it.

How about if we change the question to, "What is the probability of snowing within the next 2 hours from now? What is the probability of snowing within the next twelve months?

Apparently, the question becomes clearer. The answer became more obvious, easier, and impeccable. The response makes more sense and is easier to formulate. It facilitates the identification of other risks and their corresponding response plans. If probability of snowing is zero, then there is no risk. If probability is 50% and consequence is zero, then also there is no risk. When the assessment of both impact and probability is zero, the risk is zero. Since risk points to the future, when the duration from now (future timeline) considered is zero, then there is no risk. You will find a similar and more specific discussion in sections 7.10 to 7.13.

Risk is about the future. Remember that from now and the future there is a timeline. The timeline duration to the future has to have a value. Threat and Opportunity is about the future. Unless time travel becomes a reality, then this conceptual principle will remain. If that happens, then perhaps, I will call it FRISKs for future risks, and PRISKs from past risks. Excuse me for deviating almost absurdly but it is fun thinking about possibilities.

Another item to remember is this: when risk (threat and/or opportunity) does happen, it is no longer risk. If the risk is a threat, we should call it an issue or a persistent problem. If the risk is an opportunity, we can call it reward, benefit, advantage, or windfall. Although what I explained above is a lot of information to some, taking time to understand the risk concept presents a better point of view. Understanding the time component of risks will make you a better project risk manager.

1.7.   Black Swan Events

Black swan events are so fascinating that they are a common source of discussion in many risk management forums. The variety of perspectives coming from all directions never ceases to amaze. To a risk manager, 'black swan' phenomena are highly unlikely events that have massive impacts on a business or society on the rare occasions they occur. It means that the event is unexpected, but is of huge consequence (Ferguson, 2014).

There is no scientific way at present to predict black swan events reasonably and acceptably. I tend to question the result of the research, which suggested that by exploiting many types of data, risk managers can help prevent (or at least contain) the damage related to black swan events and other risky blind spots. I have no idea how any data can be useful without the process of correlation.

Black swan events cannot be accurately quantified or calculated. They are unknown unknowns.

The interesting part mentioned is the use of integrated data to point to potential risk. The mere mention of integrated data underlines correlation; i.e. we have to associate correctly one datum to the next, or one set of information to the others, for them to be of value.

That can prove rather impossible when we have nothing to start with. How do we start working on something we do not know? We can only begin to scratch the surface of knowledge once knowing starts.

Unknown unknowns (black swans) might be in the room, for all we know, but we just cannot see them until circumstances make them visible. Once we see that the risk exists, we would surmise that it no longer qualifies as a black swan event, because we are now aware of the risk, and the element of surprise is no longer there. It is now the normal type of risk that many risk managers are already familiar with, the known unknowns.

Bill Pieroni, Chief Operating Officer at insurance giant Marsh, contends that the best way to manage risk, even black swans is to use big data. He explains that some events occur with more and more regularity, suggesting that some seemingly unknowable events are in fact, becoming more or less predictable. He claims that this big data will give way to shades-of-grey swans.

Perhaps he is talking about the transition from being unknown to more or less known. I always say that to a person in the present age and time, black swan events can only be addressed by intuition, despite being labeled as one of the cognitive biases that underlie human flaws in decision-making.

We can all agree that if anyone has the right perspective, understanding, and tools to process universal data, and integrate them into some coherent information, prediction of a black swan event is theoretically possible. The problem in this concept is that nobody has found a way to make it practically possible. Ergo, contrary to what the author implies, real-world application of Pieroni's ideas is still impossible.

The risk universe is immense, yet each component, regardless of how small it might be, can affect the results. If we put a bracket to what data we analyze, then we do not have the whole picture. If we do not put a bracket of limitation to what we evaluate, then we are analyzing infinity and we will not arrive at an answer. We are talking about a great and expansive risk network that trumps common comprehension.

I imagine that many risk drivers actually lie so far outside the boundaries of what we tend to consider that it is futile to predict a potential outcome. Tracing the cause of a black swan event that has already happened can lead us to the most seemingly insignificant occurrence.

It is easy to posit real life example of how some insignificant event results in a big event, spawning other effects in never ending fashion. Some of you might even trace a problem to the time when a specific person was born, arguing that if he had not come into being, things would have turned out differently. The iterations are endless.

Jack Whittaker won a $314.9 Million Powerball jackpot, the biggest jackpot at the time of the drawing in December 2002. Eight months after his win, someone stole $545,000 from his vehicle while he patronized a West Virginia strip club called the Pink Pony. In 2004, the 18-year-old boyfriend of Whittaker's granddaughter was found dead in his home.

Three months later, in December 2004, Whittaker's granddaughter, Brandi Bragg died at a friend's home. In July 2009, Whittaker's daughter, Ginger Whittaker Bragg, was dead. Aside from these personal tragedies, Whittaker had a number of lawsuits filed against him for including bouncing a $1.5 million worth of checks to cover gambling losses. Strippers and alcohol were among the beneficiaries of his winnings (Koplowitz, 2012).

Lottery winner Jeffrey Dampier, a 26-year-old, won $20 million in the Illinois lottery. He was kidnapped and murdered. The culprits were his sister-in-law and her boyfriend.

Jack and Jeffrey, driven by unknown past events, ended up winning the lottery. The push and pull of the things they do before that fateful event resulted in them being in the exact place at the exact time necessary to get that winning ticket. The same is true also concerning their subsequent misfortunes.

At the time of winning, these potential misfortunes were black swan events. They were not expected. Nobody could have reliably predicted the events. The swans will remain black for the near future.

Nassim Nicholas Taleb introduced black swan events in his 2001 book Fooled by Randomness. Taleb regards almost all major scientific discoveries, historical events, and artistic accomplishments as "black swans"—undirected and unpredicted. He gives the rise of the Internet, the personal computer, World War I, the dissolution of the Soviet Union, and the September 2001 attacks as examples of black swan events (Taleb, 2010).

However, many other events such as floods, droughts, epidemics, and other disasters are either improbable, unpredictable, or both. This "non-computability" of rare events is not compatible with scientific methods. The result, says Taleb, is that people develop a psychological bias and "collective blindness" to them. The very fact that such rare but major events are, by definition, outliers makes them dangerous (Bloch, 2013).

 Based on Taleb's book, black swan events have the following criteria:

- The event is a surprise (to the observer).
- The event has a major effect.
- The first recorded instance is rationalized in hindsight as if it was expected. It means that relevant data could have been available for consideration, but was unaccounted for in the risk mitigation process.

For all the criteria items above, one must notice that risk is relative to the observer. Some of us will say that they have seen it all coming to the two winners/losers, even capturing kidnapping and money stolen in the risk register. Unfortunately, the two individuals, who in this case are our observers, were blind to the potential events. As such, the respective event is a surprise, resulting in a major consequence and now rationalized by hindsight. The results fully qualified as Black Swans.

Osama Bin Laden and his close associates, including those who hijacked the planes, knew far in advanced about the risk events. To the terrorists, they were opportunities. The passengers who came to know about the plan realized the risks before the plan reached its conclusion. To them, the risks are threats. It is for a similar reason that at present times, some people call them heroes, and martyrs, while majorities call them terrorists. A person's perception is always relative to his objectives.

To Osama, close associates, the hijackers, the passengers, and perhaps some sympathizers, the events of September 11, 2001 were not black swan events. They were all identified risks.

To the rest of America and the world, to all of us outside the parenthesis of disclosure, the risk events were black swans, or unknown-unknowns.

This is a reality of risk that all risk practitioners should understand. As such, companies should strive to bring all stakeholders to see risk on the same footing, so that they can appreciate it from the same perspective. This is where we have opportunities and threats, gains and losses.

Irving W. Berger, in his 2013 Wall Street Journal article, pointed to the ability of working across data sets and silos (separate storages of data) as the key to help risk managers get early clues when dealing with hard-to-predict, high-impact black swan events. Overcoming silo mentality is a mindset of sharing information between data sets. It happens when certain group or division shares their information with others. When projects worked in silo, most of the data become useless, unable to relate to other relevant data outside the silo. This type of mentality will reduce efficiency in the overall operation, reduce morale, and may contribute to the demise of a productive company culture. In that context, he is saying that there is much science in managing black swans.

The phrase "science in managing black swans" can be contentious, as there is none yet. I guess it is a statement anticipating a future where the science to successfully predict these events becomes available. The core of any black swan discussion these days is finding a way to identify it by using big data, so that risk managers can manage the risk the moment black swans become known. The intention is practically removing the black swan status.

There is great potential for successfully foretelling black swan events through science. We are not there yet, but it is bound to happen. If those unknown events suddenly become visible, known, and predictable through the science of data analytics, then they cease to be black swans.

They move from unknown-unknown to known-unknown to known-known. Unfortunately, today's methods and tool sets are still in their infancy despite the relative leaps in our thinking process, systems, structures, and technologies. As such, the science for managing black swans is still under development. I do agree that, at present, the science is still not there.

"…when experts investigate catastrophic black swan events, be they airline crashes, financial crises, or terrorist attacks, they often find that we failed to anticipate them even when the needed information was present because the data was spread across different organizations and was never properly brought together... In addition to having a solid foundation in statistics, math, data engineering and computer science, data scientists must also have expertise in some particular industry or business domain, so they can properly identify the important problems to solve in a given area and the kinds of answers one should be looking for. Domain expertise is also needed to be able to draw the proper conclusions from their analysis, and to communicate their findings to business leaders in their own terms (Wladawsky-Berger, 2013)."

If an observer does not know and has no expectation of the risk whatsoever, the event to him/her is unknown. In the same sense, the assessment of the impact component of risk is also relative to the observer's goals and interests. An event that might be major to one group can be a non-event to another group. A threat to one can be an opportunity to another depending on the individual intentions. It is prudent not to make a general statement.

Take the disappearance of Malaysian Air MH370. The Malaysian plane incident means little to a great number of people but it means almost their own life to a handful of relatives. The disappearance of that plane is an event the majority of the population did not expect, an event that the family members of those who disappeared with the plane did not expect. The impact is major to them but probably not to you. The event is definitely a black swan to several people on the individual level.

As repeated multiple times in various professional discussions, black swan events to one might be a known risk to another. Who among us can surely tell that there is no one who knows the real story behind the mysterious disappearance? Maybe somewhere, there is.

Since risk is relative to the observer, the elements and attributes of risk are also relative to the observer. Impact and probability are relative to the objective. A person 1000 kilometers away from an atomic blast will not suffer the same immediate consequence as the person 10 kilometers away. The probability of a person being able to save a little boy from an accident when he suddenly runs across a busy highway is a lot higher if the person is a few feet away from the child than when he is a hundred feet away.

Distance is one relative measurement of risk but there numerous unit of measures that can come into consideration. On top of that, the risk analyst should also consider that observers are relative to another observer. I believe that the core of the black swan discussion is in finding a way to identify it, so that we can manage it. The intention is practically removing its black swan status.

Lack of knowledge is different from absence of knowledge.

A mathematical genius might be one of the passengers in that missing Malaysian airline, but he could not have known that he would disappear with all the other passengers on that day.

When one say he does not know, it does not mean he does not search for knowledge.

If one does not know the risk, one should do one's best to identify and know the risk. Trying to know has a boundary. The observer's own interest heavily influence the effort he exerts. The company he represents delimits his actions. In this sense, we would have to prequalify the common phrase "I do not know," for it can mean other things.

When a person says they do not know, it can mean they are not interested in knowing. It can also mean that they are not aware of the process governing the risk management infrastructure and risk framework. It could mean that despite their knowledge in risk management, they are not able to identify the potential risks, other than what is already on the register.

When the unknown eventually happens, we will hear people say, "Honestly, I did not know this was going to happen."

Theoretically, if somewhere in this world, somebody knows about a risk unknown to another observer, he should communicate the information promptly. This is part of using the big or larger data concept. This risk attitude would significantly enhance risk identification.

The sad thing about the whole situation is that the observer's interests and objectives are their greatest obstacles and limitations.

Donald Rumsfeld, former US Secretary of Defense aptly put it in a 2009 interview (also included in his book):

"There are known-knowns. These are things we know that we know. There are known-unknowns. That is to say, there are things that we know we do not know. There are also unknown unknowns. There are things we don't know we don't know."

Risk management also uses intuition among its arsenal. It uses intuition as a method or a tool because there is more to intuition than we commonly perceive. Intuition is a product of mental data analytics. Something happens inside the human brain in which processing of certain information results in a decision intended to manage the unknown.

As the 1918 Physics Nobel Prize recipient Max Planck for his work on Quantum Theory said, "Science cannot solve the ultimate mystery of nature and that is because, in the last analysis, we ourselves are part of nature and therefore part of the mystery that we are trying to solve. I regard consciousness as fundamental. I regard matter as derivative from consciousness. We cannot get behind consciousness.

"Everything that we talk about, everything that we regard as existing, postulates consciousness (Planck, 1858-1947)."

TIP Nobody can consciously manage a black swan.

How can we say we have prepared for a black swan when we do not even know it is coming?

It is only through good fortune that when one has prepared for another event, the action accidentally also fully, or even partially, addresses a black swan.

We can describe the accidental situation above in the following example:

A passenger missed boarding the plane to address a nagging domestic concern and escaped the fate of the missing Malaysian plane.

Somebody spilled coffee on his shirt and so he was late going to the World Trade Center, effectively avoiding death by terrorist attack.

There are many stories like these, especially on the individual level. They have avoided their individual black swans without knowing it, and avoidance is one method of managing risk.

In conclusion, we should withhold judgment when someone talks passionately about the possibility of identifying and predicting black swans in the very near future.

By virtue of his inquisitive nature, and insatiable appetite to search for more knowledge, man will eventually find a way to predict future events accurately.

The ability to tap into unimaginable huge amount of data, and correlating them with confidence, holds great promise of finally breaking the mystery of the unknown-unknown.

Businesses will accomplish this through partnership, joint venture, resource sharing, collaboration, and cooperation.

Chapter 2

Risk-based Management

2.1.   Risk-based Management Process

The whole gamut of risk-based management activities an individual or a business do revolves around six fundamental processes. It starts with a plan on how to manage potential risk. Included in this plan are information covering the five processes; i.e. risk identification, quality assessment, risk quantification, response, monitoring, and control (Figure 7).

All of the active and existing risk management frameworks I have come across to date practically have the same fundamental processes, even if they are sometimes described differently. PMBOK is simply precise while offering flexibility in execution.

Our discussion in the following sections closely adheres to the PMBOK formulation. The governing logic is the same and the effort scalable whether applied by an individual or a big business enterprise. A person's daily trip to his workplace 60 kilometers away probably does not require a written risk management plan in contrast with a complex multi-billion dollar project. The first one is too simple for paper works compared to the latter where documentation is mandatory requirement.

Given a multi-million dollars project, risk identification has to be relatively early. If a construction project is for three years, project management is only primarily concerned with the risks popping up within that three years period from start. These inclusive risks are the project's main responsibility.

Simply put, any risk identified outside the period is another's group responsibility. Those risks will not affect the project objectives. Did you see the relevance of the word relatively early? A risk register holds the list of identified risks, actively maintained until the completion of the final deliverable.

Identifying risk early works best. For a three-year project, risks of same rating identified during the first year give the project a better handle than risks identified in the last six months. Generally, the closer we approach the delivery date, the lesser our influence is, to influence and manage change. Included in risk identification process are categorization, iteration, alignment, review of objectives, tools, methods, SWOT, history, current events, issues, problems, constraints, assumptions, and several others. The manner in which the attributes complement each other will dictate the success of the risk-based plan.

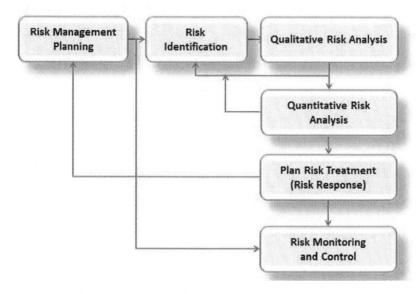

Figure 7 - Project Risk-based Management Process

Performing qualitative assessment is the evaluation of risk attributes for the purpose of prioritization. The most common characteristics considered are probability, consequence, time proximity, risk source, risk factors, and others. Items considered during qualification acceptably overlap that of risk identification.

The two processes are too close together in many aspects that they are almost a singular process. After all, who has the capacity to identify risk without thinking about its attributes? It is in this juncture that the risk analyst must ensure that his information is of good and reliable quality. Otherwise, most of the downstream risk-based management activities become fruitless.

Quantitative risk assessment deals with numbers and quantities. It is a way of communicating the criticality of risks.

The process helps highlight in more concrete terms the effect on each objective in case the risks become a reality. Main schedule drivers, risk drivers, dynamic critical path, risk sensitivities, probabilities, and contingencies are some of the useful information derived from this essential process.

Risk response plan lays out the suitable action to each of the priority listed in the risk register. A clear and concise assignment of responsibility, authority, and ownership is very important to increase the chances of success. Anticipate any secondary risk originating from the responses and be ready to give them the corresponding remedial plan. Identify and assess all residual risks.

The final process is monitoring and controlling of risks. These two come together all the time. Monitoring without control is exercise in futility. When executing an approved risk-based plan, a good risk-based management practitioner wants it implemented correctly and effectively using optimum resources. Track all risks regularly in order to appreciate current developments. Observe changes in priority, relevance, constraints, assumptions, and at times, objectives. Maintain a good recording system but avoid getting lost in the data.

2.2. Introduction to Risk-based Management

Project risk management, as defined by the PMBOK Guide – Fifth Edition and the Practice Standard for Risk Management "includes the processes of conducting risk management planning, identification, analysis, response planning, and controlling risk on a project. PMBOK is the acronym for Project Management Book of Knowledge. It is a book, which presents a set of standard terminology and guidelines (a body of knowledge) for project management. The fifth edition (copyright 2013) is the document resulting from work overseen by the Project Management Institute (Source: PMI).

The objectives of project risk management are to increase likelihood and impact of positive events, and decrease the likelihood and impact of negative events in the project (PMBOK-5th Edition, 2013)."

Project risk management is risk-based project management. Health risk management is risk-based health management. Program risk management is risk-based program management. It is all practically the same animal. Risk management is the core process operating within each management type, categorized by overall purpose, function, and objectives.

In all aspects, risk-based management identifies risk management as the core value of the management function. It aims to identify and prioritize risks in advance of their occurrence, and provide action-oriented information to managers. This orientation requires consideration of events that may or may not occur. Risk is described in terms of likelihood or probability, impacts or consequences (PMI, Project Risk Management Definition/Principles and Concepts, 2009).

A risk-based decision made in a not too distant past that reused in a similar situation in the present is still risk-based. It is probably not necessary to undergo another formal risk assessment and quantification to come up with the same decision. It is, however, prudent to document all decisions and for businesses to makes such reporting mandatory. We will go over this particular requirement as we go through the Four Cs (4Cs) of planning in Section 3.12

TIP Plans and risks go hand in hand because managing risks is part of every plan. The two of them pertain to the future.

In a big project setting, where there are many stakeholders, the documentation requirement becomes more stringent and mandatory for good reasons. One of the 4Cs of planning requires that all plans be committed on paper. This particular requirement is scalable depending on the agreement of all stakeholders. Risk-based management and decision-making on the individual level, as applied to a person's normal day-to-day affairs, is a different story.

In this case, there would be no need to do paperwork or to use the same formality required by a big organization. If one is crossing the street, a duly signed document is not required. As demonstrated, the risk-based process can be successfully scaled-down to what makes sense.

2.3. We Are All Risk Managers

We are all risk managers. All of us are more or less aware of certain risks. The purpose of life is actually managing risk. Risk is in front of us and risk management is in the very fabric of our daily life.

Risk management is the only thing we do for a living, the very reason why our company or client pays us, the reason why we go to work every day.

In this sense, we are all risk managers as we support our very existence. We survive each daily rigor because we are already unconsciously competence of what we do through years of experience and training. If for some reason we are unable to appreciate this intriguing concept of oneness of purpose, then I guess we are all familiar with risk, but we still really do not know it well enough.

What I am driving at is the concept that all categories of management are risk-based management. Project Management, by virtue of the first premise becomes Risk Management. When we take care of ourselves, or our projects, we are managing risks. We do it all the time because it is a very risky world out there.

Many great concepts come from various directions, with some lines meeting

30

to create similar points and some diverging and contrasting. This is where management, risk management, and risk-based management meet.

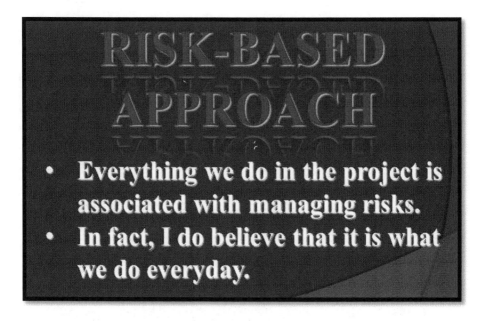

Figure 8 - Risk-based Approach

2.4.   What is Risk-based Management?

The word "management" in business means the process of coordinating the efforts of people to accomplish goals and objectives by using available resources efficiently and effectively. Management is comprised of planning, organizing, staffing, leading or directing, and controlling an organization or initiative to accomplish a goal. Resourcing encompasses the deployment and manipulation of human resources, financial resources, technological resources, and natural resources (Wikipedia, 2013).

According to Business Dictionary, "management" is the organization and coordination of the activities of a business in order to achieve defined objectives. Management is often included as a factor of production along with, machines, materials, and money. According to the management guru Peter Drucker (1909-2005), the basic task of management includes both marketing and innovation.

Here is another one. Management is the organizational process that includes strategic planning, setting objectives, managing resources, deploying the human and financial assets needed to achieve objectives, and measuring results. Management also includes recording and storing facts and information for later use or for others within the organization. Management functions are not limited to managers and supervisors. Every member of the organization has some management and reporting functions as part of their job (UNCW, 2013).

The curious thing in all the aforementioned definitions (and all the many other definitions I have read elsewhere) is that there was no mention of risk, risk-based, or risk management anywhere, yet the mere mention of the word "goals" or "objectives" automatically summons risk into the general equation. This is in spite of the fact that there is not even a singular allusion that risk is the core of management.

A survey conducted in 2011 by PM Solutions Group reveals that organizations, on average, manage $200 million in projects each year, and, in the course of that year, these organizations will realize that more than a third of their projects – $74 million – faced the risk of failing. The jobs and businesses themselves might be in jeopardy with unmitigated risks. An active recovery plan is required (Smith J. , 2012).

It is quite easy to say, therefore, that in view of the original or older definition of management, there is now an absolute need to put the word "risk" somewhere before the word "management" in order to underline the core value of what management is really about. This leads to the incorporation of the words "risk management", and "risk-based management" in today's management literature. Let us make the hidden more obvious.

All decision-making and management processes are risk-based down to the activity level. If I am a fire fighter trying to put out a fire and manage the situation such that the conflagration will not spread to the next row of houses, my decisions on what to do next each time is dictated by a risk-based thinking approach.

Regardless of whether the process is more formal, as required in small to mega-projects, or scaled down to what we usually do personally on a daily basis, any intelligent decisions we make are risk-based. The simplicity of this approach is that it comes forward naturally.

The basis of risk-based management is strong. Anchoring the idea of risk-based management to ISO 31000 or PMBOK for example, will definitely help bring the approach into proper perspective. ISO 31000:2009, Risk management – Principles and guidelines, provides principles, framework, and a process for managing risk (Source: ISO 31000 Website).

To those who question the existence of the term risk-based management, there is definitely a style, a concept, an approach, a method, and a term. It has been part of the business jargon for years. Here are some of the definitions offered for risk-based management found on the web, on day-to-day discussions, and on various forums.

Risk-based is a management approach that looks at scientific inputs to decision-making by relying on numerical assessments of probabilities and impacts (O.Renn, 2002). It is a well-structured, documented, and implemented system necessary for effective management and control of critical or risk-exposed operation in one integrated and efficient system. Risk may be related to life, environment, market, and contractual or regulatory requirements, normally also combined with financial risk (LloydRegisterConsulting, 2013).

According to LCE-Life Cycle Engineering (2013), it uses a risk-based asset management strategy that couples risk management, standard work, and condition-based maintenance. It properly applies resources centered on process criticality, while ensuring that proper controls are put in place and reliability analysis is used to ensure continuous improvement.

An effective risk-based management system includes an enterprise asset management or resource solution that properly catalogs asset attribute data, a functional hierarchy, criticality analysis, risk and failure analysis, control plans, reliability analysis, and continuous improvement (LCE, 2013).

2.5. Imagining Risks, Benchmarks, and Innovations

I can almost imagine risk as a hollow trapezoidal solid floating in space while hundreds in attendance (with varying coordinate in space) observe and try to describe it. Each spectator has a different perspective right from the get-go. Unless each one manages to see the other's perspective, an agreement becomes impossible.

For risk-based management to work properly in an organization, management has to be willing to listen. The question often thrown on the table is to whom should management listen? How can management be sure they are getting the right information? There is no certain answer to this, but a discerning manager can listen to everyone on duty and identify the real substance.

What do you think should be the approach of an open-minded management? Should we be worried that a management receptive to new and different ideas or opinions will prevent a risk framework from being effective? We always hear about streamlining a management process as we begin a new project because we all want to increase efficiency and productivity.

Streamlining and standardizing processes are there to reduce many of the problematic risks that plagued management years ago. They bring repeatability, uniformity, and good quality to the table. However, when one well-meaning risk manager gives some serious thought to it, he might see innovation and creativity as inapplicable to such a system.

Innovative ideas are initiatives that tend to run contrary to streamlining and standardizing approaches, processes, and methodologies. Innovation and creativity promote change. Streamlining and standardization underline fixed benchmarks. Each one can undermine the other if the proponents are not careful. The two objectives run in opposite directions.

It is a good reminder to all of us that management does not always have a sharp dividing line between stages and processes, despite a given structure and an implementation framework. What we see many times are blurred boundaries that can easily become grey areas.

Take as an example the blurring of boundaries between public service and private interest in the health profession (Hudson, 2012), between sectors in a national context (LSE/NCVO/ESRC, 2009), in professional identities (Whitchurch, 2009), and in organizational hierarchies (Marchington, M. et al, 2006).

Blurred boundaries should be one of the most summoned risk-based considerations during the assessment process. Blurred boundaries are risk and contentious spots. It is a region where even an intelligent person falls prey to subjective perception. It is where we tend to make assumptions,

The famous poem titled "Job Responsibility" (Osgood, 2009) had successfully pointed to it. Here are some relevant stanzas we could all reflect on.

> "There was a most important job that needed to be done,
>
> And no reason not to do it, there was absolutely none.
>
> But in vital matters such as this, the thing you have to ask
>
> Is who exactly will it be who'll carry out the task?
>
> "But nobody told anybody that we are aware of,
>
> That he would be in charge of seeing it was taken care of.

And nobody took it on himself to follow through,

And do what everybody thought that somebody would do.

"Somebody should have done the job

And Everybody should have,

But in the end Nobody did

What Anybody could have."

Chapter 3

Risk-based Planning and Scheduling

3.1.   Introduction to Risk-based Planning

The foundation of a good risk-based execution is a good risk-based plan. A risk-based plan calls for a sound plan that has considered all high priority potential risks. It is for this reason that such a plan becomes risk-based.

The project manager has to have full understanding of planning and scheduling fundamentals, concepts, governing standards, benchmarks, accepted procedures, work instructions, and all other essentials revolving around the two processes. It is important to know that the risk-based approach to planning is not limited to a particular group, role, position, or department. It does not belong to only a few individuals or companies. It is useful in all aspects of undertakings.

In this chapter, we will try to develop and improve our appreciation of the importance of risk-based planning and scheduling in a project setting, as well as in general application, including your personal situation. The terms "plan" and "schedule" in this book mean "risk-based plan" and "risk-based schedule.

Let us explore the answers to the following basic questions:

- What is an integrated schedule? Read section 3.10 and reflect.

  Your answer should not vary much regardless of whether you answer the question as an individual, a project manager, project controls director, a contractor manager or the client. As an individual planning a tour, traveling from Calgary to Las Vegas, to Alaska, to Florida and back, how would you schedule your trip? It would be unusual to consider each leg of the trip separately without considering how the others influence the whole thing and how the risk associated with each leg affects the each, most especially the return date. If this is your way of thinking, then you have the basic understanding of a risk-based integrated schedule.

- How does an integrated schedule relate to Critical Path Method (CPM) calculation? Read section 3.5 and reflect.

The critical path method is project management tool applied to network scheduling activities to determine what drives and controls the entire project's completion time. The simple trip schedule of Calgary to Florida and back is an example of critical path. In this case, there is no branching network unless one delves into the details of each leg. Delay to any of travel legs will delay the return trip to Calgary because each one sits on the primary critical path. The entire travel is analogous to a construction project where the delay of one critical activity delays the finish date of the entire project. The overall project's critical path becomes visible only when one looks at the integrated schedule.

- What is a critical path? (See preceding paragraph and section 3.5 for explanation)

- Why should an activity lying on the critical path given more priority?

A delay in any activity along the primary critical path delays the whole project. Even a single day increase in the duration of one activity is enough to push the end day out. For this reason, the focus for mitigation must lie along this path. It is very important to prevent and mitigate the risks affecting and/or associated with the activities along the path.

Other questions to ask:
- What is a CPM schedule?
- What are some tips for better and more efficient scheduling?
- What is a schedule risk?
- What is the standard or prescribed schedule quality?
- What is a schedule hierarchy?
- What are the levels of schedule hierarchy (level of schedule)?

- What is a project definition? Where can you get this information?
- How do we understand the various schedule hierarchies (Level of Schedule)?
- How can we tie together the planning and scheduling processes?
- How are they relevant to the other knowledge areas?

3.2.   The Story of Two Bulls (Strategy and Wisdom)

A colleague in the oil and gas industry was trying to be funny that day and was delivering another one of his patented jokes. I do not usually take notice because I find myself always busy with work but the story resonated differently so I came closer, to his surprise, I started taking notes. This bull story somehow relates to business strategy and acumen. I want to remember it and now I am sharing it to you.

> "Two bulls were walking side by side one day. The young one was full of enthusiasm. The older one, who was wiser, looked at other bull and shook its head. The two suddenly came across a herd of cows.
>
> The young bull said, "Let's charge down this hillside right now and have our wicked way with a couple of those cows.
>
> The old bull replies, "No, how about we stroll gently down this hillside, so they won't get scared and run away. Let us be friendly and know them better so we can then have a good time with them all for a year.""

This story is a good analogy that highlights the importance of planning over impulse when making decisions. A sure and steady pace get the goal. Instead of hastily doing what comes to mind first and being content with average return, the better way is to plan patiently, consider the risks, and schedule soundly to optimize the goal. Such is your risk-based planning and scheduling.

3.3.   Risk-based Planning

According to Business Dictionary, planning is a basic management function involving formulation of one or more detailed plans to achieve an optimum balance of needs or demands with the available resources. The planning process identifies the goals or objectives to be achieved, formulates strategies to achieve them, arranges or creates the means required, and implements, directs, and monitors all steps in their proper sequence.

A risk-based plan is a plan inspected and scrutinized both qualitatively and quantitatively, and adjusted using acceptable risk management processes. Upon risk quantification of the plan and the schedule, a risk-based baseline of the plan and the schedule is ratified and set.

The risk-based plan is an input to develop the risk-based baseline schedule.

Project planning is a participative process between project team members used to identify the activities needed in order to complete a certain scope of goals while considering their interdependencies.

According to purpose, planning is the process of establishing an acceptable course of action ("plan") to execute a project in an effective manner through the review of project scope and objectives (Plotnick, 2004).

In organizations, planning is a management process focused on defining objectives and deliverables. To meet these deliverables, management has to develop management and execution plans (Wikipedia, Wiki\Planning, 2014).

It is important to emphasize that, although not shown here as a discrete process, project execution and other plans under its umbrella, are the results of the project's planning effort.

3.4. Risk-based Scheduling

Scheduling is the assignment of desired start and finish times to each activity inside the overall timeline benchmarked to complete the project. It involves the process of converting a risk-based plan into a risk-based schedule. It is the collection of activities needed to implement a plan (AACE, AACE 14R-90 Responsibility and Required Skilld for Project Planning, 2013).

TIP A risk-based schedule is not possible without pulling together a risk-based plan.

It is the process of defining activities, durations, and relationship logic to implement the project plan, and the process of monitoring, updating, and communicating the dates of each activity.

The risk-based schedule reflects the scope, current state, forecast, impact of present and future changes, project strategy, priorities, deliverables, sequences, and the potential of success (Plotnick, 2004).

Figure 9 - Planning and Scheduling Quandary

3.5. Critical Path Method (CPM)

There are various definitions of a critical path. One describes it as a network of linked schedule activities that determine and control the entire project's completion time. Delay to any of the activities sitting on the primary critical path will delay the finish date of the whole project. Any activity sitting on the path is critical even if its duration is only one day.

Imagine a crowd of people trying to get into a singular door of a computer store on Black Friday. Within that crowd is a primary line of 200-people. The door can accommodate one person at a time. The others form secondary lines branching out hoping to get into the main line if someone leaves. If the store can serve only 200 people then that main queue is like the critical path of a schedule that controls completion at the end of the day. If additional persons find their way into the queue, delay to the day's schedule is the most likely consequence.

Identifying critical activities and critical paths uses three ways; i.e. using the longest path, total float equal or less than zero, or whatever the contract defines it to be.

The default and most commonly used critical path definition uses the longest path. The scheduling tool identifies critical activities without specifying any total float value but by merely saying "Yes" to the longest path filter.

The second method most frequent use is to filter critical activities by specifying a total float equal to zero.

The third one depends on how the governing contract defines critical. If the agreement says that all activities with Total Float less than 10 days are critical, then it is. All parties must respect that. Remember that the properties of near critical will follow the same gist.

Critical Path is a measure of schedule flexibility, usually termed as total float. On any network path, flexibility is the positive difference between early and late dates. Activities on critical path are critical activities (PMI, Project Risk Management, 2013).

Be careful of relative critical path. This is the critical path relative to some select points of constrain only. This is not the overall project's critical path.

The real critical path of an overall schedule is one generated by the calculation of a schedule that has no constraint, a schedule that flows freely.

Anything that prevents the forward and backward passes calculation makes the resulting critical path dubious and questionable. Unless the exercise is to study a what-if scenario identifying the schedule drivers that pushes certain dates, a relative critical path can end up misleading the whole team.

A constrained activity limits the full appreciation of the overall critical path. It creates a barrier that prevents the normal logical schedule flow. It can mislead planners and schedulers to the wrong overall critical path. It causes missed opportunities and poor risk management decisions if not handled properly.

3.6. Risk-based Schedule Development

Project schedule development is an iterative process that determines the planned start and finish dates of project activities. The process is continuous throughout the project as work progresses (PMI, Schedule Development Overview, 2013).

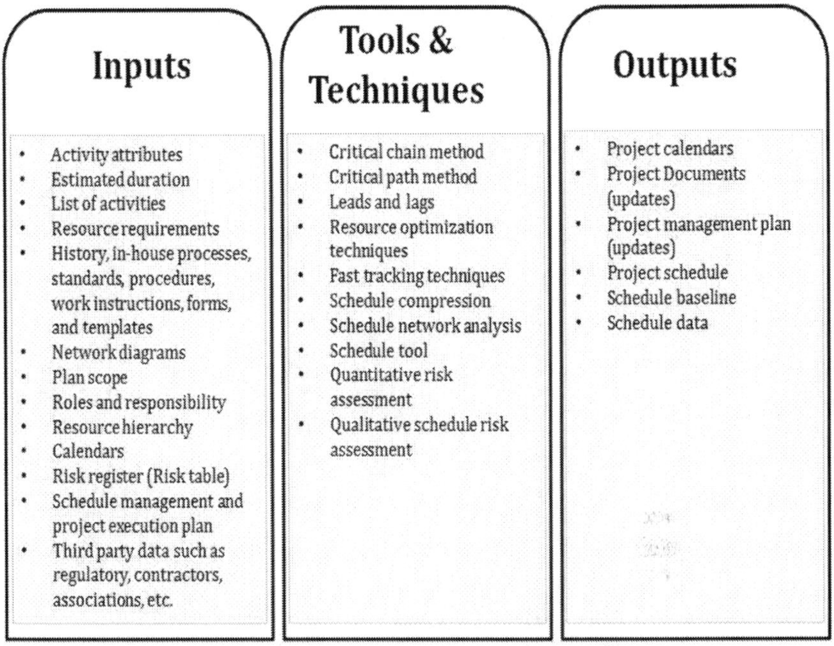

Inputs	Tools & Techniques	Outputs
• Activity attributes • Estimated duration • List of activities • Resource requirements • History, in-house processes, standards, procedures, work instructions, forms, and templates • Network diagrams • Plan scope • Roles and responsibility • Resource hierarchy • Calendars • Risk register (Risk table) • Schedule management and project execution plan • Third party data such as regulatory, contractors, associations, etc.	• Critical chain method • Critical path method • Leads and lags • Resource optimization techniques • Fast tracking techniques • Schedule compression • Schedule network analysis • Schedule tool • Quantitative risk assessment • Qualitative schedule risk assessment	• Project calendars • Project Documents (updates) • Project management plan (updates) • Project schedule • Schedule baseline • Schedule data

Figure 10 - Develop a Schedule

3.7.   Risk-based Schedule Management and Control

The process of risk-based schedule management and control represents how the project remains in control despite scheduling changes.

It is the part of the project's integrated change control process concerned with determining the current state of the project schedule, influencing the factors that create schedule change, recording and validating changes to the schedule, and managing the changes as they occur.

Proper controls not only rely on present information but the past, e.g. history, standards, procedures, and previous work performance. The past provides valuable nuances to decision-making and overall projection. It gives objectives and deliverables better meaning.

Risk-based management tracks and manages changes to the schedule. "Who can disagree with the need to evolve?." I agree to a certain extent. Sometimes, changes to the input and output processes is needed. One needs to evolve when when presented with a new challenge that a current risk process or combination of processes cannot effectively resolve or respond to.

Inputs	Tools & Techniques	Outputs
• History, in-house processes, standards, procedures, work instructions, forms, and templates • Project calendars • Project management plan • Risk-based schedule • Schedule data • Actual work performance	• Leads and lags • Modeling techniques • Performance reviews • Project management software • Resource optimization techniques • Schedule compression • Scheduling tool	• Change requests • Organizational process assets updates • Project documents updates • Project management plan updates • Schedule forecasts • Work performance information

Figure 11 - Schedule Management and Control

3.8.   Scope in Planning and Scheduling

 A risk-based plan is required before a risk-based schedule is developed.

The basis of schedule (or schedule basis) and methodologies is a plan that serves as the main source of information in building the schedule, which in turn takes relevant information from all the other project execution documents, such as the construction execution plan, procurement management plan, modularization plan, contracting plan, risk management plan, and several others.

Once the execution schedule is developed, it has to be monitored and controlled to make sure that the implementation goes according to plan. Major deviation from the plan requires management of change documentation and risk assessment.

Continuous collaboration and closed-loop communication is necessary for effective management to take place.

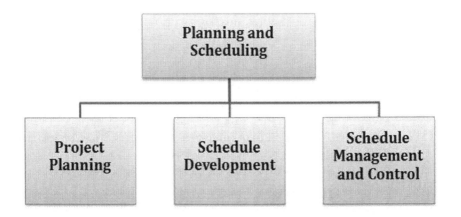

Figure 12 - Planning and Scheduling Processes

3.9. Planning and Scheduling Using Safety Lenses

All of us have seen the aftermath of those who defied the traffic sign "Drive slowly! Do not exceed the speed limits" or "Slow down, dangerous curve" (see Figure 13). As you drive on the highway, you begin to recognize that many drivers just ignore the speed limit and drive 10, 20, or sometimes 30 kilometers per hour over the limit. Everyone knows that speed kills, and seeing someone traveling above the limit makes us question how any intelligent person can commit such a reckless act. It is one of the number one ways to cause or get into a car accident.

There are 150,000 collisions, 350 traffic deaths, and 20,000 injuries every year in Alberta, Canada (AMA, 2011). You might be living somewhere in this world and you have different numbers. Your statistics might be worse or better. The thing is, behind this statistics are faces of families and friends, the communities, and workplaces. They are all negatively affected and there is an urgent need to understand and do something. If one thinks about it long enough, he will realize that the solution to this harmful and deadly consequence is risk-based management.

What do you think is the root cause of speeding? Why are people taking to the road and speeding? Are they chasing something? Why are they talking on their mobile phone and texting? Why can't they wait? Why can't they make the call before boarding their vehicles? What is too important to parents as to jeopardize the life of their precious passengers by speeding, and talking, and texting? I have asked these questions many times and came up with an explanation as to why, and that is without even receiving a formal reply from anyone. It just simply crossed my mind.

Poor planning and scheduling or their absence, is the root of many accidents, and human-made disasters.

Figure 13 - Vehicle Speeding Accidents

While teaching project teams the subject of planning and scheduling in an in-house course, the answers came flowing and they made my jaw fell. Here are some of the reasons why people are speeding. These are just a few.

1) People are running late
   - So they push the pedal to the metal
   - So they make shortcut
   - So they jump the queue
   - So they call while driving to cancel an appointment
   - So they call while driving to say they'll be late
   - So they don't know what to do except speed up
   - And many others (think about it)

2) People are impatient to drive behind another vehicle
   - So they overtake the vehicle impulsively
   - So they honk, yell, and swear
   - So they don't observe safe distance
   - So they try to annoy the other driver by bad gestures
   - So they put their headlight to high beam
   - So they get distracted
   - And many others (think about it)

3) People are tired or impaired
   - So they try to be there before they fall asleep
   - So they can be there to rest before the next appointment
   - So they commit driving miscalculation
   - And some others (think about it)

The purpose of bringing the reader's attention to this seemingly ordinary day-to-day issue on speeding is because they are all preventable. They are preventable through a good understanding of planning and scheduling. A person who has an interview the next morning will plan his activities including contingencies. He will schedule and execute them firmly surely. He will set his wake-up alarm clock to 5:30 AM if his interview is 9:00 AM not 8:00 AM, knowing that it is 50 kilometers away through traffic zones.

Any thinking man will consider congestions, some what-if accident situations, and build his buffer zone from there. These are all to make sure he can still be there on time no matter what he encounters.

By doing this, he minimizes stress. He avoids speeding, potentially saving lives and properties. He will not be a slave to his emotion when road activities go against him. He knows how to overtake a vehicle safely in wet, dry, or icy road because he has a plan. He has alternate routes in case of bottlenecks, guided by a good sense of direction and logic. Planning and scheduling is the core of risk-based management.

3.10. Integrated Risk-based Schedule

You might have an idea or two of what an integrated schedule is. However, if you compare notes with other planning and scheduling professionals, you will quickly learn that they have another definition in mind.

In this section, we will attempt to establish the mandatory minimum requirements of an integrated schedule such that anyone can confidently say when evaluating a schedule that, "Aha! Yes, this is an integrated schedule!"

When we speak about an integrated schedule, we can quickly conclude that this schedule is the result of an integrated plan. Webster's Dictionary defines the word integrated as "include, incorporated, combining dissimilar things, or bring together functions, or processes that are normally separate."

An ideal integrated project schedule is a risk-based, resource loaded, intuitive and good quality schedule (based on agreed metrics) aligned to project plan that is WBS organized and connected, or linked to all associated and relevant project activities in a singular precedence diagram network.

The degree of integration shall depend on which Checkpoint (Gate) the project is at the time of assessment (for illustration, see Figure 90).

For example, based on experience, schedule maturity at DBM is far less if we compare it come EDS. Resource loaded schedule is not required in Checkpoint 2 (G2) in many cases. Engineering resource loading might be required in equally number of cases as it matures the fastest. Resource loading is required in Checkpoint 3 (G3) or EDS. All control schedules must be resource loaded, as a minimum, with work hours and with commodities.

Cost loading is usually avoided for reason of confidentiality but some companies do so, under special arrangement.

Integrated schedule might mean including cost loading to some industry construction players. Majority handles cost separately using a different tool.

In the project controls world, supported by its existing standards, procedures, guidelines, best practices, and experiences, the following eleven criteria can be used to define an integrated risk-based schedule:

- The schedule has to bring all stakeholders on the same page where agreed information is effectively communicated
- It should use the same tool in developing and maintaining the scheduling database.
- All interdependent project schedules (silos) should be in the same scheduling database or schema (co-located)
- All interdependent project schedules should be linked together vertically and horizontally; i.e. across phases, areas, sub-areas and sub-projects.
- If one schedule resides in a different database, the scheduler must make the necessary logical connections by other means. Remember that it is challenging (if not impossible) to run a critical path assessment on a disjointed or disconnected schedule.
- The approved official baselines should be available within the same scheduling database for immediate comparison to the current. Both the contractor and the client who will execute the project, and who will monitor progress respectively own the established baseline. The two parties officially sign off, make necessary arrangements, and officially declare a contract schedule baseline, a risk-based schedule as per contract agreement.
- An integrated schedule should practically have the same level of detail throughout the different project phases. If it is a Level 3 schedule, then the rest follows.

- The scheduling tool should have streamlined and standardized codes and structures, and an official reporting format.
- The schedule or group of interrelated schedules should be representative of the total scope of the project.
- The schedule should be resource-loaded. The loaded resources (usually in work hours) should be in alignment with the latest baseline estimate. Alignment between the execution schedule and the execution estimate is an important and fundamental requirement. The schedule approved for execution has to talk with the execution estimate before an integrated execution baseline schedule is approved (Frago, DBM Schedule Development Workshop, 2015). These are available at a time around the end of Engineering Design Specification stage, a part of front-end engineering (FEED).
- Loading cost values in the schedule as part of integration is not mandatory in majority of current cases. It would require a buy-in from other stakeholders in order to pursue this manner of full integration. Other team members might see this kind of loading as a risk exposure of cost information.
- Key milestones and the overall sequence should line up with all the key document information (project management and execution plan, project charter, basis of schedule, and other relevant documents).
- Checkpoint review and regulatory milestones should be included in the schedule.
- The data in all inter-related component of the schedule needs to be of the same data date. Project information shall be on the same point of reference for all updates to cascade properly and all forecasts to come across accurately.
- Make sure that all Users Preference Setting (UPS) and Administrative Setting of the tool is correct and uniformly set on all projects.

3.11. Common Pitfalls in Planning and Scheduling

There are numerous mistakes and misconceptions about the process of plan and schedule management. It would probably take a whole book just to list them one by one. For this section, we would look at some of them closely.

Common mistakes are to:

- Analyze plan and schedule without considering assumptions and constraints

- Create a schedule without deep consideration of resource commitments
- Execute an unapproved plan and schedule
- Execute work without a plan to guide the project
- Fail to assess any of the following seven planning and scheduling attributes: content, level of definition, achievability, clarity, accuracy, completeness, and integration
- Fail to follow and monitor checklist requirements of inputs and outputs. We need a complete set of input data to come up with the most useful set of output information.
- Not asking the right questions (see Section 3.13 to 3.16)
- Fail to implement remedial action to identified upcoming risk
- Fail to monitor new and emerging risks
- Fail to use a continuous collaboration process
- Holding on to outdated pet heuristics with a closed mindset (for instance, the belief that commissioning and start-up should begin only when construction is 70% complete)
- Ignore or fail to track changes
- Ignore or discount the human element of planning and scheduling, such as the need to establish good relationships with other team members
- Ignore risk indicators
- Ignore schedule quality
- Love the project too much, resulting in unconscious blind disregards to the signs of risk
- Not do enough to address the origins of current issues and fail to realize that these same issues can be the root cause of future risks
- Plan and schedule without a good control system
- Have a poor understanding of the integrated project management processes
- Refuse to undertake risk assessment, seeing the process as guesswork
- Rely too heavily on the tool (computer jockey)
- Rely on status meetings, listening to reports that evaluate progress solely by percentage complete, closed and not closed, in progress and not started, done and not done
- Skip the execution audit. It is good to hold an execution audit within the first six months of execution right after sanctioning the project. Skipping an execution audit makes the project lose an opportunity to assess if plan and schedule implementation is

doing well. One must remember that identifying a problem sooner gives the project a better management handle.

- Think that an implementation framework is not important
- Think that schedule management is the scheduler's responsibility
- Think that the schedule is the plan
- Work in a vacuum

3.12. Four C's of Planning

I found an old notebook in my drawer recently, flipped through the pages, and found a subject called the 4Cs of Planning. It is from a 2004 Administrative Control System course notebook I still have. The foundational principles of the 4Cs are so simple to follow that I have used them frequently when explaining what planning is all about, despite not knowing who developed the concept.

All I know is this: it makes sense. I have adopted it and am now sharing the principle with you.

3.13. Clarify Objectives

Having objectives is important, but if objectives are unclear, that is worse than having no objectives at all.

This incites confusion and causes project turmoil. Ask yourself:

- What is the goal of the project?
- What does the client need?
- What is the most important element of the goal?
- When will this project be complete?
- When will these activities occur?
- When will these tasks occur?
- What is the cost? How much is the total cost?

3.14. Codify Requirements

Codifying requirements points to how the project organizes, sorts, and integrates its resources and information. What is the use of knowing that all resources are available if we do not know where to assign them? What good is it in knowing that we have a complete scope of activities if we do not have a structured plan laid out in a logical order? What will happen if we do not know which equipment should be part of a certain construction work package? Ask yourself:

- What are the major work items?

- What is the adopted Work Breakdown Structure (WBS)?
- How can we define and break the plan to manageable pieces?
- What are the major work items?
- How can we measure success and failure?
- Can I stop the work on the project?
- What are the resources needed to accomplish the goal?
- How do I monitor the progress?
- How will I know I am on schedule? (Key Milestones)
- How do I stop the work on the project?
- How do I manage the changes needed? (Note that asking people to change anything is a major task!)

3.15. Identify Contingencies

Contingency reserves are time buffers or time reserves in a project schedule to account for risks that might delay the end deliverable. In cost management, contingency is a reserve to address cost uncertainty. It is part of the cost baseline allocated to respond to identified risks if they happen (PMI, Reserve Analysis, 2013).

Donning the PMBOK hat, the two basic attributes used to influence and control risk are its probability of occurring (addressing the project's risk appetite) and its consequence (addressing the project's risk tolerance). Ask yourself:

- What is the cost breakdown structure (CBS)?
- What are the risks?
- How do I assess and treat risks?
- What is the schedule contingency?
- What is the total cost of the project?
- What is the contingency of the overall project?
- If each phase is a separate budget with a separate owner, what is the contingency of each phase (i.e. engineering, fabrication, modularization, and construction)?

3.16. Commit Plans on Paper

Small to large organization should strive to follow this last of the 4C guide. The rule that a plan is not a plan unless it is committed on paper makes proper sense. Why would an entity seeking profit start any work unless there is a buy-in from all stakeholders and a clear plan of action in place?

A project goes above the individual level of thinking. It is not acceptable to just think about installing a set of compressors, including ancillary equipment and auxiliaries, and commencing construction work right after. Never work without an approved plan because it will create heartache for all. It is not like a trip to Vegas that one can decide on anytime. Documenting a plan protects the client, the contractors, and the government. Ask yourself:

- How do I get a buy-in and subsequent approval?
- Does the project have a buy-in of all stakeholders?
- Does the project have an approved project charter and execution plan?
- How do I develop and prepare the project baseline?
- Does the project have an approved baseline?
- What should the project use to monitor progress?
- Did the project hold an interactive planning (IAP) session?
- Where is IAP the minutes of meeting?
- Where is the list of action items from the IAP session?

3.17. Schedule Hierarchy or Levels of Schedule

Schedules, like plans, become more and more defined as the project traverses the phases from initiating and scoping to execution and closeout. The plan and schedule are more defined downstream than upstream in the project life cycle.

Divide the project into the usual phase checkpoints such as scoping/idea generation (Checkpoint 1), planning and designing (Checkpoint 2), execution/plan implementation (Checkpoint 3), closeout (Checkpoint 4) and post project review (Checkpoint 5). There will be less detail in Checkpoint 1 than Checkpoint 3 or 4.

The work breakdown structure (WBS) controls the details.

Level 1 - Management Summary Schedule (Checkpoint 1)

- Schedule consists of summary bars and major key milestones showing projects, sub-projects, major areas, and project phases.

Level 2 - Master Schedule (Checkpoint 2)

- Schedule consists of activities down to the discipline level such as civil, piping, mechanical, electrical, structural, and others.

Level 3 - Execution Schedule (Checkpoint 3)

- Schedule has details that down to work packages. E.g. engineering work package, modularization work package, and construction work package.

Level 4 - Detail Schedule (Checkpoint 3 to 4)

- Schedule is down to a "field installation work package" (FIWP) level. This is best illustrated by the one espoused by the workface planning concept sponsored by Construction Owners Association of Alberta (COAA) (Insight-WFP, 2014). You can visit their website (http://www.coaa.ab.ca) to learn more.

Level 5 - Task Schedule (Checkpoint 3 to 4)

- Schedule is down to the task level, possibly very short duration tasks (compared to the length of the project or phase)

- Includes systematic instructions on how to accomplish activities such as foundation installation (set forms, pre-tie rebar, set rebar, pour concrete, and remove forms) or even lower.

- Special purpose schedule such as a maintenance turn-around (shutdown) schedule, drop-dead schedule, or expediting schedule are good examples.

3.18. Basis of Schedule (BOS)

The basis of the risk-based schedule (also referred to as schedule basis and methodology) is a document that describes the critical and most important risks, issues, assumptions, and strategies considered. The BOS is part of the execution plan and is a direct critical input in the development of the schedule.

Encompassed in the BOS are information about the adopted strategies, methodologies, assumptions, constraints, rationales, key deliverables, interfaces, schedule administration, templates, reporting protocol, references, responsibility table, precautions, calendars, tool set, and others as needed. This is to provide a sound and achievable risk-based schedule aligned to the baseline estimate.

3.19. Schedule Driven Project

One IPA benchmarking article mentioned an IPA study presented in March 2010 annual meeting of the Industry Benchmarking Consortium (IPA, 2010) how frequently small, site-based projects fail to meet objectives. The study divided the projects into two groups, cost-driven and schedule-driven. The question came up whether there are real benefits to grouping a project into the two categories regardless of project size.

TIP In the project management world, we accomplish and perform a schedule driven project using an overruling and dominant control of time. The risk-based process involved revolves around the final timeline, timeframe, scheduled key and critical dates. It is a management mandate to make time the key condition of project's success. It becomes the heavier consideration when making project management decisions. It means that time is the essence. The project schedule is highly prioritized over and above other project elements such as cost, resources, quality, and risks. It is unfortunate that in many instances, quality is the first to go.

Project people should be wary using the term haphazardly as many are not familiar with it, even within the same industry. An inexperienced person will end up giving a different meaning than intended.

For example, we asked Peter Guessing (not his real name) how he interprets the term "schedule driven" mandate applied to his project. Just like several others, he came up with the same all-encompassing connotation that in his project cost and spending will not be a problem.

A few others tuned in and said it means sky is the limit. The project can spend higher than normal as long as the project meets the delivery dates. In short, the business is willing to pay.

A project geared to reduce carbon emissions and sulfur contents is a good example. If the project misses the effective date or dates of a critical regulatory requirement, then the law or statute applies promptly, resulting in court injunction, huge penalty, unproductivity, financial losses, construction stoppage, or even the closure of a large operating facility, resulting in unemployment.

If management floats the term schedule-driven without explaining what it really means, other members might expect something different. A schedule-driven project has a general default definition but it is prudent to provide more specifics by defining some boundaries to be effective.

A strategic balance needs to be set despite the mandate. Focusing on one leg of the iron triangle all throughout the project duration can derail overall success.

3.20. Schedule Risks

Project risks are uncertain events or conditions that, if they occur, have a positive or a negative effect on at least one project objective, such as time, cost, scope, quality, and others (PMI, Project Risk Management Definition/Principles and Concepts, 2009).

We can say, therefore, that a schedule risk is as an uncertain event or condition that, if it occurs, has a positive or a negative effect on the project's schedule.

Schedule risk analysis examines the risk to the project and specifies how they might affect the schedule, how this translates to cost, and how the total cost is affected.

Examples of the tools and applications used for quantitative risk analysis are:

- @RISK
- Pertmaster
- Oracle Primavera Risk Analysis (OPRA), previously Pertmaster
- Deltek Acumen Risk
- Crystal Ball

3.21. Categorizing Projects by Capital Cost

A good way to group projects to enhance the risk-based management approach is to categorize the projects according to their size in terms of the projected budget (see Sections 3.22 to 3.25). The division below is a view of what it can be like in 2014 for a big corporation with annual net income around the $2 billion mark.

Note that when looking at these projects using an in-house lens, the cost bracketing of the category might be relative to the size of the organization. What is small for one major player in the industry can be large to another.

A small business can categorize its projects quite differently. It will probably see what are considered by large corporations as small projects as something completely out of this world. Categorizing projects according to size is relative to the organization's perspective. Sections 3.22 to 3.25 are example of categories of a multi-billion dollar corporation.

3.22. Mega-Projects

- Total estimated cost is greater than $750 Million dollars.

3.23. Large-size Projects

- Total estimated cost is greater than $250 Million dollars but less than $750 Million.

3.24. Medium-size Projects

- Total estimated cost is greater than $50 Million dollars but less than $250 Million.

3.25. Small Projects

- Total estimated cost is less than $50 Million dollars.

Chapter 4

How to Prepare for SQRA

4.1.   Introduction to Proper SQRA Preparation

Schedule Quantitative Risk Analysis (SQRA) is a critical component in the overall assessment of any major project. Carrying out such analysis is primarily used for endeavors that are of great significance to a business venture, such as a multi-billion dollar construction project, a high profile government regulatory compliance project, a very complex sustaining project, or an exceedingly visible project sponsored by the company's most powerful and influential stakeholders.

Performing a Monte Carlo simulation is the core of SQRA. Several commercial applications such as Oracle Primavera Risk Analysis or OPRA (previously called Pertmaster), Crystal Ball, @Risk, Risk Simulator, and Acumen Risk are some of the applications in use across various industries.

Through a meticulous, mathematical, and methodical process of risk modeling, a project manager will be able to identify, calculate, assess, and predict the following:

- Achievability of the overall schedule or, in other words, the probability of your project being completed on schedule and within budget
- Achievability of specific deterministic milestones and deliverables
- Overall Probability versus Schedule Date distribution
- Specific probability of each key activity and milestone
- Overall schedule contingency
- Schedule contingency of each major stage or phase
- Critical schedule drivers
- Critical risk drivers
- Duration/risk sensitivities
- Cruciality (a combination of Criticality and Duration Sensitivity index)
- Schedule criticality and tasks that remains on the critical path
- Schedule quality
- Completeness of the schedule

- Impact of schedule changes and updates
- Duration sensitivity
- All other useful derivative information as the project decides

Any project manager worth his/her salt will say that failure is not an option. Therefore, it is vital to validate the achievability of what we know as the project management triple constraints (cost, time, and scope). PMBOK (2009) further improved the concept.

The advanced illustration of the iron triangle (Wikipedia, Project Management Triangle, 2013) shows two superimposed triangles with opposing apexes creating a six-point star where each point represents the constraints to be monitored, and managed. The two points I would like to delve into in detail are time and quality. Note that the project schedule represents the time management component of the project.

I will show the readers how to prepare for the SQRA process and what planning inputs are needed to improve success. By providing the recommended list of quality benchmarks and explaining the rationale of using those quality metrics to mitigate time-bound risks against the potential consequences of a poor quality schedule, I expect all practitioners to gain complete understanding of the overall philosophies involved.

A good manager who ignores or intentionally skips SQRA loses a great opportunity to manage even better. Regardless of the apparent challenges revolving around the subjectivity of the process, with right, logical, and intelligent inputs, SQRA will give the project a sound basis when making a difficult choice. It will provide a solid foundation when announcing a "Go or No Go" project decision.

Although SQRA is one of the best practices in project management, it must be borne in mind that not every project requires this process. The resources needed to perform the quantitative risk process and the potential return value will determine whether to do one.

A simple small to large project or portfolio of say, a few thousand to a few million dollars might not need to perform this process. A qualitative risk assessment through a simple risk register is usually enough.

The correctness, accuracy, completeness, and usefulness of a Schedule Quantitative Risk Analysis (SQRA) will depend heavily on the quality of planning data used for input, or more plainly, the quality of the project schedule.

The rule is simple. All of us have heard it before. Garbage in is garbage out or

GIGO (Wikipedia, Garbage in, Garbage Out, 2013). It is an old rule of thumb, and one of the main reasons why an analyst needs to perform the qualitative process before the quantitative one.

TIP A good quality schedule is a critical prerequisite for a successful quantitative exercise.

The reader will become more familiar with the term "minimum schedule quality" at the end of this chapter. One will learn the fundamental requirements and approaches to SQRA by following the guidelines described.

Being able to acknowledge how and why certain schedule quality criteria are critical and important will ultimately influence how risk models are prepared. The relationship of SQRA and schedule quality is undeniable.

It is for this reason that the quality of schedule input can turn out to be the project's number one risk driver.

4.2.   SQRA Preparation Guideline

The overall schedule network starts with one constrained start milestone and end in one finish milestone that is not constrained.

Imagine a spider web that starts from one point; with the network slowly expanding intricately through the timeline and gradually receding to a singular milestone at the end (see Figure 14 and Figure 15).

Changing the data date to equal the project start date can also do the trick instead of constraining the start milestones.

Avoid constraining any activity unless necessary. There should be good reason in every constraint. If there is no good reason for a constraint, remove it. All constraints must be approved and agreed-to by all schedule stakeholders. There should be no hard constraint except the one mentioned in the project start date. A hard constraint is an expression of 100% certainty. The fact that the project needs to consider is nobody on this earth can predict that an activity will happen at a particular date with one hundred percent certainty.

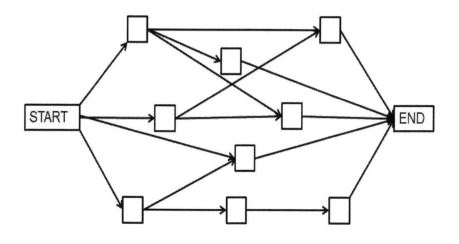

Figure 14 - Level 1 Integrated Schedule Precedence Diagram

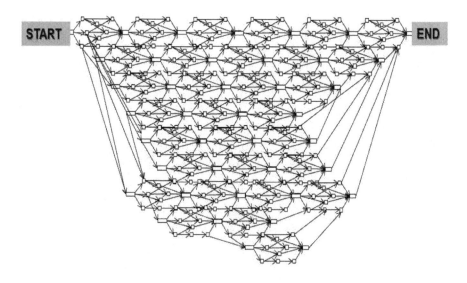

Figure 15 - Level 3 Integrated Schedule Precedence Diagram

Constraints limit the team's options. A project manager should determine whether there are unrealistic constraints that may cause risk to prevent the possibility of project success. Constraints are not risks, but they may cause risks. Who imposed the constraints is not the main concern in a high-level review of constraints (Mulcahy, Risk Management Tricks of the Trade for Project Managers, 2013)

The scheduler should be careful in assigning constraint to an activity just basing on assumptions. It must be borne in mind that assumptions are happenings that we believe will happen with no previous indication. It is not a result of a thorough investigation or a reasonable thinking process. An intelligent Project Manager should test the rationality of every assumption because it has a definite impact to the success and failure of the project. An assumption is something that has a high probability of occurring. In many ways, making an assumption is like risk identification. If it is, make sure to label it as risk and include in the quantification process.

Note that a milestone activity does not contribute to the risk calculation. Changing a normal activity to a milestone activity, we are in effect saying that this activity will not be a schedule driver. It becomes a marker because there is no effort associated with that milestone.

Tie the schedule logically from start to end. To ensure that there is no schedule disconnect, the logic should flow freely and calculation set to retained logic. There should be no broken link (Figure 15).

The project can constrain a select milestone only if it is a project goal and should not tie to any activity in the schedule. It will be a flag for judging the success of the schedule when doing analysis. In a sense, it is not really part of the schedule but a marker. Example: Milestone No. 1 = EDS Complete would be a constrained activity without any logic link. It sits in the schedule but as a marker.

It is important to remember that a schedule answers the question "when?" and should always have a beginning and an end. A start milestone has no end date, while a finish milestone has no start date. Both of them do not have duration or resources. Although an important fixture of scheduling, they are more of a checklist.

Note that all of the constraints added in the schedule will be considered in the risk analysis calculation except "As Late as Possible" (ALAP) relationships (see Section 4.8), which will be ignored by the tool. Consider only activities outside the control of the project. These includes external party supplied materials, hardware, or software.

They are activities or milestones tied to appropriate activities in the schedule.

In the analysis, these activities represent delivery constraints defined by the uncertainty distribution associated with the delivery date. This is more of an exception than a rule.

Minimize hammock-type level of effort (LOE) activities in the schedule as much as possible. Do not convert them to activities when translating to OPRA. Make sure that the project schedule was set to "Retained Logic." This is also a good setting to flush out the out-of-sequence activities, which could derail the risk analysis calculation.

Do not use more calendars in the project schedule than practicable. Avoid naming calendars differently even though they have the same attributes. There should be no actualized dates beyond the data date. All dates beyond the data date of the schedule are invalid dates.

Remove all expected finish dates for activities that have not yet started. An expected finish date assignment should be done only on an activity that has already started.

If an activity needs to be included in the risk analysis, it must be an activity, not a milestone. It is important to emphasize here that a milestone carries no risk input. Avoid external links. External links uploaded to OPRA will act like mandatory constraints. It is important that the project manager establish what I have called a "Ready for Schedule Quantitative Risk-Criteria" (RSQRA-C). This is a list of schedule quality benchmarks representing the minimum schedule quality (MSQ) requirements.

This is an excellent approach geared to remove as much inherent risk as possible in the project schedule. By removing a substantial amount of inherent risks, a project can reduce high risks that are already affecting or have potential to affect the schedule. The end goal is to improve the project's overall chance of being on time.

It is a good idea to do schedule clean-ups on a daily basis while working in the live schedule. The RSQRA-C should be approved and agreed to by all stakeholders before it can be used to govern the questions surrounding "limit and values" of schedule quality. Make sure that schedule coding follows your company's standard scheduling global codes. This includes your resources and calendars.

4.3.   Planning Inputs Required for a Successful SQRA

Relevant and driving planning documents must be ready as reference three (3) to four (4) weeks before quantitative risk analysis workshop. These critical documents provide necessary information in formulating a result.

The documents required are:

- List of schedule's key and critical milestones
- Participative planning minutes of meeting and attendance sheet, including action plans. These documents ensure that all schedule stakeholders were involved in the planning process and support the developed schedule
- Input sheet, also called risk interview worksheet (see Figure 16). This typical worksheet designed for traditional duration ranging and risk analysis review helps a lot. It provides an outstanding perspective on why the subject matter expert (SME) and/or stakeholders provided the 3-point estimate values they have given.

	A	B	C	D	E	F	G	H	I	J	K	L	M	N	O	P
	Activity ID	Activity Name	Rem Dur	Start	Finish	Budgeted Labor Units	Remaining Labor Units	At Completion Labor Units	Min Duration	Most Likely	Max Duration	Resources	Budgeted Nonlabor Units	Rem Nonlabor Units	At Comp Nonlabor Units	Short Description of Risk (if any)
2	Batangas Upgrader-Phase 1															
3	Batangas Upgrader-Stages															
4	Detailed Engineering			19-Apr-10 A	29-Nov-10											
5	Project Management															
6	BATS-1230	Building Permit	15	28-Sep-10	21-Oct-10				15	15	20					
7	WR: Well Manifold Module															
8	BATS-1255	Bid Clarifications - Well Ma	6	15-Jul-10	26-Jul-10				6	6	8					
9	BATS-1260	RFP - Well Manifold Module	10	06-Aug-10	20-Aug-10				7	10	15					
10	WR: VFD Building Module															
11	BATS-1270	RFQ - VFD Building Module	10	03-Aug-10	17-Aug-10				8	10	15					
12	BATS-1290	TBE / RFP - VFD Building M	10	15-Sep-10	29-Sep-10				6	10	15					
13	Process / Value Improving Practices															
14	4-BATS-1220	P&ID IFC (Module)	10	24-Jun-10 A	23-Jul-10				10	10	10					
15	4-BATS-1220	LDT IFC (Module)	10	30-Jun-10 A	23-Jul-10				10	10	10					
16	4-BATS-1240	P&ID IFC (Off-Module)	8	26-Jul-10	06-Aug-10				8	8	13					
17	4-BATS-1260	LDT IFC (Off-Module)	8	26-Jul-10	06-Aug-10				8	8	13					
18	4-BATS-1280	Shutdown Key IFC	10	09-Aug-10	23-Aug-10				10	10	15					
19	4-BATS-1300	Control Philosophy IFC	10	16-Aug-10	30-Aug-10				10	10	15					

Figure 16 - Risk Analysis Interview Sheet

- The XER (Primavera native file) of the deterministic schedule is preferred over a file located in a common database or folder. This file contains the schedule for risk analysis. The submission is best through an official e-mail transmittal to document the official transmittal. In this way, there will be no confusion as to what file will be analyzed. This ensures that the schedule data do not change because of someone modifying the same source file while quantification is going on. It is very important that the project stakeholders have reviewed the submitted schedule. It has to have their buy in. Try to use the schedule with the latest update for the risk analysis to be much more meaningful.

DO NOT USE A STALE SCHEDULE! Use the most current schedule as the risk model. Doing a risk analysis on a schedule that is already more than one update behind is not good. More than two updates behind is worst.

Why would anyone in his right mind run the risk quantification exercise on an old schedule? How would the analyst handle hundreds of remaining activities already actualized? There is no acceptable way out of this situation even if the analyst made sure that all actualized activities are sitting on their right dates before SQRA commences. These activities will move during iteration. Actualized activities are not supposed to move because they are now certain. It is for this reason, that the latest version of the current schedule is the best model to use when running SQRA.

These are rhetorical questions and you must know the answer. Unfortunately, you will be surprised with what is really going on. Many projects keep violating this best practice for whatever reason.

- If the project has already undertaken schedule quantitative risk analysis on their own, the duly designated risk analyst has to double-check the results. He has to get the OPRA PLAN file for inspection, the narrative report of the risk analysis done, including tornados, duration sensitivity, criticality, cruciality, SSI, criticality distribution profile, and duration distribution charts for the whole project, and select key activities under assessment. Ensure that the risk analysis was according to governing standards and procedures of the organization.
- Approved basis of schedule (schedule basis and methodology)
- Schedule check report based on the business' established minimum schedule quality criteria. If these are not yet available to your project organization as a benchmark, then it is about time to get them!
- Approved estimate summary
- Approved basis of estimate
- Approved detailed estimate
- Latest/updated risk register
- Approved/updated project charter
- Latest/updated project execution plan
- Project kick-off presentation
- Latest project monthly report
- Assumption log and constraint log

4.4.   Who Are Required to Participate?

Project stakeholders or their duly designated representatives (delegates) are the best participants in SQRA. They have the authority to give inputs in behalf of the group they belong. They are there to answer whatever clarifying question might come up during the SQRA facilitated process.

Stakeholders who have the power to decide and influential objectively on matters involving their individual discipline or expertise are invited.

Some SQRA facilitators try to avoid inviting managers and directors from the session because the perception is they end up babying the project, mixing bias into their inputs. Front-end specialists and experts often come up with excellent objective feedbacks.

If management participates, it is more to balance overall perspective, help facilitate collaboration, provide relevant management information, and encourage free speech among the front-end leaders and disciplines. It is suggested that the planner/scheduler, senior risk specialist, and risk manager facilitates the session. They develop a strategy on how to extract the best information.

List of SQRA stakeholders

- Engineering Leads
- Procurement Leads
- Contracting Leads
- Controls Specialists
- Planning and Scheduling Specialists
- Construction Foremen
- Modularization Foremen
- Fabrication Foremen
- Senior Risk Specialist or Risk Manager (facilitate or guide the facilitator)
- Project Manager
- Engineering Manager
- Project Controls Manager
- Risk Manager
- Safety Manager
- Others, as needed

Item 15, others essentially points to a list of additional and relevant project

67

personnel who can provide valuable input on any risks associated with and/or affecting the schedule; e.g. regulatory specialists, camp coordinators, contractor representative, union representatives, progress specialists, commissioning and start up leads, and so on. Whoever can fill that existing information gap is a potential invitee.

4.5.   Minimum Schedule Quality (MSQ)

Ready for Schedule Quantitative Risk Analysis Criteria (RSQRA-C) is a list of select schedule quality benchmarks or metrics that need to be satisfied before carrying out schedule quantitative risk analysis. The criteria represent the minimum schedule quality requirement needed to produce a reliable SQRA result.

By attaining or exceeding the set schedule quality, the business or the project will, in effect, prevent or mitigate most of the high inherent schedule risks. Risk prevention and risk reduction are two best techniques of achieving the project objectives.

TIP   The schedule serves as the input data to SQRA. The higher its quality, the more reliable the quantified risk result will be and vice-versa.

4.6.   Hard or Mandatory Constraints

Hard constraints are firm, compulsory, or two-way constraints applied to remaining schedule activities; i.e. "Must Start On" or "Must Finish On" constraints.

Imposing a date in the schedule can delay the start and finish date for no good reason. It interrupts network logic.

The number of mandatory constraint, with the exception of the project start date, should be equal to ZERO. Avoiding mandatory constraints is best practice. It is important to flag, inspect, validate, and explain any mandatory constraint

If the explanation of the schedule owner is acceptable or the constraint is part of the schedule risk model, the risk analyst excuses the activity count pertaining thereto.

Do not consider completed, summary and LOE activities because they no longer add value to the forecast. Include only normal activities and milestones that are planned and in-progress.

Consider using soft constraints instead of mandatory if constraints are necessary. This quality benchmark uses hard count of activities, not percent. Release all constraints along the critical path of a schedule.

Even one mandatory constraint indiscriminately set in place can change the whole complexion of the project schedule. It will generate its own critical path while excluding other activities that might be more or equally critical and important.

It is the same as adding 100% certainty to an activity and completely defeating the SQRA process.

Do review Section 3.5 of this book for additional information.

4.7.   Soft Constraints

Soft constraints are one-way constraints applied to remaining scheduling activities; i.e. Start No Earlier Than or Finish No Later Than. Soft Constraints is acceptable if used as part of the risk model, are agreed-to assumptions, reliable information, and/or an expression of contractual commitment. Use them sparingly.

The number of Soft Constraints should not be more than ten (<10) but preferably less than five (<5). Ideal number of soft constraints is ZERO. If explanation is acceptable, exclude the activity count pertaining thereto.

A narrative explanation of soft constraints is in the schedule assumption table. They are best included in a planning document called Schedule Basis and Methodology or often called, Basis of Schedule (BOS).

Soft constraints affect CPM calculation but it is not as impactful as hard constraints. Review the resulting critical path of a schedule with constraints carefully.

There is also a tendency to bring rigidness into the schedule resulting in possible loss of opportunities. Limiting the earliest date an activity can begin on is tantamount to removing that opportunity.

The imposition of the date will ignore an opening to do the work earlier. Limiting the latest date an activity can finish on is tantamount to removing the flexibility of the schedule to flow.

The imposition of the date will ignore an opening to do the work later even if it is for the schedule's benefit.

All soft constraints must be explained and reflected upon in a schedule assumption table, which is best included in a planning document called the schedule basis and methodology, or often called the basis of schedule (BOS).

4.8.　As Late As Possible

As late as possible is a special type of soft constraint that forces the activity to start as late as possible without impact to Early or Late dates applied to remaining activities. ALAP is unlike other soft constraints.

The others fix an activity to a single direction while the ALAP permits the activity to slide to both directions dependent on its governing successor activity.

Tasks are scheduled as-late-as-possible (ALAP) based upon the target end date. ALAP also refers to activities with Zero Free Float (ZFF). Further discussion is widely available in the net between ZFF, and ALAP.

In a well-crafted schedule, one cannot start activities earlier than their early start and cannot finish later than their late finish without affecting the critical path. Actual times should fall into this envelope.

The contractors want to finish non-critical activities as early as possible, and paid a lot sooner. In addition, there is no blame for the delay. The owner wants them to finish non-critical activities as late as possible to lessen the risk of change.

Usually intuitive resource leveling dictates the contractors spread out the non-critical activities anyway. For these reasons it is recommended to give the contractors as much access to float as possible but also that they schedule non-critical activities at the "last responsible moment" (McManus, 2009. AACE Forum on Early dates and Late dates).

As Late as Possible constraints in this case does not affect the calculation of the Quantitative Risk Analysis but affects and works against critical path method (CPM) in a regular scheduling work environment.

OPRA tool ignores ALAP. Risk simulation, and calculation releases the ALAP constraints. Some other risk analysis application considers ALAP in its calculation. The analyst must be aware of these differences between tools.

ALAP should be avoided as much as you can, selectively used, and with intelligence.

The number of Soft Constraints should not be more than ten (<10) but preferably less than five (<5). Ideal number of ALAP is ZERO.

If part of an overall strategy, use them sparingly.

All soft constraints must be explained and reflected in a schedule assumption table which is best included in a planning document called Schedule Basis and Methodology or often called, Basis of Schedule (BOS).

While not considered as overriding as hard constraints nor the soft constraints mentioned earlier, ALAP impact CPM calculation in P6.

ALAP can create an artificial critical path in a schedule as shown in the example.

Initially, Activity E has no ALAP constraint in Figure 17. To demonstrate the effect of an ALAP, Activity E is constrained (see Figure 18).

When calculated, the critical path shifted from A-B-C-F-G to A-B-C-E-F-G. We can now see that Activity E is in the critical path.

ALAP changed the complexion of the schedule. It produces an artificial critical path.

Blanket assignment of ALAP constraints changes the dates of the activities belonging to the existing critical path. It shows the longest path (LP) without ALAP.

The whole schedule becomes critical. The float disappears by targeting the late dates (Figure 19 and Figure 20).

When the identification of the critical path becomes questionable, the project loses an effective handle to effective management. There will be missed opportunities and plenty of wasted resources.

People will end up concentrating on activities that are least important. Non-driving activities will be falsely identified as driving activities. Confusion and chaos will eventually take over.

Projects will spend time and resources on activities and work packages that are not really critical while real drivers continue to deteriorate and become more serious.

Great losses become serious consequences.

A runner going in the opposite direction will never win a race even if he has more stamina and runs the fastest. Project managers must exercise great care in allowing ALAP in the guise of just in time strategy or satisfying construction required at site (RAS) dates. Without selective and intelligent application, it can bring in troubles!

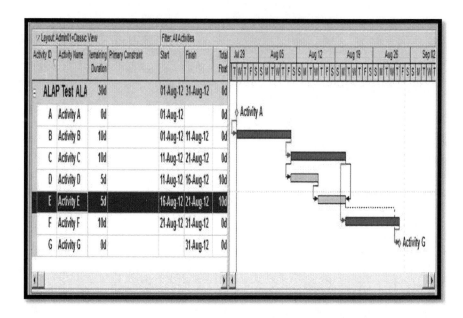

Figure 17 - Schedule ABC without ALAP Constraint

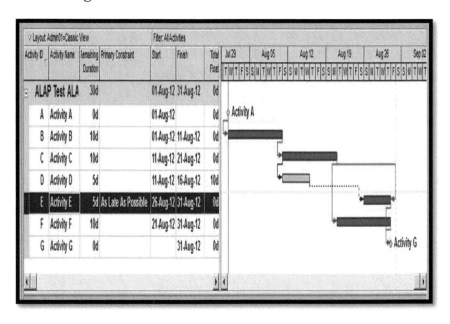

Figure 18 - Schedule ABC with ALAP Constraint

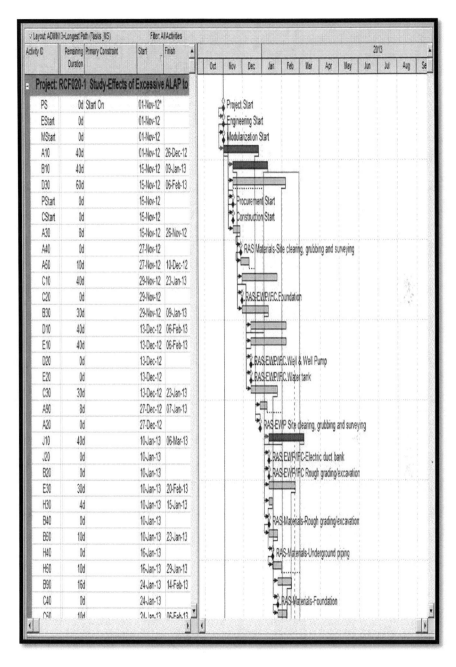

Figure 19 - Project RCF020-1 Shows LP without ALAP

73

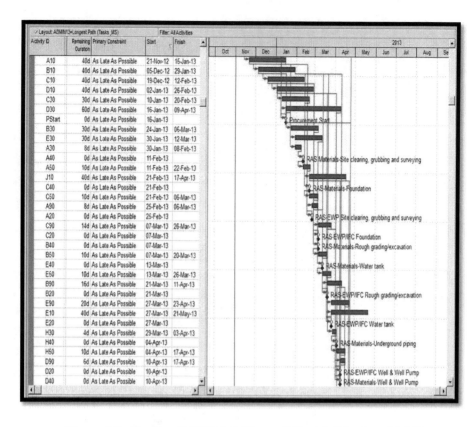

Figure 20 - Project RCF020-1 Shows LP with Blanket ALAP

ALAP constrains and intentionally delays activities without delaying their successor activities. This is risky, as any delay in delivery will then delay work activities. When dealing material delivery using ALAP, give special concern to owner-supplied materials. The scheduler must verify the reasonableness of all durations. Using a production analogy, work-in-progress (WIP) are minimized and not incurring costs earlier than necessary.

From the project manager's viewpoint, there is better focus at the critical start of the project because there are simply not as many tasks scheduled to start. Improper use of ALAP can result in a difficult court claim for the one who uses it. It increases the probability of not being able to complete critical packages in a timely manner and can trick the project into doing non-critical activities first.

All tasks are critical once you are in tracking mode. An increase in duration of any task will push out the project end date by an increased amount.

Student syndrome: This refers to the phenomenon that many people will only start seriously working on a task just at the last possible moment before a deadline (Wikipedia, Student Syndrome, 2014). This leads to wasting any buffers built into individual task duration estimates (Goldratt, 1997).

Simply said, student syndrome is procrastination. The project can use up all valuable free float without even realizing it, because the activity is not yet on the radar. With the float already gone, the tasks must be perfect, and the delivery dates achieved at all cost. Any little change in the situation can now result in medium to major delay.

Relying on "As Late as Possible" dates means that the schedule will have an increased probability of not being able to complete (provided it is not impossible to achieve) on time since there is no more room for anything being late. This is a very risky thing to do. Instead, define a "deadline" date for the completion milestones and schedule. Let the scheduling tool computes. If the date is not viable, the project has to change the plan.

ALAP absorbs only the float (free float). It does not affect successor activities but successor activities affect them. However, in Microsoft Project, it does. It sucks the free float and the total float as well, delaying the successor activities in the process (Harris, 2013).

There are some useful notes to remember before assigning ALAP. These reminders are valuable to project schedulers who directly work on the schedule. See below:

Guidelines to remember before assigning ALAP:

1) Avoid using blanket application of ALAP. Consider this constraint as rarely used except in special situations. Use them wisely, intelligently and "*fit for purpose.*"
2) Evaluate your target objective first before employing ALAP. Always remember that ALAP sucks the float out from the path. It can change the existing critical path(s) and can introduce new challenges to existing strategies.
3) Ensure that the project's objective is specific before applying ALAP. Otherwise, a too general application of ALAP will result in something the project never really intended.
4) ALAP scheduling for convenience will not benefit the project in the end.
5) What comes after ALAP is usually activity delay, as the float is no longer available to play with.
6) Excessive use of ALAP is not a good scheduling practice. It sets the project up for failure.

7) ALAP can result in difficult court claims for the one who is using it.
8) Contractors love to use ALAP when submitting their proposed baseline schedule. They use optimistic schedule when proposing and executing. Clients/owners organization must exercise due diligence in accepting such a schedule. Ensure to test schedule quality first to validate achievability.
9) As much as possible, use ALAP only on non-resource loaded activities such as waiting time, delivery time, documents preparation, and the like. Limit using ALAP on activities requiring direct resources.

4.9. Missing Predecessors

This pertains to an activity that does not have any predecessor. The point of an activity bar that has missing predecessor is an open end. It can be part of a dangler count.

The number of missing predecessors should not be greater than one (< 1); i.e. if the project has not started yet. This means that the number of activities with missing predecessors should be equal to ZERO if the project has already started (project start was already actualized).

The basic rule on schedule dependency, with the exception of the project start, is that every activity in the network diagram should have a predecessor.

Missing predecessors are open-ended deficiencies that cause time and risk analysis calculations to be erroneous.

Open-ends are indications of missing scope, and incomplete or missing planning inputs. Properly tie all activities with open-ends, preferably within the same schedule.

Best practice recommends that the number of normal and valid remaining activities with missing predecessor should be equal to ZERO. It is important to flag, inspect, validate, and explain any open-end.

If the explanation of the schedule owner is acceptable, the risk analyst excuses the activity count pertaining thereto.

Do not consider completed, summary and LOE activities because they no longer add value to the forecast. Include only normal activities and milestones that are planned and in-progress.

4.10. Missing Successors

This pertains to an activity that does not have any successor. The point of an activity bar that has missing successor is an open end. It can also be part of a dangler count.

The number of Missing Successors should not be greater than one (< 1). It means that the only activity allowed with missing successor is one. It is the project end date, after which, there is none.

Missing successors are open-ended deficiencies that cause time and risk analysis calculations to be erroneous. Open-ends are indications of missing scope, and incomplete or missing planning inputs. Properly tie all activities with open-ends, preferably within the same schedule.

Best practice recommends that the number of normal and valid remaining activities with missing successor should be equal to ZERO. It is important to flag, inspect, validate, and explain any open-end. If the explanation of the schedule owner is acceptable, the risk analyst excuses the activity count pertaining thereto.

Do not consider completed, summary and LOE activities because they no longer add value to the forecast. Include only normal activities and milestones that are planned and in-progress.

4.11. Open Start Danglers

Open start danglers are activities where the only predecessor is either Finish-to-Finish or Start-to-Finish resulting in an open start to the activity. They are dangling activities. The number of open start danglers should equal zero. Appropriately tie all schedule activities at each end to avoid danglers.

In Figure 21, Activity A is connected finish-to-finish (FF) relationship to Activity B. However, Activity B remains a dangler. It needs to have a predecessor Activity C connected to its start date in order to complete the proper logic link.

The critical path will not pass through an open start dangler activity because its logical links are incomplete. Nothing is driving the start date of the activity. There is no path to another activity. It is like dead end. The path will traverse towards the FF connected end, skipping activity B to go straight to A. Danglers are activities that usually have large total float, a reflection of their questionably diminished role in the network.

One can use OPRA or Deltek Acumen Fuse, among other tools, to detect danglers. At this time, Primavera cannot detect this deficiency, nor is it generated in the P6 Log Report.

Solution for this type of dangler is to tie both ends of any activity. Activity B below has to have a predecessor. This is an important requirement in OPRA to accurately calculate and iterate all risk inputs and provide a reliable output.

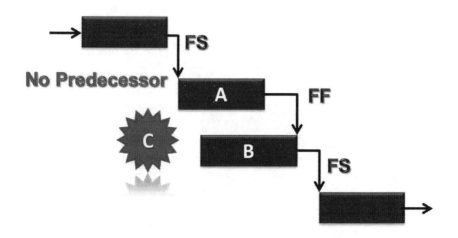

Figure 21 - Example of an Open Start Dangler

4.12. Open Finish Danglers

Open finish danglers are activities where the only successor is either a start-to-finish or start-to-start resulting in an open finish to the activity. They are dangling activities. The number of open finish danglers should equal zero. Appropriately tie all schedule activities at each end to avoid danglers.

In Figure 22, Activity A is connected using start-to-start (SS) relationship to Activity B. However, Activity A remains a dangler. It needs to have a successor Activity C connected to its start date in order to complete the proper logic.

The critical path will not pass through an open finish dangler activity because its logical links are incomplete. Activity A is not driving anything. There is no path to another downstream activity. No activity is relying on its timely completion. The path will traverse towards the SS connected end and skip activity A to go straight to A's predecessor. Danglers are activities that usually have large total float, a reflection of their questionably diminished role in the network.

One can use OPRA or Deltek Acumen Fuse, among other tools, to detect danglers. At this time, Primavera cannot detect this deficiency, nor is it generated in the P6 Log Report.

Solution for this type of dangler is to tie both ends of any activity. Activity A below has to have a successor. This is an important requirement in OPRA to accurately calculate and iterate all risk inputs and provide a reliable output.

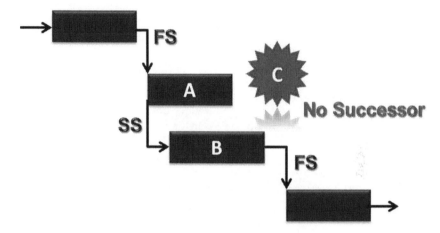

Figure 22 - Example of an Open Finish Dangler

4.13. Negative Float

A negative float means the total float is less than zero. There should not be any negative float in the schedule because it indicates delays, a strong warning that successfully achieving the schedule is not possible.

Therefore, the number of activities with negative float should be zero too. It is important to flag, inspect, validate, and explain the presence of any activities with negative float. When the schedule has negative float, it is an indication that certain deliverables are late.

The final take will depend on what path is affected. If the last deliverables, such as first oil or final turn over, cascade forward into a critical path generated by negative float, then the possibility of project delay becomes more real.

Negative float can be the result of an artificially induced, accelerated, and constrained schedule (see relative critical path in Section 3.5). Assessment based on constrained completion dates are not good representation of an overall critical path. Such constraints must not become a permanent fixture in the schedule.

This what-if methodology is excellent in determining activities impacted by the constraint dates but its usefulness is limited only to the constrained objective.

The schedule is primarily an output more than an input during the schedule development process. The role can reverse when continuous collaboration becomes heavier during the execution phase. In that time, the schedule becomes distinctly both. It becomes an input to planning and an output of planning.

Do not consider completed, summary and LOE activities because they no longer add value to the forecast. Include only normal activities and milestones that are planned and in-progress.

4.14. Out of Sequence Activities

Out of Sequence refers to actualized activities before their successors were completed. The total number of out of sequence activities should be equal to zero. Any number above the benchmark is unacceptable. Correct the culprit activity logic right away. Ensure that calculation of the scheduling tool schedule is set to retained logic.

This quality benchmark counts the number activities, not percent. Even just one out of sequence activity can push certain downstream dates out by a wide margin, for what seems to be no apparent reason. When out of sequence is not controlled, the calculation of the critical path is in error. Management of the schedule becomes difficult unless the offending activity logic is rooted out and corrected.

TIP To identify out of sequence activities, the scheduling tool should be set to "retained logic."

4.15. Excessive Float

This refers to activities with an excessive total float relative the overall project remaining duration or the overall project phase duration. The former points to the whole project, from the start milestones to the last finish milestones, while the latter refers to the duration of each major phase within the project, like engineering, procurement, modularization, fabrication, construction, and commissioning.

The schedule details affect the interpretation of this benchmark. The specific stage of development in the project lifecycle guides metric formulations.

It is imperative that project governance adjust the benchmark parameters according to what make sense.

In consideration of the phase duration approach, and at the EDS stage of schedule development, the recommended benchmarks are as follows:

- Excessive total float is a float greater than 20% of the overall project remaining duration.
- The number of activities with excessive total float should not exceed three. Ideal is ZERO.
- This quality benchmark counts the number activities, not percent.
- Do not consider completed, summary and *LOE* activities because they no longer add value to the forecast. Include only normal activities and milestones that are planned and in-progress.

Looking at the phase duration approach, and at the DBM stage of schedule development, the recommended benchmarks are as follows:

- Excessive total float is a float greater than 30% of the overall project remaining duration.
- The number of activities with excessive total float should not exceed three. Ideal is ZERO.
- This quality benchmark counts the number activities, not percent.

Do not consider completed, summary and *LOE* activities because they no longer add value to the forecast. Include only normal activities and milestones that are planned and in-progress. It is important to flag, inspect, validate, and explain why any activity has excessive total float.

If the explanation of the scheduler is acceptable, the risk analyst excuses the activity count pertaining thereto.

Activities or activity paths with high amounts of float typically arise due to constrained activities or other much longer competing critical paths. The situation is further aggravated if the constraints applied have no merits to them.

Activities installed haphazardly without much thought adds to the problem. The project should consider schedule optimization for paths with a total finish float of more than three months for large to mega projects, two months for medium to large projects and a month for small to medium projects.

The final decision whether to optimization depends on the business representatives or the individuals who own the business. How they see their business influences their action plan. Review Section 3.21 to 3.25 and reflect.

TIP

The project should pursue the opportunity to move and add activities into that big float region without affecting the project completion date.

4.16. Milestone to Activity Ratio

Milestone to Activity (M/A) ratio refers to the number of remaining milestones divided by the total number of remaining active milestones and normal activities.

Example:

Number of Milestones = 50

Number of Normal Tasks = 3000

M/A = 2%

Quality Assessment Result = Passed

This number should not be greater than 10%, or a ratio of 1:10, for projects with greater than 200 activities. For projects with less than 200 activities, the number of milestones starts with five, but does not exceed twenty. If the ratio is greater than 1:10 (10%), then the schedule has too many milestones. The greater the number of milestones, the more updates needed. It adds to the clutters and possibility of scheduling confusion. The 10% demarcation should meet the milestones requirement of any schedule. If the ration resulted in more than 10%, other milestones have to go.

Some project management professionals I spoke with were willing to accept up to 20% milestones and higher. Some said that there is no limitation to the number of milestones, as long as the project needs them. I absolutely do not agree with them. Ten percent is more than enough with very few exceptions. This ratio is an influential metric that tells us whether such fundamental premises of the schedule as "date output" are preserved.

Do not consider completed, summary and LOE activities because they no longer add value to the forecast. Include only normal activities and milestones that are planned and in-progress. It is important to flag, inspect, validate, and explain why any activity has exceeded the ratio limitation guide. If the explanation of the scheduler is acceptable, the risk analyst excuses the activity count pertaining thereto.

 Too many milestones indicate that the schedule is becoming more of a checklist, undermining the recommended fundamental "output philosophy." The milestone to activity benchmark hopes to prevent the project from approving a schedule that is more of a checklist than a logic driven one.

By having too many milestones, the project might be erroneously reflecting what was supposed to be resource-loaded activities as milestones instead of normal activities, completely missing the added opportunity of using resource distribution as a handle in schedule management. The ratio guide will strike the proper balance between milestones and the resource-loaded activities they represent.

A milestone activity is a marker in time representing key deliverables, approvals, key interphases, or the culmination of major work packages. It contains no resources in it. As such, there is no effort associated with them. Therefore, it has no real contribution to the generated schedule output resulting from the calculation of resource and duration inputs. So why would the project want too many milestones incorporated in the schedule? Projects should control the number of milestones they create in their schedule.

4.17. Links to Activity Ratio

Links to activity (L/A) ration points to the number of logical links or relationship ties per remaining activities. The suggested ratio is between two and three, or ideally two and a half (2.5). Logic density™ is another name formulated by Deltek for this ratio.

Review the schedule logics of activities contributing to the ratio of less than two (< 2.0). These activities require additional logic links. A ratio of four (<=4) is the threshold allowed. Logic density above this threshold (> 4.0) is an indication that excessive and compound relationship ties exist within the schedule.

Do not consider completed, summary and LOE activities because they no longer add value to the forecast. Include only normal activities and milestones that are planned and in-progress. It is important to flag, inspect, validate, and explain why any activity has gone beyond the L/A ratio limitation. If the explanation of the scheduler is acceptable, the risk analyst excuses the activity count pertaining thereto.

The schedule becomes unnecessarily complex by having too many unneeded relationships. This makes the schedule a lot harder to understand and manage. Therefore, some control should be set in place. As the L/A ratio increases, logic redundancy increases and the chance of error increases, affecting the schedule's critical path calculation. If that happens, the outcome of SQRA is in question. As such, identifying and removing redundant logics (Figure 23) using the L/A ratio.

Using Acumen Fuse, the analyst can fix high logic density using redundancy index™ (RI) benchmark and logic analysis. If your project has this kind of analytic tool, use it.

According to some scheduling professionals, RI is a better measure to use than L/A ratio. I see it as just a matter of preference borne out of exposure. The added bonus of using a tool such as Deltek Acumen Fuse is that the planners and schedulers can automatically clean and remove all redundant logic and export the clean schedule back to the main scheduling tool to replace the previous one in just a few minutes.

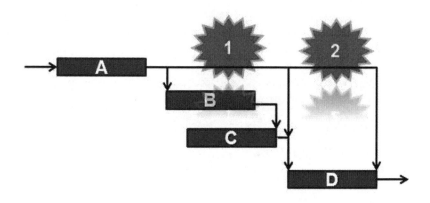

Figure 23 - Redundant Logic 1 and 2

4.18. Activities with External Links

These are activities with relationships tied to activities outside the subject schedule. It can be the links between activities of an open project to another project and sub-project in the same database, or an external database.

If we import an EPC schedule for analysis from a contractor database into our own, receiving an XER that does not include the engineering and procurement (EP) schedule, we will have external links!

Do not consider completed, summary and LOE activities because they no longer add value to the forecast. Include only normal activities and milestones that are planned and in-progress. It is important to flag, inspect, validate, and explain why any the schedule have external links.

If the explanation of the scheduler is acceptable (seldom does), the risk analyst excuses the activity count pertaining thereto.

OPRA will question external links. P6 can identify and flag external links by using a combination of layout and filter. Deltek Acumen Fuse (Schedule Analytic) can do the same.

If there are several sub-projects comprising the whole project, with logic links connecting each area, it is good practice to open all of them when making the analysis. Otherwise, the links to the unopened projects are external links.

Connections to them will display as activities with constrained dates, making the schedule unable to flow freely. The analyst should avoid this from happening.

A successful SQRA depends greatly on the ability of the subject schedule to flow based on sound logic during iteration and simulation. To prevent external links, bring all activities as part of a singular project file, either as representative activities or milestones.

4.19. FS Negative Lags

This metric refers to all activities in the schedule using Finish to Start (FS) Activity Relationships with negative lag (Figure 24). Finish-to-start means that a successor activity can only start if and only if its predecessor finishes.

It pushes the start date of a driven activity out when the completion date of the first activity pushes out. It puts the second activity completely at the mercy of the first activity.

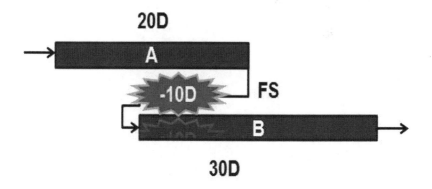

Figure 24 - *FS* Relationship with -10D Lag

The total number of remaining activities using FS relationships with negative lag should equal to zero. FS negative lags or leads adjust the successor start date relative to the FS logic link applied. It can result in critical path calculation error when the successor tries to start before the start of the predecessor.

This usually happens when the negative lag becomes greater than the updated duration of the predecessor activity (Figure 25).

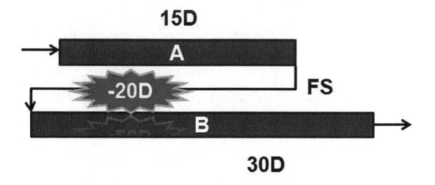

Figure 25 - *FS* with -20D Lag or Invalid Negative Lag

The 2006 AACE International Transaction, PS.02 white paper-"The Great Negative Lag Debate" by Winter, Douglas, Calvey, and McDonald, provided some insights into the pros and cons of using negative lags.

A good example of a project situation using FS negative lag is as follow. The supervisor who is in charge of a building structure said, "I will start installing the leave-out steels two weeks prior to the pipe installation being complete.

The foreman has decided that two weeks prior to the piping discipline concluding their work, he will mobilize his steel workforce to start work on the remaining steel members."

The problem with using negative lag is the common knowledge that any lag is not transparent. A lag is not normally visible. It revolves around the start of the successor work based on a forecasted duration and completion rather than the normal push of the predecessor. Updating can result in an invalid negative lag.

Unless the finish date is with 100% certainty, negative lags can create the issue just described. The reality to accept is that there is really nobody who can predict that something will happen exactly as planned.

4.20. SS Negative Lags

This metric refers to all activities in the schedule using Start to Start (SS)

Activity Relationships with negative lag (Figure 26). Start-to-start relationship means that a successor activity can only start if and only if its predecessor starts.

Delaying the start of driving activity pushes the start date of driven activity out. It puts the start date of second activity completely at the mercy of the first activity. Relationship like this should be revisited to check if absolutely needed. Usually, the successor activity is better tied to another more relevant and logical activity.

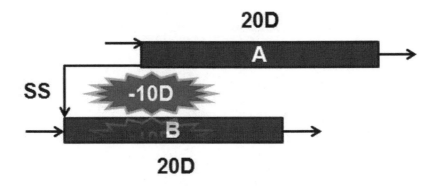

Figure 26 - *SS* relationship with -10D Lag

The total number of remaining activities using SS relationships with negative lag should be equal to zero. It is not recommended practice to use negative lags.

Total count of this metric includes normal activities and milestones that are planned and in-progress. Completed activities are generally ignored unless lags are connected to those completed activities. Be aware that Primavera has special default setting that plays a big role in how lags are handled and calculated.

The activity count should only include normal activities and milestones that are planned and in-progress.

A schedule that falls above the benchmark is suspect. It has to undergo validation.

If to be retained as-is, it should be explained.

TIP
SS relationship with negative lag is not necessary. Negative lag can be expressed using positive lag (Figure 27).

By reversing the sequence of activities, the scheduler can use a positive lag instead.

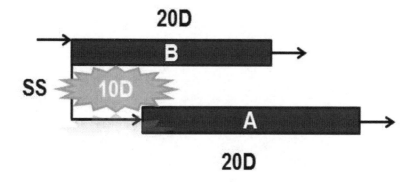

Figure 27 - Equivalent Logic of *SS* (-10D Lag)

Positive lag makes the lag concept easier to understand and the schedule less complicated to managers, especially during critical path tracing.

They will question why the critical path passed through certain activities with SS negative lags. The explanation and discussion that will ensue can be long.

The foreman-in-charge of pouring the foundation said, "I will pour concrete four weeks prior to the compressor set date."

He has decided that four weeks prior to the compressor being set on the foundation, he will start his pour.

The statement is good but expressing it with a logic using negative lag is better avoided because it can be expressed a lot better using positive lag.

Lags expressed as normal activities are more acceptable in many cases. Lags are now visible when expressed as regular activities. It makes the schedule more manageable.

4.21. FF Negative lags

This metric refers to all activities in the schedule using Finish to Finish (FF) Activity Relationships with negative lag (Figure 28).

Finish-to-finish means that a successor activity can only finish if and only if its predecessor finishes.

Extending the driving activity pushes the driven activity out. It puts the second activity completely at the mercy of the first activity.

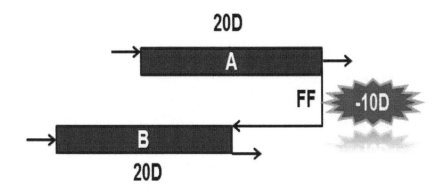

Figure 28 - *FF* Relationship with -10D Lag

The total number of remaining activities using FF relationships with negative lag should equal to zero. Do not count completed, summary and LOE activities. They do not add value to forecast.

The activity count should only include normal activities and milestones that are planned and in-progress.

FF relationship with negative lag (Figure 26) is not necessary. Negative lag can be expressed using positive lag (Figure 29). By reversing the sequence of activities, the scheduler can use a positive lag instead.

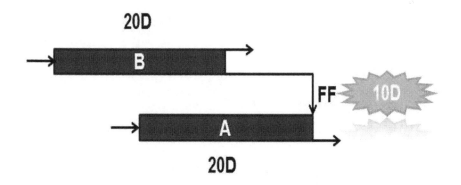

Figure 29 - *FF* (-10 lag) Expressed as Positive Lag

Positive lag makes the lag concept easier to understand and the schedule less complicated to managers, especially during critical path tracing. Includes normal activities and milestones that are planned and in-progress.

The 2006 AACE International Transaction, PS.02 write-up-"The Great Negative Lag Debate" by Winter, Douglas, Calvey, and McDonald, provided some insights into the pros and cons of using negative lags.

Here is an example of a FF negative lag situation.

The Piping/Instrumentation Engineer said- "I will complete and issue the line designation table (LDT IFC) twenty days (20D) before the 90% Model Review is scheduled to complete.

The Engineers have decided that five working weeks prior to the scheduled completion of the 90% Model Review, they will complete their LDT EWP/IFC.

The statement is good but expressing it in a schedule with a logic using positive lag is better (Figure 29). Express lags as normal activities. Normal activities are visible. They make the schedule more manageable.

One must be aware that when the duration of predecessor considerably decreased to equal or less than the assigned negative lag, the logic becomes unreasonable and has to change, as shown in Figure 30.

This is where a positive lag becomes the solution (Figure 28).

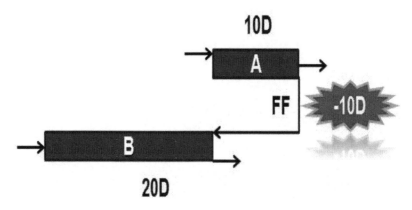

Figure 30 - Duration of Predecessor Decreased Considerably

4.22. SF Relationship

SF Relationships refers to Start to Finish (SF) logic links between activities.

The total number of remaining activities using SF relationship should equal zero. The activity count should only include normal activities and milestones that are planned and in-progress.

The use of "Start-to-Finish" (SF) logical link is not common. They have an unusual effect to activities. It is rare that the successor happens before the predecessor.

It is poor practice to use this type of activity relationship. Many get confused explaining to people what SF indicates. It is right to avoid using the SF relationship as much as possible.

An example of SF relationship provides a good perspective. Very few example of SF applied with common sense comes across projects. A number of scheduler uses it to massage the schedule to come up with an adjusted forecast date. Workforce schedule of an operating plant uses SF more frequently than other application.

Example:

Tony, the Head Operator of a production plant is about to end his 7 am to 3 pm duty and is waiting for his relief. Ben, the person coming in to replace him is due to work from 3 pm to 11 pm shift. Tony will not be able to leave unless Ben starts his shift. The relationship demonstrated between Ben (Predecessor) and Tony (Successor) is an excellent example of SF logic, i.e. the predecessor Ben has to start first before the successor Tony can finish.

4.23. Consequences of Poor Schedule Quality

- Schedule is counter-intuitive, disconnected, or disjointed.
- Poor project management and control.
- Flawed schedule quantitative risk analysis.
- Wrong critical path
- Wrong probability calculation
- Miscommunication and communication breakdown
- Inaccurate if not missing inputs to plan
- Negative effect on productivity
- Adverse effect on achievability
- Unclear scheduling strategy
- Unclear results and expectations
- Lost opportunity to manage the project better
- Increases the threat to project objectives
- Creates confusions
- Work strategy can become ineffective

- Flaws in resource distribution analysis
- Managing resources more challenging
- Resource leveling will be in error
- False risk and performance indicators generated
- Wrong progress report
- Unable to assess scope and schedule achievability accurately
- Project misalignment
- Scope is less clear
- Missing scope, schedule is incomplete

Chapter 5

Schedule Quantitative Risk Analysis

5.1. Introduction to SQRA

CPM scheduling software like Primavera Project Management (P6), MS Project, or other programs application feature when it comes to risk analysis is quite limited. This is why several other applications cater to the specialized requirement of risk quantification. The deterministic schedule we see using our plain scheduling tools like Primavera and Microsoft Project can only give the following information.

- They predict a single completion date and cost.
- They use single values for activity durations and costs.
- They do not really take uncertainty and risks into account.

Schedule quantitative risk analysis quantifies the overall probability or chance of completing a project on time and on budget. The quantification process uses various distribution profiles, like a three point estimate for duration and costs (for example, using min, most likely, and max). The three points estimate method is what many call the traditional method of quantification. It looks at risk events and estimate uncertainties. These are two distinct elements of a three-point estimate (Figure 31 and Figure 32).

An estimate is a projected value of a certain quantity like labor hours, number of elbows, fittings, bolts and nuts using scientific methods available. Adding to this uncertainty is the uncertainty brought about by risk events if they are to happen; e.g. cable pulling estimate during the winter months of December to February will take longer than when the activity will occur during the summer months of July to August. A good project risk analyst recognizes them using the project schedule.

Accurate modeling is required if a risk analyst does not want to unnecessarily slant the results. Uncertainties are captured using risk factors and their accompanying ranges. Risk events come from the risk register and issue logs. It is good practice to consider positive and negative risks as equally important. The schedule reviewer should consider at least two types of risks. One is the inherent risks, often referred to as systemic risks. The second one is project-specific risks.

This chapter will revisit the fundamentals of risk, risk probability, and impact. An introduction to qualitative and quantitative risk analysis is included to provide a preview to some of the schedule analytics and generated reports. An explanation of the key benefits associated with the proper management of risks highlights the practical application of risk-based management.

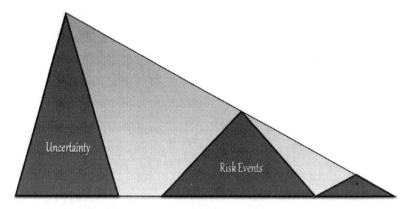

Figure 31 - Components of a Three-Point Estimate

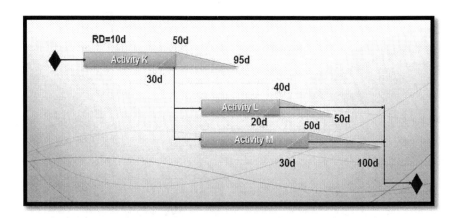

Figure 32 - Gantt Showing Dynamics of the 3-Point Estimate

5.2. Let Us Picture Risk

Mark is boarding a plane and heard one passenger in front of him remarks jokingly that the chance of the plane reaching its destination is 50% (Figure 33).

It is just a joke but the statement demonstrates the probability component of risk. Probability is the certainty of something happening.

Since risk is the effect of uncertainty on objective, the objective of reaching the destination is only 50% certain. Another way of looking at it is by saying it is 50% uncertain.

What can be some of the possible consequences a passenger might be thinking? A new passenger might be anxious and entertain the thought of the plane crashing. A less experienced passenger might entertain the thought that plane might be diverted to another place due to some emergency or threat.

A more experienced passenger might say that no real risk is present and that the plane will reach the destination on time. The perspective of an observer depends largely on the specific risk identified, plus his knowledge and experience on the subject.

Figure 33 - Probability Surrounding Air Travel

5.3. Visual Example of Impact

Figure 34 shows a collapsed bridge, the consequence of water a surge brought about by a typhoon and heavy rains that went on for days. The risk of the bridge collapsing was identified a year before. A key risk indicator is the erosion of its foundation from previous storms and floods.

95

The consequence of the bridge finally failing brought other major consequence such as death, property damage, disruption to commerce and education, transport issues, health problems, etc.

Figure 34 - A Collapsed Bridge after a Strong Typhoon

The burned down busses shown in Figure 35 are the consequence of an alleged rebel coercive tactic of collecting tax from a large operating plant in one South East Asian country. The group doused the busses with gasoline, and then ignited them using rocket propelled grenades (RPGs).

The risk manager or safety officer is aware of the threat, but has dismissed the probability of the event occurring. Fortunately, there were no casualties. The key risk indicator (KRI) is the fact that there were numerous sightings of the group within a ten kilometers radius of the plant six to nine months before the burning incident happened.

The burning incident disrupted bus service to and from work. It incurred additional costs to plant management when forced to provide security and military escorts. Some employees resigned for fear of their life. Rumors also circulated that the company had succumbed to the demands of the group's progressive taxation in order to prevent further losses. Management paid additional pay incentives to employees to allay their fears. This type of risk is quite common in many countries of the world and companies learn to manage their way through, one way or another.

Figure 35 - Rebels Burned Company Busses

5.4. Visualizing Risk Probability

One way to visualize risks is to look at the picture of a situation or the situation itself. Hold it in front of you and imagine that you are there. If you are actually in there, ask yourself why? What is your purpose of being there? Are you there in behalf of an enterprise? Are you there to help or to document what is happening? What are the boundaries dictating your actions? What can you give? Are you a neutral observer whose interest is for the general good?

Figure 36 shows portions of a flooded metropolitan. What do you see? What is it to you? If you are on a sturdy boat taking this picture, the possibility is small that you will consequently end up in the water. In any case, that is still a risk you might want to consider. The fact that some people are in dirty floodwater, conjure up the risks of diseases eventually contracted by them. You can calculate that such a probability is high. Thinking about risk in terms of probability should be easy enough as long as you think about the consequence within the framework of your objectives or the objectives of the entity you represents.

Figure 36 - Flooding Scenario in Asia

5.5.   Monte Carlo and Latin Hypercube Simulation

Monte Carlo (MC) simulation is the name given to a method of analysis that runs iterations to produce a statistical result. This is opposed to deriving a function that would give the required result (often an almost impossible task in anything but the simplest of plans).

Latin Hypercube (LH) simulation is a stratified method of sampling a distribution that gives outcomes nearer the theoretical values of the input distribution with less iteration.

The efficacy of Monte Carlo (MC) or Latin Hypercube (LH) has nothing to do with the type of model, (e.g. cost estimate or schedule). It is practically just a question of how much time it takes to reach stability and coming up with the results.

Generally, LH stabilizes results quicker than MC. However, a Monte Carlo simulation of a schedule with few activities could stabilize quicker than a Latin Hypercube simulation of a cost estimate or schedule having many input ranges.

Monte Carlo takes the three points estimate representation of each activity (represented by the triangle), and divides it up into equal segments. The tool samples a random segment in each iteration. Randomness, makes it less likely but possible that the same sample segment is selected more than once.

Each iteration is a "what-if" scenario of the project. One thousand iterations are like looking at 1000 project scenarios.

This means that a thousand iterations are like looking at the same project one thousand times, with a different situation each time. The value of each three points range can skew the overall distribution of the result.

Latin Hypercube does the same, but without repeating previously sampled values. Each sample is unique. To conclude, the black box sampling method provides a better representation of the risk model. It is also relatively faster even though we are really talking only time units in seconds.

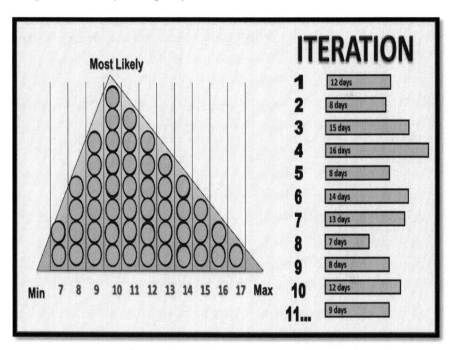

Figure 37 - Monte Carlo versus Latin Hypercube Iteration

5.6. Risk Analysis Tools and Techniques

The PMBOK Guide briefly explains the tools that can be used for qualitative risk assessment. An aspiring risk manager can use risk probability and impact assessment, probability and impact matrices, risk data quality assessment, risk categorization, risk urgency assessment, and expert judgment (PMI, Project Risk Management Overview, 2013).

Many risk practitioners adopt the processes described in Figure 7.

The result of quantitative risk analysis depends largely on the data gathering and representation techniques, because these affect the quality of the input data. Quantitative risk analysis and modelling techniques can use any tool designed for the purpose, like OPRA (previously Pertmaster), Crystal Ball, @Risk, the Decision Tools, Neural Tools, and others.

5.7.   Risk Management Application and Benefits

Since risk management caters to cost, schedule, quality, safety, and other project deliverables, we can use the process to accelerate the schedule, reduce costs, and still achieve main objectives.

The project can put available resources together and increase confidence by creating a more realistic budget and schedule, using the quantitative results as reckoning points.

TIP   Another benefit is the ability to identify main risks, enabling the project to work on a formula geared to reducing risk exposures by revealing hidden critical paths. Last but not the least, scope and contract management becomes more effective and less subjective.

5.8.   Understanding Contingency

Quantitative risk analysis generates distribution charts. Visual illustration of schedule contingency using the information and chart below will give a better appreciation of the concept.

Schedule data date = 07-Jul-2009

Maximum duration   = 431 days - 12-Sep-2010 Chance: P100

Risk simulated finish = 404 days - 16-Aug-2010 Chance: P50

Deterministic duration= 399 days - 05-Aug-2010 Chance: <P11

Project risk standard = P50

We measure risk dates differences from the deterministic end date. The difference between XYZ Upgrader Project Risk Standard P50 and the deterministic date is termed schedule contingency (Frago, Schedule Risk Analysis Report (Final) of XYZ Upgrader Project, July 2010).

Looking at the distribution chart, there are eleven days, or 1.57 weeks, contingency needed to achieve the P70 date. Determining the value to add or subtract from the base schedule (or cost) in order to achieve the desired probability of under run or over run is straightforward. The amount of time (or money) added or subtracted from the base schedule is termed as schedule (or cost) contingency (Wendling, 1999).

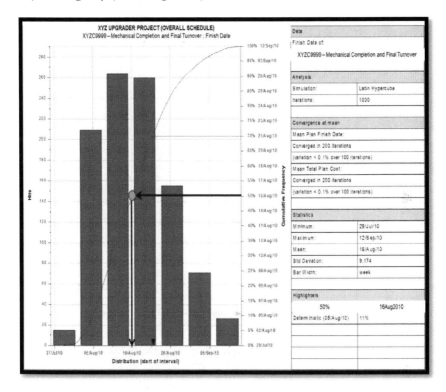

Figure 38 - Probability Distribution Showing P50 Date

5.9.   Approach to Duration Ranging

Everyone in the risk management community knows what schedule quantitative risk analysis is. It is what the majority of us in project management call the traditional method of quantification. One day, I decided to ask a group of subject matter experts this.

"What do you think is the best approach to duration ranging?"

I have done and facilitated so many three-point activity duration estimating sessions that I have already lost count. Regardless of how many, though, I still ask myself, "Am I doing the three-point estimate correctly?"

There is a growing opinion from some risk management professionals that the "duration range" should only take into account estimation of uncertainties, not risk events. Let us take the activity called "piling installation". It is an activity with 20 days duration. Most probably, it will take 20 days, but it can be 25 days at maximum and 18 days at minimum.

This three-point spread is solely because of estimating uncertainty.

This means that the activity should not be tied to a risk event (or events) taking place. According to them, risk events should be taken into account separately using the risk register (risk scoring). Duration ranging should stick within the range and averages of the work itself based on normal conditions and not on assumptions of abnormal conditions taking place.

5.10.   Relative Values between Three Points

How about duration ranging? How should we monitor the validity of the three-point estimate? Should the risk analyst allow the following flawed values?

1) Most likely duration equals minimum duration; i.e. ML =MIN
2) Most likely duration equals maximum duration; i.e. ML=MAX
3) Most Likely Duration is less than Minimum Duration; i.e. ML < MIN
4) Most Likely is greater than Maximum Duration; i.e. ML > MAX
5) Most Likely is equal to Minimum and Maximum Duration; i.e. ML=MIN=MAX
6) Most Likely is different from the Remaining Duration; i.e. ML NE RD

These relative values are quite common when facilitating a risk session or running the risk analysis itself. Default Most Likely (ML) value of each activity considered is equal to the activity's remaining duration. The default was borne out of the basic principle of schedule development that calls for the schedule to represent the "most likely."

In many cases, projects end up giving any of the numerous flawed inputs stated above. When this happens, the activity on focus is not a P50, or the Most Likely. When ML is not equal to RD, depending on the differential value, and the frequency, the schedule is saying whether it is aggressive or lax.

Once all the values are in, the risk analysis tool runs the simulation. It will calculate the inputs versus the network backdrop, providing the result or generate either a warning, or an error. The errors and/or warnings usually boil down to preceding items 1 to 6.

A subject matter resource who inputs a value that has ML=MIN is trying to say that the remaining duration is flawed and does not represent the expected value of P50. When he brings the minimum value to equal the most likely value, he is saying that finishing the activity on time using the remaining duration has less probability. It will be a bigger challenge than when the ML stays as is, and the minimum value opens up to the left of any specific duration range. He thinks that the remaining duration of the activity is the earliest possible duration. As such, the remaining duration of the activity is actually nowhere near the most likely deterministic duration value.

Conversely, when ML=MAX, it means that there is no way the activity will complete later than what is shown in the remaining duration of the activity. It can also be interpreted the Most Likely value as too pessimistic and needs to be recalibrated to a lesser value. The facilitator has to clarify from the subject matter experts (SME) the rationale and act accordingly. By saying so, the project is assuring that the deterministic value is the same as maximum.

Does this make sense? Something is not quite right if one thinks about it for a moment. If two of the three values were equal, would it still be a 3-point range? What is a good perspective? Are we going to allow this? If yes, why should we allow this?

Many risk analysts still consider the right triangle distribution as a valid distribution. Fortunately, the SQRA tool can successfully do the calculation. In other words, there is technically no problem. The facilitator should try to avoid such a distribution scenario because it is not a good reflection of the possible ranges and can be self-defeating. Such distribution is unrealistic and impossible.

Items 3 and 4 will come out as error. Calculation will stop. The Most Likely value lying outside the confines of minimum and maximum values is unacceptable. Calculation will not proceed unless the issue fixed.

Calculation stops because values relationships do not make sense.

When the Most Likely duration equals the Minimum and Maximum or ML=MIN=MAX, the warning message comes up. This kind of entry is the same as no entry at all if ML=RD. Since there is no duration range provided, it has practically no input to provide. You can ignore the warnings.

A popular distribution is called the TRIGEN (P10/P90). This is a distribution profile where the minimum represents, for example a P10 and your maximum a P90. The calculation brings into consideration what risk practitioners call "outliers", values which describes the remaining 10% outside the P10/P90 points.

When a subject matter expert provides duration input ranges based on their experience, the assumption considered is that their minimum and maximum value inputs are not true reflections of the actual minimum and maximum. Rationale:

TIP Even the experts have not experienced the real minimum and maximum values in their lifetime. To compensate for the blind spot, we opt for P10/P90 to consider outliers.

5.11. Three-Point References

It will be beneficial for anyone performing a three-point estimate to review the information and data quality of the following documents:

1) Basis of estimate
2) Detailed Estimate
3) Estimate Summary

This provides a good understanding on how the duration of an activity or work package came about. It is mandatory that the facilitator is familiar with the estimate, because crosschecking the resource inputs is essential.

Removing the unfounded biases during duration ranging will address some of the dreaded systemic schedule risk.

Note the relevant project stage or phase and how they can help validate the duration estimate and the ranges. Be familiar with the estimate classes adopted for the particular stage.

Understand that knowledge of the estimate basis is a big plus; e.g. number of crew per day, number of hours per day, composition of mixed crews, work assumptions, work strategies, rules for fabrication and construction, and others.

5.12. Avoid Double Dipping

Double dipping is a common problem in three-point estimating involving risk event consideration.

The participating disciplines and stakeholders tend to come up with risk events already captured in the risk register. The risk analyst should be constantly aware of this. In addition to the documents listed in Section 5.11 is the latest and up to date project risk register.

The problem happens when risk events that were qualified and quantified using the risk register are now again part of the discussion in SQRA.

> **TIP**
> Only those risks not found in the risk register, or in the risk register but not yet evaluated, are best included in the schedule risk analysis.

Three common methods of quantifications:

- By identifying new and relevant risks and incorporating then into the approved risk matrix table of the risk analysis tool. Tying and correlating each risk to the impacted activities or work packages follows.
- Using traditional approach or commonly called three-point estimating. Review and simulation of specially selected activities according to agreed-to criteria using duration range as input.
- Record the risks considered in a common project register and do separate empirical calculations to come up with the dollar or duration value.

5.13. Quality of Input Data

The correctness, accuracy, completeness, and usefulness of a Schedule Quantitative Risk Analysis (SQRA) shall depend heavily on the quality of planning data used for input or plainly, the quality of the project schedule."

As I have highlighted in the first part of this write-up, a good quality schedule is required to come up with good quantitative results. It is the root of it all. Good quality begets good management that begets good result.

I have written a guide called "How to Prepare for Schedule Quantitative Risk Analysis" which focuses particularly on the ready for SQRA criteria (Frago, 2013) where I discussed comprehensively the effects of schedule quality on the process of quantitative risk analysis.

It is a sad paradox to conclude that many ill-prepared project schedules are victims of time constraints. A schedule is supposed to manage time effectively, yet, developing one to the right quality becomes impossible in favor of expediency. "We have to submit the baseline tomorrow for our gate review. There's no time to address all of the schedule's flaws and inherent risks. This will do," says the project control manager. As a consequence, a poor quality schedule becomes the project's Achilles heel. Too bad!

Figure 39 - Management of Schedule Quality

There are several semi-automatic quality assessment tools available in the industry today. They can help the project manager gain more insight into the very fiber of their schedule.

A product called Deltek-Acumen Fuse, for example, can provide a powerful dashboard style presentation of schedule quality based on any in-house or industry standard benchmark criteria (Reference: Jul-2013, How to Understand Acumen Fuse Score by Rufran C. Frago, Slideshare and 2013, Guide to Acumen Fuse Scoring by Tom Polen of Deltek Acumen Fuse, YouTube and Deltek Acumen presentation).

5.14. Validating the Project Schedule

Validating the project schedule is essential before anyone embarks into full-fledged SQRA. The schedule has to be the right specimen. This touches on the significance of good schedule quality as a decent starting point towards schedule quality validation.

Upon quality validation and subsequent SQRA, the project has to approve a baseline for execution. Ideally, all the stakeholders have to vet and sign the baseline schedule. If this is not possible, then all the most influential and powerful schedule stakeholders must complete the sign-off. The project stakeholder register will provide the information as to who should be involved.

Ideally, it should have the information as who among the stakeholders have more influence, the power to make a decision. It will be very contentious if any schedule stakeholder argues that the analysis is unacceptable because the summarized project schedule does not reflect the detailed schedule.

5.15. Issues with Calendars

The calendar is a contentious element of a schedule. The challenge here is that we are often not talking about one or two calendars. The project, through the schedulers, has a nasty habit of creating numerous calendars. In fact, I reviewed one major project a few years back that had 11 calendars.

The contractors prepared the sub-projects separately, thinking that each one will have a different calendar. The good thing is that, upon closer inspection, five of the eleven calendars were practically the same.

Upon conversion of the five to a singular calendar, I still had to convince the project that the remaining seven calendars were just too much. Fortunately, the project finally decided to use just one or two calendars. Too many calendars complicate the schedule. It has to be just right.

5.16. Baseline Schedule

I strongly espouse the rule that the baseline schedule should never be built in isolation. It should represent the "most likely" schedule with no built-in risk. Doing this will limit vulnerability to double-dipping risk inputs.

One should remember that risk is something that might or might not happen in the future. The project watches for triggers ushering the schedule risks, but does not include them in the baseline.

Every risk has a trigger before it happens, and that is the only time the risk action owner should activate the corresponding response plan (i.e. to avoid, transfer, mitigate, or accept if it's a threat or to exploit, share, enhance, or accept if the risk is an opportunity). For additional clarity about these strategies, see PMBOK 4th Edition, Chapter 11, page 303-305, Section 11.5.2 Plan Risk Responses: Tools and Techniques.

5.17. Use of Schedule Filter

One of the more popular approaches I have used embarking into duration ranging was to filter the schedule's critical and normal, identifying about 300 to 500 activities in the process. From these, we filter out activities with relatively short duration such as those with RD<=3D. To exclude less critical activities, I change the filter to define the schedule's degree of criticality. The following can be set: TF<10D, or perhaps TF<15D, whichever will give a count of about 150 to 300 activities, (or whatever acceptable representative statistical target number of activities suits the project). All of these will depend largely on the level of schedule. There is also a danger that some activities did not fall into our criteria. These activities might have substantial potential to change because of risk factors that could influence the result.

5.18. Problem with Using Static Paths

The issue I always have in the back of my mind using the filter approach of identifying critical paths is this:

TIP Critical paths are more dynamic in nature than static. It constantly changes with each schedule update even activities with high criticality can switch path. Some might even end up as non-critical.

What we can filter from our P6 schedule are static critical paths. They are practically just a snapshot of the path in time. That snapshot is equivalent to a singular iteration run, using our risk analysis tool. Never rely on this indicator with blind confidence. Always crosscheck with periodic schedule risk analysis.

The importance given by many project managers on static path is one of the reasons why they fail to have a good handle of their projects. The path is good only at the moment of inspection and do not offer even a short standing influence on the overall deliverables. If this is the right way, I can merely pick any 200 activities because anyone of them can be critical the next time we look. What a downer! It seems very ineffective and absurd to focus on the critical path produced by a singular run.

Know that running the schedule risk analysis is the better method of identifying schedule criticality. In fact, SQRA simulates all scenarios. In a way, the number of iteration equals the number of what-ifs. A 5000-iteration equals 5000 what-ifs. Iteration is equal to one scenario. Five thousand (5,000) iterations are like looking at the same project in different scenarios, a 5000 times.

5.19. Integrated Assessment is a Must

It is important to underline that proper schedule risk quantification requires an integrated schedule. An integrated schedule has all the practical elements under consideration to be within the same deterministic network during calculation with all essential relationships preserved. One major indicators of a schedule that is not integrated is the presence of external links. Read section 4.18 to digest its relevance.

If the project schedule has ten key deliverables to assess and analyze, there is no need to generate ten PLAN files or disconnect relationships in an effort to zero-in on one deliverable. Use a single PLAN file to ensure that everyone deals with only one version of the truth.

5.20. Very High Level Summary (VHLS)

Back in 2009, a fellow AACE member demonstrated his preferred way of risk modeling. He asked the project team to prepare a model of the whole schedule, but with no more than 25 activities. The thought of simplifying a multi-billion dollar project that way brought a quick frown. It seems illogical and naïve so I was quick to push back.

I implored him, "Good risk management relies on the presence of details. Enough details to make a good decision. If I am to convert a large schedule of, say 20,000 activities into 25 representative activities, will that be a good representation? I don't think so!" As he was not able to answer the question confidently in the affirmative, I felt that he was wasting time.

He tried to explain that the focus is to look only for those critical activities driving the completion date. The targets are those that fall along the primary and secondary critical paths, plus those activities not necessarily on the critical path but tagged as high schedule risks.

TIP Another reason he offers as to why having a small number of summary activities is preferable is to minimize the effect of the Central Limit Theorem (CLT). It is simpler and ensures a more productive workshop process. The method will not require importing from the scheduling tool (e.g. Primavera or MS Project) into a risk assessment tool such as OPRA.

This suggested simplified method puts an end to the capacious risk models that beginners to the industry employ. It is expected to isolate the real points of concern from the noise by creating a simple and very high level summary (VHLS) (Reference: Aug-2009, Iron Triangle Analysis (Methods and Concept) Discussion Thread Started and Facilitated by Rufran C. Frago, look for full commentary made by other participants).

5.21. Medium Level Summary

A schedule risk Medium Level Summary (MLS) model of major projects is one that consists of about 100 to 300 sensible medium level activities. This model makes more sense than a VHLS. MLS activities represent the overall project schedules longest path/critical, near critical and high-risk activities. I have applied the criteria to a Level 3 schedule (see Section 3.17) where the count of remaining normal activities is greater than 3000.

$$\frac{5\%}{3\%} \quad Nm$$

Where:

Nm is the number of remaining normal activities in the model.

Nd is the number of remaining normal activities in the detailed schedule.

A good number of risk analysts in the construction industry have expressed their preference for using a separate and summarized schedule model, compared to the use of the detailed and overly complex schedule. They believe that they achieve a better and more acceptable result. It takes more time, but the separate model will also permit the risk analyst to advance his overall understanding of how the project schedule is established.

The identification of very few activities using the static primary and secondary critical path only will not fly. It seems like a good idea at first to newcomers, but as soon as one understands that static critical paths are not reliable, then it will not be so appealing.

TIP The critical path is dynamic and will probably change path as soon as the project updates the schedule. With the exception of some activities with high criticality, the path is constantly changing. What the scheduler filters from his/her schedule and what many initially perceive as critical are just static critical paths, which are practically just snapshots of moments in time. This is only equivalent to one of the 1000 or more iterations carried out by OPRA (previously Pertmaster) or any of the other risk modeling tools available.

5.22. Summary Model

Other analysts opined that summarizing the schedule is building a completely different schedule. It is quite doubtful that a junior or intermediate planner/scheduler could successfully do it.

It takes years of experience in the science of planning and scheduling before one is able to do so. Inexperience can unintentionally bring into the summarized project schedule the following: transfer errors, omissions, flawed relationships, personal biases, and other issues. The summarized schedule can end up completely departing from the details.

Think about this: if VHLS is the kind of simplification that we want to do, I can merely select any 15 to 30 activities. I need not bother filtering the critical activities, because they might not be critical any more after the first schedule update.

As such, a 15 to 25-activity summary of a multi-billion dollar mega-project will not be sufficient. This is a "very high level summary" (VHLS) and can make many risk managers a bit uncomfortable. I disagree with the notion of creating a too simplistic schedule risk model.

TIP Risk management hinges very closely on details to be effective, and a VHLS does not provide enough. If I am to decide, VHLS will be out the window.

5.23. Fit for Purpose Model

We start with the objectives, followed by the methods. The process, although independent of the tool, should govern the use of the tool.

The modeling method should be "fit for purpose." In view of that, there can really be no standard way of doing it. The best anyone can do is to have some guidelines in place, then pick the best approach that satisfies the project's goals. It means that each project will have to come up with a unique set of criteria.

Since one of the fundamental and glaring attributes of a project is being a unique endeavor, fit-for-purpose approach makes the most sense. Unfortunately, that line of thinking puts into question the need for project benchmarks.

If one thinks about a new project relying heavily on benchmarked information of similar projects executed during the past years, there is a good chance that doing so might become the organization's pitfall. Why would it be?

TIP It can happen because of the basic premise that each project is unique. By logic, they might not be comparable.

Many organizations use benchmarks more often, i.e. clients and contractors alike, as an excuse not to conduct a full-blown quantitative risk analysis.

Using benchmark instead of going into risk quantification specific to the current project is common.

The project gravitates towards the tabulated results of their in-house or third party consultant database even without understanding the attributes of each benchmark.

Are there built in risks in the benchmark? Is the benchmark applicable for use in North America? ...in North Africa? ...in Singapore? etc... What assumptions were considered in this benchmark? Was this benchmark normalized? How was it normalized? What factors were taken out?

I have seen a number of projects using such approach derailed for leaning too much to the repeatability idea of project execution.

⚠ Using benchmark information without knowing their detailed attributes introduces unwelcome surprises. The information is a line on the sand that serves as reference. The unfortunate truth however, is that a project by virtue of its unique attributes, is actually not repeatable. In most instances, it does remain a line on the sand. In this sense, a benchmark is not a target.

One of the accepted online definitions of repeatability is the ability of an operator to repeat consistently the same measurement of the same part using the same gauge under the same conditions (Minitab, 2015). It is clear that the ability to repeat is more operation in nature.

Are project management practitioners relying on a different degree of sameness and consistency as the definition of repeatability described by the aforementioned?

⚠ General project practices can be repeatable but not the results. This kind of thinking, believing that a project can be repeatable to a degree similar to a manufacturing assembly line is easily the root cause of many project failures.

Projects and operation differ primarily in that operations are ongoing and repetitive, while projects are temporary and unique (PMBOK® Third Edition, 2004).

It is for the above reasons that I would recommend an integrated quantitative risk analysis for any substantially high-risk project.

Figure 40 - Fit for Purpose Approach

5.24. Proponents of VHLS Schedule Model

In fairness to the proponents of the VHLS methodology, I did ask a few of them to explain their rationale.

Proponent #1 replied:

"I take the whole project schedule and make sure it is up to date. Calculate the schedule to identify the critical paths (CP). Note that CP depends on how the project has defined it. Retain only the primary critical paths and those that the project believes are high risks work packages. After this is done, I ask the scheduler to delete everything else that falls outside the set criteria."

Proponent #2 replied:

"Using the VHLS method in SQRA is preferable if the quality of the overall schedule is not good. Take for example a big schedule of 10,000+ activities with a bunch of open-ends and dangling activities. These are indications of missing scopes and wrong logic ties. In my honest opinion, it is much better to build a representative summary schedule that reflects the real execution strategy and sequence. I want a model having the correct logic that will permit the unhampered, unconstrained flow of the schedule."

Proponent #3 replied:

"My consideration of the VHLS revolves around the availability of time. I ask the project whether there is enough time to do the risk analysis. It is apparent that a summary schedule will take a smaller amount of time and simplify the model. Going through the facilitation process will be a breeze."

Proponent #4 replied:

"One of my friends in the risk management profession related he has performed SQRA using the summary schedule approach, while their contractor performed a schedule risk using the detailed schedule. The results were similar and comparable. The difference was that the contractors work required over three weeks involving more than two subject matter experts to facilitate while the summary approach only took a week and one person."

Many project managers say that summarizing the schedule is not that hard. Proponents #1 to #3 and especially Proponent #4 have suggested it.

Re-creating a schedule through a representative summary requires someone with very strong planning, scheduling, and risk modeling knowledge and skills. He/she should be able to visualize the overall execution strategy and capture it. It is reaching the main objective by traversing above the details, through the timeline on a zip line. Recreating a schedule cannot be overly simplistic or else we end up kidding ourselves. Facilitating the 3-point estimate risk session using a summary schedule will be quite challenging. The disciplines might end up losing their independence, expertise, and confidence because the summary becomes too general.

5.25. Mega-Projects Should Stay Away from VHLS

It is okay to support a summary schedule that offers enough meat for risk assessment. Some of us have done summary schedule on some occasions in the past. As I mature in the risk management profession, I admit that I tend to stay away from making too many simplifications, such as VHLS of a very detailed schedule. Did you not notice that more information gets lost as the distance between each summary level increases? Try creating a level 1 schedule from a level 5 construction schedule. It is like reflecting an 8000-activity schedule into a one-activity schedule. Does that make sense? Will it be useful as a schedule risk model?

With due respect to those who love the very high-level summary version of a schedule as the risk quantification model, here are some of the reasons why I cannot embrace the method completely.

One must remember that summaries are high-level representation of the details. The higher the level, the harder it is to have acceptable logical links between activities in a schedule. In such situations, a scheduling person uses more SS and FF scheduling relationships that rely heavily on lags and constraints. This decreases the quality of the schedule immensely. Excessive use of these SS, FF, and lags introduces inherent risks, while the constraints add unfounded certainty that welcomes error into the model.

TIP Summary schedule tends to rely heavily on constrains and lags. This is not desirable. Lags behave like normal but hidden activities. This is not saying that the detailed schedule does not have its share of lags (Section 4). The difference to consider here is the magnitude of the lags involved and the quality of the schedule.

When this happens, we encounter the problem that it is better for some of lags to be visible, expressed as normal activities.

Take note that Primavera (P6) and OPRA (previously called Pertmaster) consider the lag calendar in the calculation. The impact to the schedule or the risk model, depending on the tool's setting, will be immense.

The risk analyst who goes through the quantification process blindly and unaware of the setup will have a problem because the imported dates will change and disagree with the detailed schedule.

TIP In several forums, I have always conveyed this rule of thumb: "The higher the level of the schedule, the greater the number of unknowns."

"And why is that?" you will ask.

The simple answer is this. If we fly above a forest, we would not know exactly what is happening under the trees. Effective risk management requires details, and a VHLS certainly does not have enough. The project manager will

115

look at the schedule only to ask what is in there, only to realize there are several unknowns. Unless the manager knows the project's strategic objective, it will be difficult to connect the dots and decide.

If there is no unknown in the schedule, breaking it down is not necessary. If the schedule does not offer the details we want, we have to break it down to smaller pieces.

The details are there so that we can clearly see the critical bumps and potholes, the schedule drivers the project needs to address along the path of travel to our destination. Maybe we should be utilizing them, not blurring them. We have to strike an acceptable balance.

5.26. Contracts and Level of Schedule

One factor to consider is the standard level of schedule required by the contract. Regardless of how much information the project has, if the contract says that a level 3 "control schedule" has to be prepared, then it has to be. It is also the schedule subjected to risk analysis. Even if the activity data is suitable for a lower level schedule such as level 4 or 5, the responsible party must prepare a level 3.

I prefer using whatever schedule is agreed-to by all contracting parties. If we are to risk analyze an approved base/control schedule and it has 10,000 activities or more, we can proceed with what is in front of us. The number does not really matter, because all ranged values, correlations, and risk factors inputted into the select activities will always be part of the simulation/iteration. By proceeding to identify 500 long duration, critical, and near-critical activities to range, we have practically focused on the critical summary representation of the schedule.

SQRA iterates through its course considering the whole schedule and calculating the values given to the 500 activities. A thousand iteration means we are in fact looking at 1000 different project situation, or 1000 what-ifs.

As mentioned several times in the last few paragraphs, remember in all of this that when one picked the critical and near critical from the deterministic schedule, those critical and near-critical activities are activities belonging to a "static critical path".

Once simulation starts, most of those activities will indicate that they are no longer critical. We will identify valid areas of concern by tapping into the judgment of project subject matter experts and third party project management professionals. The project risk register can offer additional information as well.

The ranged values of the 500 activities are reviewed with some removed as needed.

5.27. Schedule Owner Provides the Summary Model

The owner of the schedule should be the one to clean the schedule and nobody else. To fix broken links, correct logic, change descriptions, or simplify what needs to be simplified. The repercussions of touching and summarizing a schedule can be distressing.

The peril of doing so without an agreed-to procedure is that as soon as the risk analyst touches, summarizes, and changes the schedule, the owner of the schedule, be it the client or the contractor, is already poised to disown it.

If that summarized schedule finally ever becomes the basis of the SQRA result, issues, disputes, and disagreements will likely occur between contracting parties. If that happens, the landscape will not look good.

5.28. WBS in Quantification Instead of Summary Model

If the project decides to run SQRA on the summary level, the better way is to use the WBS Summary activities. With a proper and manageable WBS structure in place, there is no need to waste valuable time rebuilding an already built schedule.

The schedule, once improved according to the minimum schedule quality requirements, can be risk analyzed with more confidence.

5.29. Optimum Size of the Schedule for SQRA

What should really be the optimum size of the schedule for risk analysis? Should it really be 150 to 300 activities? 500? 800? 1000? 2000? 3000? Again, this will bring us back to the quality of the detailed schedule because one has to understand that if the project schedule is incompetently developed, there might be no point to the summary.

My preference of using a good quality, approved detailed schedule does not mean that my eyes are closed. As long as it is not a VHLS, I believe we can prepare a good representation of the detailed schedule.

The danger for many beginners is in tying themselves too much to the tools and applications, imprisoning their works to its features. Maintaining the right perspective becomes a challenge when familiarity and monotony prevail.

The issue of risk analyst and schedulers being computer jockeys are well known.

One of my mentors always reminds, "Rufran, the right division of knowledge is 80% process and 20% tools." That is, do not to be "Tool-centric" but to be more "Process-centric." Whether this relates directly to the subject at hand is something else. I will let you decide. Who knows? Your perspective might open up more.

5.30. Running SQRA Using the Detailed Schedule

I have used available tools such as Oracle Primavera Risk Analysis (OPRA), which is previously Pertmaster (Version 6 to Version 8.7), and I have found no limitation to what it can handle. Running a project portfolio as large as 15,000 to 50,000 activities is not a problem.

As to the accuracy and practicality of running such a large model, it can be as simple as one plus one or it can be quite complex, depending on best practice such as:

1) Completeness: Is the schedule complete? Does it have the entire scope?
2) Accuracy: Did the model accurately reflect the execution plan? Do we have the same data date for all sub-projects?
3) Timeliness: Do we have time to do a comprehensive SQRA?
4) Fairness: Have we successfully removed input biases?
5) Enforceability: Did the stakeholders approve this same schedule for SQRA?
6) Methodology: Did we follow the standards and procedures governing this SQRA?
7) Inherent risks: Were there any inherent risks identified?
8) Project buy-in: Did the project accept the schedule constraints and assumptions?

5.31. ICSQRA

I strongly agree with a growing number of risk managers that the ideal method is an integrated cost and schedule quantitative risk analysis (ICSQRA). All mega-projects should strive to unite these two components in order to get the complete picture. Doing them separately can create informational gaps.

One thing that an excellent risk practitioner should remember is not to rely on just one risk model. A singular risk model limits the project from seeing the best alternatives and courses of action.

Using two or more, or even several models give the project a better view of the situation, and provides them with enough information to make the best decision.

Observing the behavior of other risk practitioners, I shake my head whenever one uses a singular model to come up with the results.

This perspective of complacency needs to change. Tweaking and adjusting the risk schedule model considering other factors will help generate all possible results.

TIP It is best to run the process several times while varying certain input information, risk factors, and assumptions.

5.32. Deterministic Schedule and Political Dates

When a project presents a schedule model for SQRA, the schedule is the deterministic schedule from which all analysis emanates. The deterministic term is quite clear. It should not confuse anybody.

A deterministic schedule is a snapshot in time. The deterministic dates, including the end of the project date, become the point of reference to which schedule contingency is measured.

The risk analysis tool will allow the iteration to proceed with a simple warning regarding the relative values I mentioned. However, it will flag an error if the MAX value is less than the ML value, the ML value is greater than the MAX, or the MIN is greater than the ML.

The analyst must exercise care in accepting values from the stakeholders/participants without understanding the frame of mind from where they came from. It is important to bring everyone to think within one frame of thoughts so that all perspectives are from the same footing. It prevents selective perception.

Selective perception refers to instances where you see what you want to see (Intaver, 2006). This occurs when one's intention is to fit or influence the estimate to fit the mandated cost limitation when preparing the project's budget.

It is also one known reasons why projects force their schedule to satisfy mandated political dates. Many project managers will force-fit cost and schedule without blinking an eye or a pushback.

Then the problem starts.

Political dates are influencing factors to consider. It is the risk practitioner's responsibility to provide the facts of the matter. If the assessment is not positive, a responsible person should be honest about it.

A risk analyst worth his salt should be able to say with firm conviction that an optimistic or a pessimistic schedule is not an effective schedule.

What will you do if the management's target finish-date conflicts with what the developed project schedule reasonably shows? If the Client has mandated and announced that the project should finish by January 30, 2014 and the project team knows the updated control schedule could no longer reasonably achieve this date, even after undergoing a thorough team review process, what is next?

Let us say the project team now has a schedule that has a deterministic date of July 1, 2014. For goodness sake, the task to do the risk assessment fell on your lap!

Figure 41 - Organizational Cultures and Politics

5.33. Which Schedule Should We Use?

At once, the question you probably ask yourself is this: Which schedule should I use? Should I use the one with the management deterministic date of January 30, 2014 or the most likely schedule with a July 1, 2014 end date? In view of this management mandate, how should the project manager and his risk manager/analyst carry on and approach the SQRA process? What is the acceptable approach to this political date?

One of my colleagues plainly said that the January 30, 2014 management date should be the target and the July 1, 2013 should be the deterministic date. The plan is left reflecting the understood delivery method and end date (i.e. the plan is not massaged to fit the management date!). Risk analysis would then report the probability of achieving both dates.

The project team would work (further) to shorten the schedule by reviewing delivery methodology, scope management, value engineering, resourcing levels, and other factors with the intent of achieving the management date objective.

The rationale is that the project management has to know the probability of achieving both the target and deterministic dates. What that project team chooses to report to its client, sponsor, and board is a team decision. The SQRA results will assist in that decision.

5.34. Schedule Contingency versus Political Date

The above logic makes sense, but I do have some questions. If the January 30, 2014 is a target date and July 1, 2014 is the deterministic date, then what dates are the project schedule contingency points?

What is the best and proper way of reflecting that in the distribution chart? In this particular situation, although seemingly acceptable, is the term "target date" an acceptable terminology?

Is there a way of reflecting this management target date on the generated distribution chart?

I tried looking for guidance but was not able to an answer. This is not really a big issue technically and is a question of communication and buy-in. The probabilities of all focused dates are all easily extractable.

If the management date prevailed, schedule contingency shall refer to that date.

The apparent difficulty lies in the basic premise that schedule contingency is the difference between the project's risk probability standard and the deterministic date.

Since the client has mandated the project should finish on January 30, 2014 and the most likely schedule ends on July 1, 2014, the contingency cannot be determined based on this formula.

In this situation, as I have described in the previous paragraph, I would suggest a second model using the management end date as the deterministic date.

If the project risk appetite is P70 corresponding to the September 30, 2014 date and the July 1, 2014 deterministic schedule turned out to be actually P50 (Most likely), then the schedule contingency is P70 minus P50, or 13 weeks.

Let us say the project modified the schedule such that the management target date is now the deterministic date. If the date is a P10 (10% probability of occurring), we can now calculate the schedule contingency as P70 minus P10 (Figure 42).

This is about 34.8 weeks (~35 weeks).

Through this, the project can be objective in laying out its case strongly to the leaders.

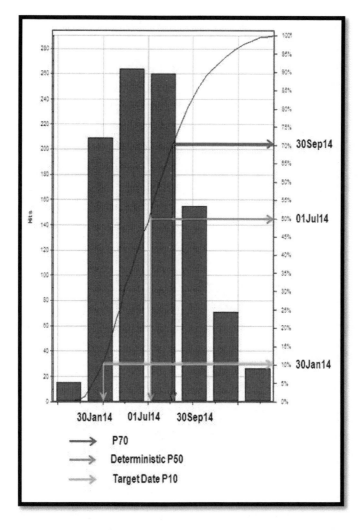

Figure 42 - Probability Distribution Showing P10, P50, and P80

Chapter 6

Importing Schedule to OPRA

6.1. Introduction to OPRA Import Process

Many risk professionals have experienced difficulties using Oracle Primavera Risk Analysis, also known as OPRA (previously called Pertmaster) in processing their sample deterministic schedule for quantification and analysis.

The persistent issues encountered, especially by new would-be risk analysts, is the discrepancy of the risk plan file and the original multi-calendar Primavera schedule after import.

If the wrong translation is not fixed, the original deterministic dates of affected activities will stay misaligned, producing erroneous results.

This chapter will attempt to present the secret key to the proper use of this tool, preventing loss of data quality, hence, an accurate risk assessment!

The detailed guide to the correct method of importing or converting Primavera project files to Oracle Primavera Risk Analysis (OPRA) is in this chapter (Section 6.6).

The reader who wants to be a risk analyst will learn how to align the OPRA schedule to the original P6 schedule. Aligning the two schedules ensure an accurate schedule quantitative risk analysis.

The goals here are to save time, increase accuracy, reliability, and optimize effort expended on schedule risk quantification.

6.2. The Problem

1) A major project schedule was imported and converted to Oracle Primavera Risk Analysis (OPRA) for schedule quantitative risk analysis (SQRA).

2) The result of the import check in OPRA (Pertmaster) revealed several large variances in the deterministic dates of the sample schedule compared to the original version.
3) The imported start and finish dates of 20 activities varied from the original deterministic dates by between 5 and 33 days.
4) In many instances, the difference between import dates and original deterministic dates were even bigger. The delay of some activities was as big as three months or more.
5) The result of schedule quantitative risk analysis is in error because the reference deterministic dates have changed. As such, the calculated schedule contingency is wrong.

6.3. Related Tools

1) Project Management (Primavera 6.1 SP1, 6.2, 6.7 SP1, 6.7 SP2, SP4, SP5, and higher)
2) Oracle Primavera Risk analysis V8, V8.7(previously called Pertmaster)

6.4. Definitions

1) The term "user" in this document is the person using the Primavera or OPRA tool. He can be the risk analyst, planner, the scheduler, the project manager, or anyone else.
2) OPRA is an acronym for the Oracle Primavera Risk Analysis tool, previously called Pertmaster.
3) SQRA is an acronym for schedule quantitative risk analysis.
4) UDF is a Primavera acronym for a User Defined Field.
5) P6 is the Primavera scheduling tool.
6) Original schedule means the P6 schedule before importing or translating to OPRA. It is usually in XER format, but can be in other format like XML.

6.5. Problem Analysis (PA)

1) Import of multiple calendar schedules to OPRA produces date discrepancies. Dates suffer translational variances compared to the original P6 schedule.
2) There is no date or duration problem encountered by any user when importing singular calendar schedules to OPRA.
3) To simulate the issue, create Project-A (Figure 43). This project has multiple calendars for each summary phase. Each

calendar has a different time period setting (i.e. working hours per day). It is an engineering, procurement, construction, and start-up (EPC/S) overall schedule that has the following calendars assigned to each phase:

- A 5-2-8 calendar for engineering (5 days on, 2 days off, at 8 hours per day)

- A 5-2-10 calendar for module and fabrication (5 days on, 2 days off, at 10 hours per day)

- A 10-4-10 calendar for construction (10 days on, 4 days off, at 10 hours per day)

- A 24/7 calendar for commissioning and start-up (7 days on continuously at 24 hours per day)

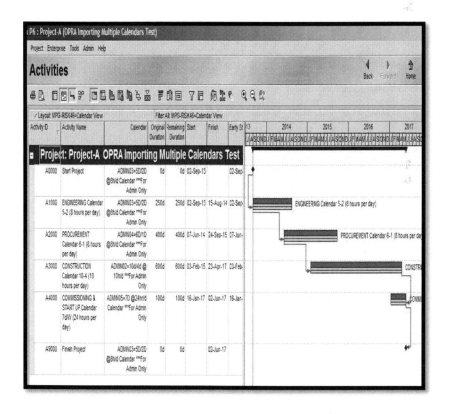

Figure 43 - Project-A Activity View

127

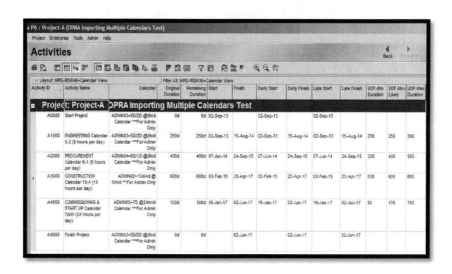

Figure 44 - Project-A Activity View Showing Duration Ranges

4) Load the schedule with optimistic, most likely, and pessimistic duration values using P6 UDFs (Figure 44).

5) After mapping in OPRA, import the schedule, including all the three-point ranges. To demonstrate the issues that came about, assign the standard 8 hour per day time-period conversion (Figure 45). Note that this setting did not work with a multi-calendar schedule.

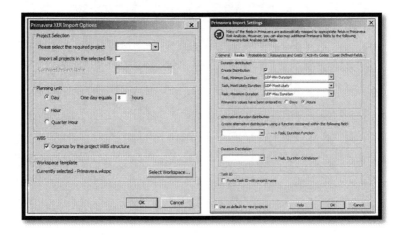

Figure 45 - OPRA Import Settings Window

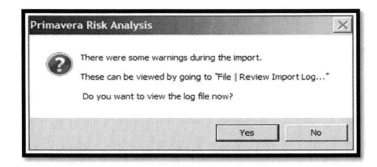

Figure 46 - OPRA Import Log Dialogue Box

Figure 47 - OPRA Import Warning Log (Notepad Text)

6) Upon pressing OK, the import process will commence. The import will generate a log after each import is completed (Figure 46). The user can then choose a directory to save it in (Figure 47).

7) Lags and leads calculation with respect to the associated calendars contributed to the issue. The differences were too high and too many. As demonstrated below, the deterministic finish date of the project has moved to the right by 114 days (Figure 48). The standard 8 hour per day setting made in item 5 resulted in several unacceptable variances.

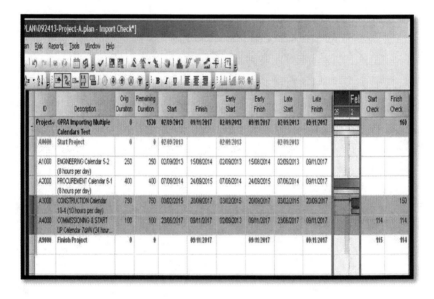

Figure 48 - Result of Import Check

8) The fundamental philosophy here is this: If the data quality is poor or wrong, the results of the SQRA will likely be in error also. This is all because of the wrong deterministic date reference points.

Observe below that some of the translated ranges are wrong, particularly activity A3000, which has durations of 400, 480, and 640 (Figure 49).

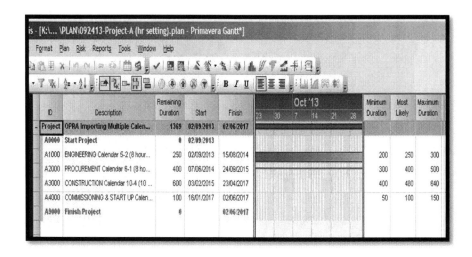

Figure 49 - Activity Window Showing Translated Min, ML, and Max

6.6. Explanation and Solution

A schedule with a singular calendar imported to OPRA did not have this problem. The translation was quite simple and straightforward. If the calendar "time period" is 8 hours per day, then the unit of conversion is the same, which is 8 hours per day.

The large variances were due to improper preparation and incorrect settings when importing a schedule with multiple calendars schedule. An adjustment to the import settings is necessary when importing a schedule with multiple calendars.

TIP
The only way multiple calendar projects can be properly imported is to convert the durations of the ranges into hours, using the right time-period setting of hours/day. The activities are then mapped each specific calendar.

We have brought all the values to the same footing for final processing and analysis. For example, an activity with a three point range of 100 days, 150 days, and 200 days for minimum, most likely, and maximum duration activity respectively, with a calendar time period of 10 hours per day, will have to be converted to hours using the aforementioned time period value.

The converted three-point range for that particular activity is as follows:

100 days × 10 hours/day =   1000 hours

$$150 \text{ days} \times 10 \text{ hours/day} = \qquad 1500 \text{ hours}$$

$$200 \text{ days} \times 10 \text{ hours/day} = \qquad 2000 \text{ hours}$$

The portion of the Project-A Primavera schedule below showing the converted day's ranges to hours will make the point clearer (Figure 50). To deal with the multiple calendars assigned to Project-A activities, we used the same calculation concept mentioned in previous paragraph. This method should eliminate the problem of high variances in start and finish dates on the OPRA schedule, compared to the original version in P6.

The ideal variance is no variance or near zero variance. Some variance between OPRA date and time and the original schedule is the result of very slight translation variances emanate from the configuration of various calendars. Durations between the two tools that are supposed to be the same value generate errors although displaying exactly the same date probably lies on the differences between hours or minutes component.

The apparent differences between durations rounded off to the nearest ten lies on the decimal component of each. It does not usually register to anyone because the value is not in plain sight. Change the time unit display in order to see such small differences.

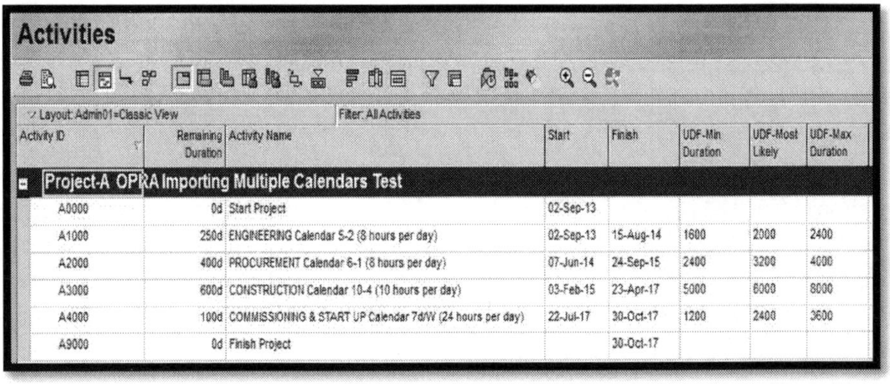

Activities

Activity ID	Remaining Duration	Activity Name	Start	Finish	UDF-Min Duration	UDF-Most Likely	UDF-Max Duration
		Project-A OPRA Importing Multiple Calendars Test					
A0000	0d	Start Project	02-Sep-13				
A1000	250d	ENGINEERING Calendar 5-2 (8 hours per day)	02-Sep-13	15-Aug-14	1600	2000	2400
A2000	400d	PROCUREMENT Calendar 6-1 (8 hours per day)	07-Jun-14	24-Sep-15	2400	3200	4000
A3000	600d	CONSTRUCTION Calendar 10-4 (10 hours per day)	03-Feb-15	23-Apr-17	5000	6000	8000
A4000	100d	COMMISSIONING & START UP Calendar 7d/W (24 hours per day)	22-Jul-17	30-Oct-17	1200	2400	3600
A9000	0d	Finish Project		30-Oct-17			

Figure 50 - Project-A Showing Converted Min, ML, and Max

Select "Hour" as the planning unit in the following OPRA dialog box (Figure 51). This setting will correct unit conversion with respect to different calendar assignments.

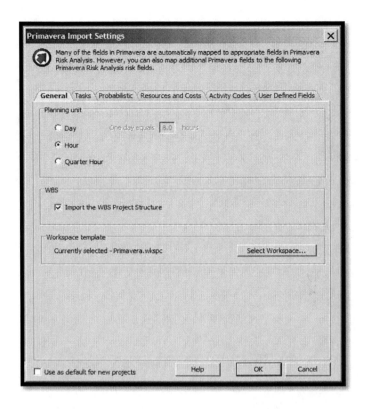

Figure 51 - OPRA Import Settings, General Tab Dialogue Box

We need to define and assign the optimistic, most likely, and pessimistic durations as user defined field (UDF) data in P6 in order to map this into OPRA during import.

Select the already defined duration range fields in the following import mapping dialog box in OPRA.

Check the button that says, "Primavera values have been entered in: "hours" (Figure 52).

If the project has the ranges corresponding to the activities in hours, then also select hours in this import settings window.

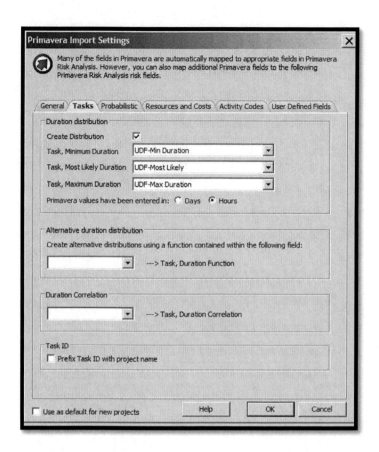

Figure 52 - OPRA Import Settings, Tasks Tab Dialogue Box

Upon pressing OK, the import process will commence. The import will generate a log after import is completed.

The user can then choose a directory to save it in (Figure 53). The folder level in the directory must not be too deep as it is known to affect the application process; slowing it down or stopping it completely. The first three levels are recommended (see Section 11.26 on the subject of directory).

It is recommended to have a file name that is shorter and simpler. Avoid unusually long file name. There's a limitation to the number of characters summed along the directory tree. The limit to the number of character allowed combined with an extremely deep level file folder stops the application program.

Figure 53 - OPRA Import Warning Log

TIP

After completing the import, save the OPRA risk plan. Click the "Import Check" tab and check for considerable variances in the activities' start, and finish dates. Compare these imported dates to the original P6 schedule deterministic dates.

In this example, there was no variance. The import and translation of Project A was successful. Figure 54 displays alignment of the start and finish dates with the original deterministic dates.

The zero variance (empty fields) on the two columns confirms good alignment to the original schedule, which is the imported XER file.

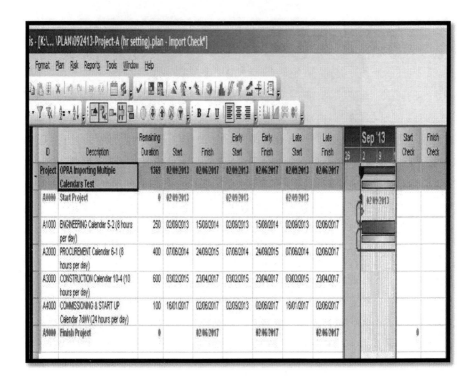

Figure 54 - Project-A Check of a Properly Imported Schedule

Once the import check passes, we can start the quantification process by running OPRA. Alignment between the original state of the schedule and the imported one indicates that it is one version of the truth.

Since the schedule data quality is excellent, the results should be reliable and indicative of the real situation.

All the take-off points and key milestones match the deterministic data.

Set the number of iterations. The recommendation is to set quantification to a minimum of 1000 iterations when doing any regular run (Figure 55).

I prefer more iteration, especially if I have enough time on my hand. Many of you will do the same in the future as you do risk quantification.

Many analysts recommend 500 to 1000 for preliminary run and 5000 or more iterations for final run. This is to get better data convergence.

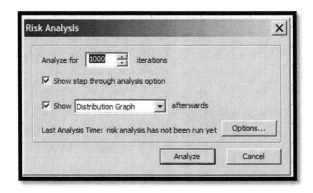

Figure 55 - Risk Analysis Dialogue Box

- Click on the Options button and choose the Risk Data tab.
- Since cost components are not part of this quantification, select Calculate Duration Sensitivity.
- Select Calculate Risk Percentiles"
- Save Resource Data" (Figure 56).

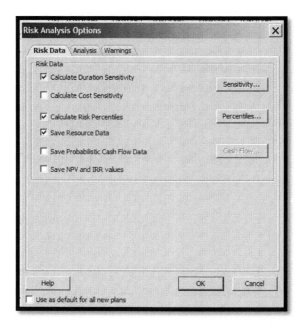

Figure 56 - OPRA Options, Risk Data Tab Dialogue Box

- Choose the Analysis tab.

- Put a check mark on Use Latin Hypercube Sampling.
- Select Show Step Through Analysis Options.
- Set Own Seed for Random Number Generator.
- Show Distribution Graphs as demonstrated below (Figure 57).

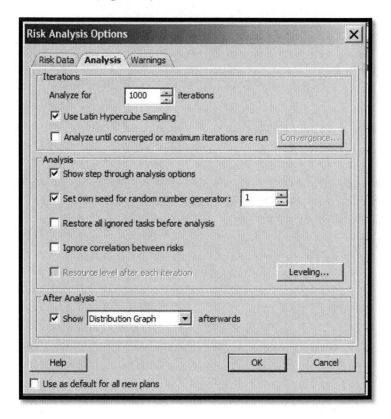

Figure 57 - OPRA Risk Options, Analysis Tab Dialogue Box

Click on the "Warnings" tab. Make sure that all buttons have a check mark (Figure 58).

Checking all the options instructs the tool to do a final prequalification of the data, ensuring that Users understand the warnings and errors.

When the messages do appear, the User has to fix the errors and address/acknowledge the warnings to proceed successfully with quantification.

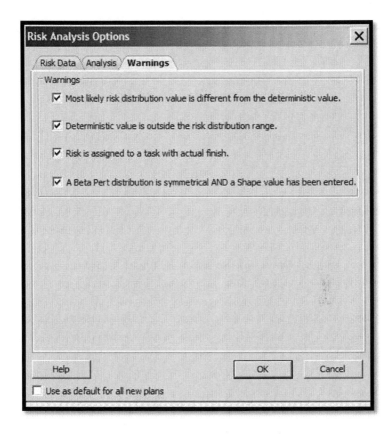

Figure 58 - OPRA Options, Warnings Tab Dialogue Box

Start the iterations by clicking OK. The tool will simulate the schedule risk model.

There might be some warnings at the end, similar to the example shown below. Read the messages and try to address the warnings if needed.

Some of the warnings might not be critical to the calculation.

Ignore and accept the warnings by clicking OK. The user has to make that call, deciding what is most reasonable. If the warning is unacceptable, address and fix the warnings (Figure 59 and Figure 60).

Example 1: Record 1 of 1, Task A3000

Warning Message: Check Distribution error, most likely value is not the same as the remaining duration.

The concept that deterministic schedules must represent the Most Likely value is the basis of the common expectation that the Remaining Duration is equal to the Most Likely. When OPRA compares the two and detects inequality, a warning flag is raised.

All Error messages should be corrected or fixed. There is no acceptable way to get around them.

Not fixing the errors stop OPRA on its track. A MostLikely Value that falls outside the Minimum and the Maximum is a good example.

Such situation is considered unacceptable by OPRA. See section 5.10 for additional information.

Action: Ignore the warning if flagged discrepancy is true. Most likely duration can be greater than or less than the deterministic activity remaining duration.

This is acceptable as long as most likely does not cross beyond the maximum and minimum of the three-point estimate.

Example 2: Record 2 of 2, Task A4000

Warning Message: Check Distribution error, remaining duration is outside the range of distribution.

This is not acceptable because the most likely crossed beyond the maximum and minimum of the three-point estimate.

See section 5.10 for additional information.

Action: Fix the root cause of the warning if flagged discrepancy is true.

Most likely duration can be greater than or less than the deterministic activity remaining duration.

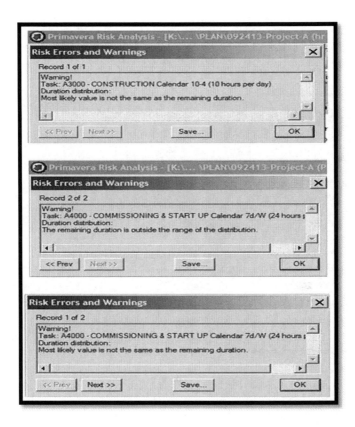

Figure 59 - Risk Errors and Warnings Windows

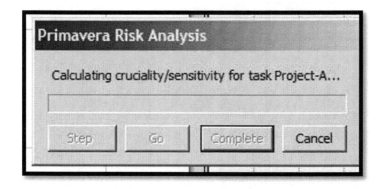

Figure 60 - Calculation Status Box

Look at the ranges. In the example below, I made sure that all the three point estimates for each ranged activity are aligned with the original deterministic schedule (Figure 61).

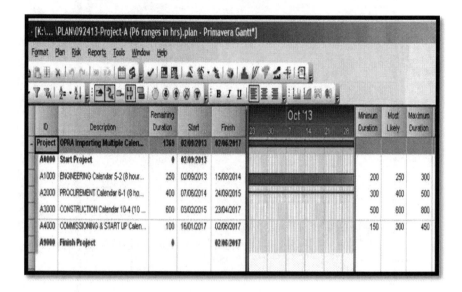

Figure 61 - Cross-check OPRA Ranges to Confirm Correct Translation

Change Planning Unit to Days (Figure 62) in order for OPRA to show the schedule using rounded off days as duration display.

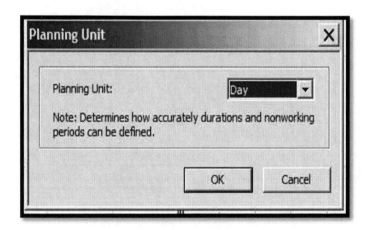

Figure 62 - Planning Unit Window

Probability Distribution charts (Figure 63, Figure 64, and Figure 65) of the entire plan. The chart represents the project end deterministic date of June 2, 2017. There is 34% probability of achieving that date.

Make sure that this date lines up with the deterministic date intended. It is also prudent to check alignment with the original Primavera schedule before importing to OPRA.

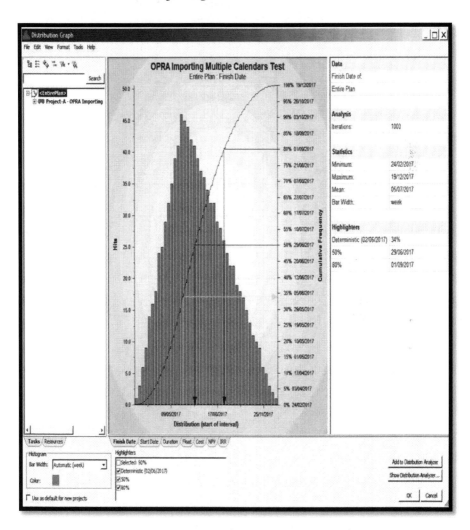

Figure 63 - Probability Distribution of Overall Schedule

The chart displayed on Figure 64 represents the completion of the engineering phase of the project. It has a deterministic date of August 15, 2014.

There is 51% probability of achieving the date.

Again, make sure that this engineering date lines up with the deterministic date intended. It is also prudent to check alignment with the original Primavera schedule before importing to OPRA.

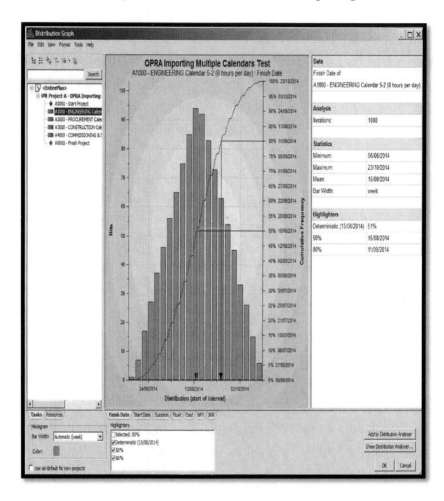

Figure 64 - Probability Distribution of the Engineering Phase

The chart displayed on Figure 65 represents the completion of the construction phase of the project. It has a deterministic date of April 23, 2017 with 34% probability of achieving the date.

We have the ability to focus on each activity in the schedule to see their corresponding probability estimate. Just filter and highlight the activity on the work breakdown hierarchy located on the left window.

Again, make sure that the construction completion date lines up with the deterministic date intended. Check alignment with the original Primavera schedule where the OPRA PLAN file originated.

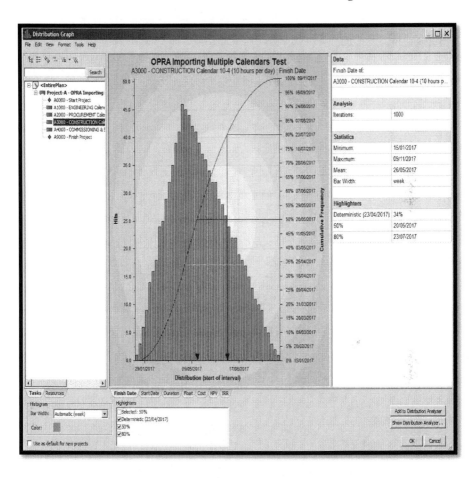

Figure 65 - Probability Distribution of the Construction Phase

Figure 66 displays a distribution analyzer curve of the entire plan. It is another form of graphical representation of an activity's deterministic date probability estimate. It is a translated histogram graph similar to the one shown on the two previous pages (see Figure 63).

The curve facilitates comparison and analysis between dates and probabilities of two or more activities in the schedule network.

145

Comparing attributes between S-curves is many times easier than between distributed histograms.

It is also an excellent window to compare the result of a current SQRA result to a previous one, especially one associated with major project checkpoints.

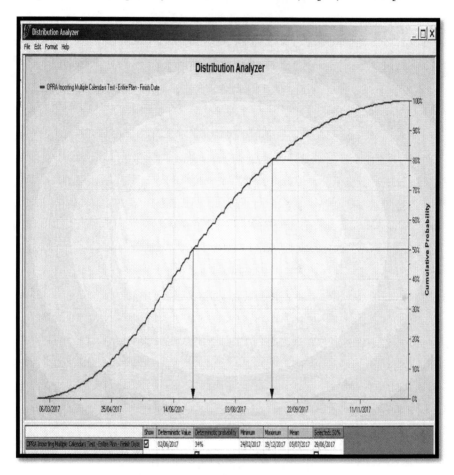

Figure 66 - Probability Distribution Analyzer

Make sure that for multiple calendar projects, the "For task durations use Time Periods associated with the task calendar" field of the Plan Options, Time tab is checked. It is the key for the calendar settings to govern instead of the default time-period shown in Figure 67.

If the User missed to set the Time tab properly, there will be error in translation. It is like translating Chinese to English without understanding the nuances of the language. Many risk analysts using the tools do not know that this setting is available to correct the discrepancies in durations and dates after import is completed.

Correcting this setting is necessary when big translation variances are discovered.

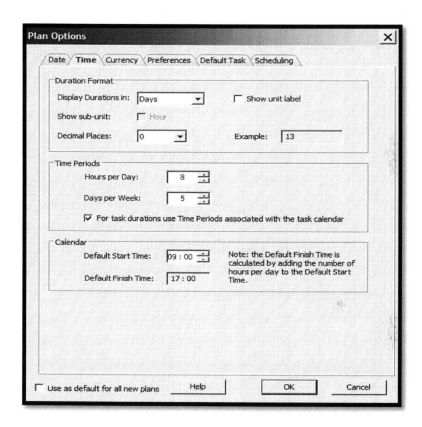

Figure 67 - Plan Options, Time Tab Dialogue Box

Chapter 7

RBM and Natural Disasters

7.1.   Introduction to RBM and Natural Disasters

According to the National Disaster Risk Reduction and Management Council (NDRRMC), the death toll from super typhoon Yolanda (International Code name Haiyan) had reached almost 6,000 by 11-Dec-2013. On that date, there were 27,022 people reported injured, while 1,779 were still missing. The disaster had reportedly affected some 2.6 million families, or about 12.1 million people in more than 12,100 villages in 44 provinces. Some 870,000 families were displaced, equivalent to around 3.9 million residents. Of those displaced, about 22,000 families, or some 94,000 people, are staying in the 386 evacuation centers.

The reported estimated damage to property was thirty-five point five (35.5) billion pesos or (825) million US dollars. This includes 18.2 billion pesos (US$ 423 million) in infrastructure and 17.3 billion pesos (US $402 million) in agriculture. The estimated damage to infrastructure included 1.2 billion pesos (US$ 27 million) in health facilities. The super typhoon destroyed at least 594,000 houses and damaged 598,000. Relief assistance of only 1.1 billion pesos (US$ 25 million) was provided to affected families as of the aforementioned date (GMANews, 2013)."

The delay of relief assistance at a time of grievous need, as described in the previous paragraph, underscores the prevailing risk management quality of the responsible government agencies. This is true for all, not only for a third world country like the Philippines. It is a no-brainer that the Philippines will always be a recipient of storms and earthquakes. The country is in the center of it all. In view of that, the Philippine government should develop an effective and viable response plan that everyone understands. They need to manage the probability (degree of certainty) and consequence (or impact) of risk to a certain extent.

As these two natural disturbances were one hundred percent (100%) certain within a year's time, the responsible government agencies must try to mitigate the impacts by using the existing breadth of national experience as a resource (read Section 7.11 and reflect). The question should be, "How can we reduce the impact, given the information already in the national archive?"

The technocrats who make decisions should then look at all the givens, while seriously considering the time element affecting all possible impacts during assessment, recommendation, planning, scheduling, and implementation process.

7.2.   Disaster Management is Risk-based Management

A project manager (or any other manager) has to understand the fundamental and mandatory integrative approach to risk management processes and knowledge areas. The long years of national experience on natural disasters are enough to convince any logical person that disaster management is also about risk management.

Looking towards the future knowing that there is a next big one is the start. Mitigating threat or enhancing opportunity consequences are main areas of control in cases where a risk practitioner has no influence on probabilities.

Underlining the connections between primary risks, secondary risks, residual risks, issues, and problems helps people realize the importance of cause and effect analysis in successfully determining the root causes and potential consequences of any event.

Sharing all these interesting principles with other professionals and disciplines should lead to more awareness, knowledge activation, and effective risk management. An excellent risk manager is able to differentiate risks, facts, issues, and problems.

7.3.   The Philippine Situation

The Philippine weather situation is a case that merits some study. Do you know that around 19 tropical cyclones enter the Philippine area of responsibility each year? Out of the 19 storms, about six to nine make landfall.

In terms of earthquake occurrence, the country experiences frequent seismic and volcanic activity. This is because it lies along the Pacific Ring of Fire. Much smaller magnitude earthquakes occur very regularly due to the meeting of major tectonic plates in the region (Sexton, 2006).

According to Wikipedia, eighteen (18) major earthquakes, as high as seven point five (7.5) on the Richter scale, have damaged the country from 2001 to 2014.

This is exactly equal to 1.5 earthquakes per year, with an average intensity of 6.44 (Wikipedia, List of Earthquakes in the Philippines, 2013).

7.4.   Super Typhoon Haiyan (2013)

One of the most powerful typhoons on record slammed into the Philippines on November 7–8, 2013 (shown in Figure 68 and Figure 69). It has recorded sustained winds of 235 kilometers (145 miles) per hour, and gusts up to 275 kilometers (170 miles) per hour. According to remote sensing data from the Joint Typhoon Warning Center, sustained winds approached 315 kph (195 mph) just three hours before landfall, with gusts up to 380 kph (235 mph).

Figure 68 - Typhoon Haiyan as Seen in Outer Space (NASA, 2013)

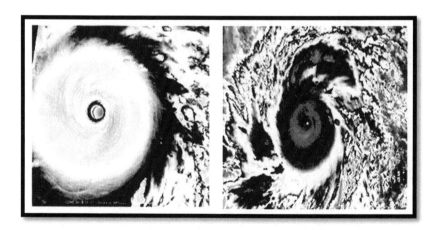

Figure 69 - View of Haiyan before Landfall (Samenow, 2013)

Haiyan's diameter was an estimated 600 kilometers (Figure 69). It practically covered the entire Philippines archipelago (Samenow, 2013).

There was absolutely no escape from its path. It is too large not to hit a good part of the country.

7.5.   Haiyan's Aftermath

Risk factors such as ethics, political will, planning, coordination, execution strategy, monitoring, and effective control, as well as many others, determined the extent of the Haiyan devastation (Figure 70).

Figure 70 - Devastation (Gilbeaux, 2013) (Measham, 2013)

While the government and other relief organization scrambled to save the living, the dead just had to wait. Many complained about the rotting corpses of their loved ones. This is a tragedy within a tragedy. Survivors expressed disbelief that assistance had not come sooner, and they feared the spread of disease. To allay the fear of the survivors, the World Health Organization declared that the bodies of victims of Typhoon Haiyan did not pose a public health risk and were not a priority. The picture in Figure 70 showed utter devastation by Haiyan (Gilbeaux, 2013) (Measham, 2013).

"The health risk to the public is negligible," the Canadian Red Cross's manager of public health and emergencies said to CBC News. "It is a myth actually. Unfortunately, there's a misunderstanding about the actual impact of dead bodies after a natural disaster" (Hildebrandt, 2013).

7.6. Philippine Earthquakes

The number of earthquakes occurring in the Philippine area of responsibility is from one point five (1.5) to three (3) per year. These occurrences have varying intensity and shock distribution. This would make any thinking person rightfully conclude that the risk of an earthquake is 100% certain on a yearly basis.

Again, we can only contemplate that the factors in our control are the consequences and impacts. A Philippine seismic and earthquake map (Figure 71) shows seismic activity distribution from 1990 to 2006 and the existing fault lines in the region where it lies, called the ring of fire (USGS, 2012) (Topinka, 1997). As was described, the cluttering of seismic activities in the archipelago is quite dense.

"Since the 1600s, there have been 106 earthquakes in the Philippines with a magnitude of more than 6.0 (Rappler, 2015)."

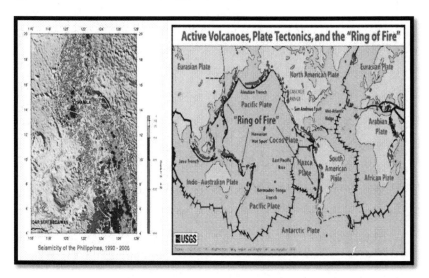

Figure 71 - Philippine Seismicity & Earthquake Map/USGS, 2010/1997

7.7. Probability and Consequences of Natural Disasters

The Philippines is a country prone to the primary risks of damaging natural forces such as typhoons and earthquakes. The grave consequences are inescapable (Figure 72).

Knowing that the probability of a typhoon or earthquake hitting the Philippines in any twelve-month period is 100% certain, it is no longer a risk but a fact. In the same vein, a realized risk is already an issue.

With all weather related risk events, where influencing the probabilities of occurrence is not possible, mitigating the consequences must be the means of control.

This tells all concerned that to manage the risks, there should be comprehensive, complete, workable, and effective contingency and response plans in place.

The government modeling its contingency to satisfy the possibility of its biggest historical disaster is prudent and wise. Response and relief funds must be flexible and transferable. It does not matter where the earthquake hits the hardest. There is no need to remind that it is the same country!

The pain of the little finger is a pain of the whole body.

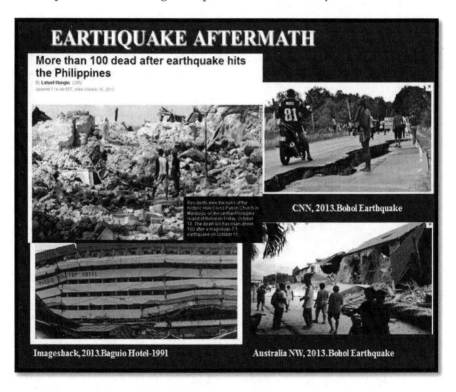

Figure 72 - Earthquake Aftermath (Mungin, 2013)

Figure 73 – Risk and Chaos

7.8.   The Risk Cycle

Any risk, if not mitigated or prevented, can result in an issue, issues, or non-issues, meaning a problem, problems, or non-problems which can result in another risk, risks, or non-risks and lead to another issue, issues, or non-issues. The cycle is the same for mitigated risks with residual risks, or one resulting in new risks, issues, or problems. When probability is one hundred percent (100%), it is already a fact. It is an assumed fact until the risk happens or not happens. Philosophers will tell you that the common check for a declaration of fact is verifiability.

When the risk finally occurs sometime in the future, the risk consequence becomes an issue or a problem. We are able to verify the fact.

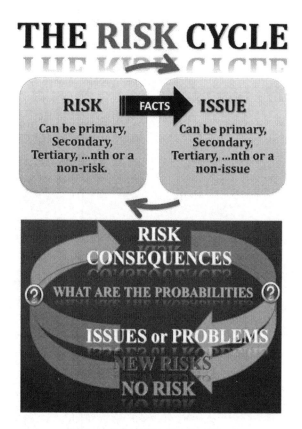

THE RISK CYCLE

RISK FACTS **ISSUE**

Can be primary, Secondary, Tertiary, ...nth or a non-risk.

Can be primary, Secondary, Tertiary, ...nth or a non-issue

RISK CONSEQUENCES

⑦ WHAT ARE THE PROBABILITIES ⑦

ISSUES or PROBLEMS

NEW RISKS

NO RISK

Figure 74 - Risk Cycle Diagram

7.9.   Use Ishikawa Diagram for Root Cause Analysis

Root cause analysis is the process of finding the event or condition that leads straight to an occurrence. It is a systematic procedure used to identify the principal possible cause of risk. In risk-based management, root cause analysis (RCA) is more useful in predicting future events.

RCA is no longer a hindsight technique of investigation but a forward-looking one. It still relies on previous experience, statistics, and more heavily on data correlation.

The Ishikawa method, often times called the Fishbone Diagram must be specifically expressed. The causes should not be a general description. Causes must be actionable and adjustable items.

It should exclude anything beyond a person's control. Root cause analysis helps produce effective recommendations for the prevention or exploitation of risks.

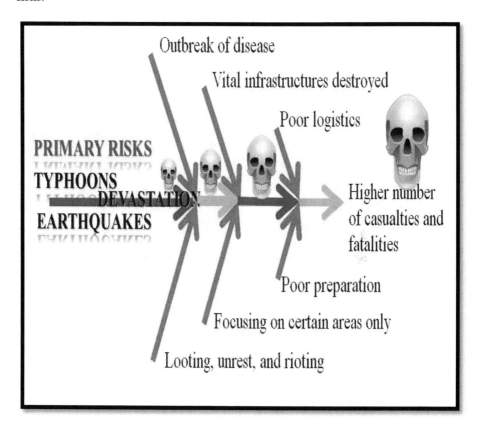

Figure 75 - Root Cause Analysis Using Ishikawa

7.10. Risk and Issues

Risk is an uncertain event or condition that, if it occurs, has a positive or negative effect on at least one business objective such as time, cost, scope, or quality (read Section 3.20 to reflect).

An issue is a negative risk that has occurred. In a logical sense, it is no longer a risk, as it is now certain and in the present. An issue can create problems that needs prompt response. An example is a forest fire. If it is happening right now, it is no longer a risk. It is already a problem. If it remains uncontrolled, and unmanaged, it becomes an issue. Others humorously define issues as problems that people learned to live with while continuously whining about it.

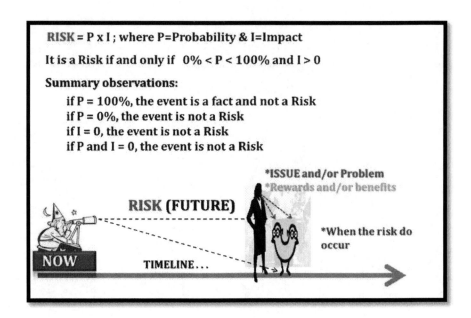

Figure 76 - Risk, Fact, Probability, Impact, Issue, and Problem

7.11. Issues and Problems

A problem is solvable while an issue is a problem that continues to become a problem, even after administering a solution or arriving at an answer. Issues take more time to fix because the solution usually does not fix the underlying problems accompanying the main one. While a problem is something that has a clear answer, the issue does not.

Both issues and problems can cause debates, arguments, and conflicts that divide or unite people. Issues are relatively larger and can be broken into smaller problems. If the problem cannot be resolved and people end up divided over it, then it becomes an issue (Phelm, 2013).

Let's go back to the forest fire. The animals scampering to safety at that time are all driven by their survival instincts much like a man suddenly faced by a life or death situation during a terrorist attack. He is also driven by instinct on how to survive.

The time to manage a life-threatening problem is so short that his actions might not qualify as management but pure luck. If he dies from a bullet wound, like those tourists who were recently attacked in Tunisia, then tough luck. If he survives, then great luck. He is probably in the right place at the right time despite being in the midst of chaos.

A problem, although not a blanket rule, usually needs quicker and prompter response, sometimes in seconds or minutes.

7.12. Risk Consequences Turn into Issues

Risk consequences can spawn a wide range of issues. In this case, poor logistics caused tremendous delay in distributing aid after the disaster. Casualties due to lack of food, water, shelter, clothing, and medical aid for several days (4 days to a week) contributed to the chaos. Similarly, poor preparation led to the government's heavy reliance on foreign aids, tools, transports, equipment, supplies, and expertise. Some issues created by these risk consequences as collated from (BBCNews, 2013) and (Katz, 2013) news articles are:

- Higher and increasing number of casualties and fatalities
- Dealing with survivors' serious physical and psychological trauma
- Extremely high relief operation cost.
- Populace reflecting on a weak and ineffective government resulting in a deteriorating reputation
- Dealing with civil unrest
- Unrealistic short term and long term recovery plan
- Poor communication management; for instance, difficulties in confirming casualties and fatalities, flawed statistical records or wrong data, or the majority of citizens in the provinces not having a clue what a "storm surge" is.
- Ineffective/inefficient collation of information
- Insufficient qualified resources to spearhead rescue, recovery, and security effort. This led to burial delays waiting for recovery and eventual identification, not enough police presence to prevent looting, and many other problems.
- Insufficient refrigerated morgue space, resulting in rotting corpses
- Outbreak of disease due to unsanitary conditions in the survivor camps
- Dealing with serious psychological trauma suffered by relatives and survivors, especially the young ones
- Overall late response by the government, epitomized by the numerous excuses as to why they fell short of expectations
- Wrong information resulting in the wrong response
- Tendency of the relief operation to focus on certain areas only
- Massive destruction resulting in a massive need for rescue, relief, and recovery
- Vital infrastructure was destroyed, including power, communication lines, roads, bridges, pier, and airports

- Poor hygiene and sanitation
- Delays due to political manoeuvrings, for instance, relief goods were repacked and branded with names and logos of a local politician, causing delays in the relief operations of charitable institution such as Red Cross.
- Underestimation of the risk
- Risk culture, for instance, evacuation orders not followed, and the government did not have sufficient contingency plans to deal with the consequence.
- Ignorance of risks, its probabilities, and its consequences
- Ill-equipped government relief agencies
- Local government was not prepared to deal with high impact risks, such as stronger typhoons and earthquakes
- Pervasive corruption in the government, like in one Asian country where natural disasters were used as front to scheme billions of dollars from its citizenry (Guzman, 2013)
- Anti-government rebels control certain areas
- No central operation command
- Assigned evacuation centres were destroyed, together with evacuees (Ehrenfreund, 2013)

7.13. Managing Risks, Issues, and Problems

Currently, in 2014, many economic soothsayers are predicting the worst economic crisis known to modern man to occur in the later part of 2015, advancing through most of 2016, a downturn expected to be worse than the recession of 2008. This projection came from known economic analysts who claimed to have accurately predicted the 2006 American real estate collapse and the 2008 worldwide economic downturn. The indicators he presented, if true to form, make sense.

On December 8, 2014, the Toronto Stock exchange had its biggest one-day drop in eighteen months as oil prices continued a sharp decline. Some industry analysts worry that it could extend into next year. The drop is bad news for the many oil and gas producers (Yew, 2014).

Reflecting on this makes one realize that identifying the risks brought about by weather conditions in a specific geography, such as in the Philippines, is already a given, and can be effectively addressed if the governments just put their minds and hearts to it. Nobody can prevent typhoons from happening, no one can control their magnitude, and no one can change their direction. A risk-based manager, therefore, has no power over the risk source, but has considerable power over the consequence of generated risks through loss reduction.

162

The governments has to learn to efficiently and successfully collaborate with private businesses, non-government offices, public sectors, existing bureaus, and ad-hoc committees to develop, plan, maintain, update, and execute necessary contingencies when identified risk are triggered.

Much like any business, government should have a well-established continuity management plan (CMP) and a strategic redeployment plan (SRP). It is great to imagine that all governments have such a plan, for if not, even an integrated government portfolio is not enough. This thinking has become more prominent in the last fifteen years because of 9-11, Hurricane Katrina, the 2008 financial crisis, the Fukushima nuclear disaster, Typhoon Haiyan, and several other major crises. The recommendation is for governments, NGOs, and businesses to set in place a plan that will permit each to optimize its resources, protect its existence, and preserve its reputation over and beyond enterprise risk management, in the event of a major disruption such as a horrendously strong typhoon. The focus deals more with the possible consequence of disruptions.

During any major disruption, a continuity management plan (CMP) might not be sufficient for restoration and survival. It is therefore mandatory to revalidate existing strategy and make the necessary changes. Over half of businesses exposed to a disastrous occurrence fail immediately (Elliott, Risk Assessment and Treatment, 2012). When an organization's survival is threatened, a strategic redeployment plan (SRP) is required. ERM, CMP, and SRP complement and supplement each other.

The use of a continuity management plan or business resiliency plan to address major potential threats to the organizational operations, (such as a financial crisis, a natural disaster, a man-made disaster, catastrophic damage to assets and facilities, or the loss of critical supplies), is growing in popularity. The goal is to build an operational plan with contingencies that allow key operations and key functions to continue if a disruption occurs (Elliott, Risk Assessment and Treatment, 2012). Citizens, business, business partners, and key stakeholders develop a renewed trust and confidence if they know that the organization has a CMP/SRP. The business survives, its reputation improves, operation continues, and relationships are more stable.

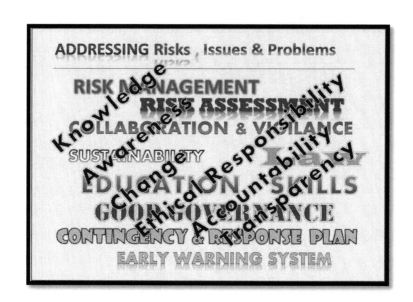

Figure 77 - Addressing Risks, Issues, and Problems

Chapter 8

Managing Cultural Diversity

8.1. Introduction to Diversity Risk-based Management

Are you an internationally trained professional working in the Canadian workplace? Are you experiencing communication challenges despite your good grasp of the English language? Do you feel that your leader and co-workers do not fully understand what you want to convey? Do you find your actions and your words get misinterpreted? Do you, through all these snags and complications, start to use the race card to make a point, maybe debate with yourself on what to do? Are you now thinking of going back to your point of origin and giving up the Canadian dream?

Perhaps it is the other way around. Are you a Canadian born or Canadian trained professional who serves under an internationally trained professional who was born and raised in another part of the world? Do you find it difficult to deal with them? Are you still wondering why he/she sometimes comes in completely from the left field?

The bottom-line objective in this chapter is simple. I hope to convince upper management in any organization to step back, look around, and start the much needed employee cultural orientation training. Lead the way in understanding various cultures. Educate employees how to cope with differences, to accept and manage diversity brought about by multiculturalism.

Managing diversity is not just for business. A person's action, speech, and manner of expression influences us one way or another as an individual. It affects our decision as a human being. It plays a big role with respect to our happiness and peace of mind. The more successful we are in managing others, the better our outlook would be. We can get more of what we want. Projects will be more fruitful. Relationships will prosper. There will be less contention because of biases. Acceptance and tolerance will govern.

I am not an expert or a social scientist, but I would like to present my experiences, studies, collaborative learning, and observations in this commentary. In my mind, if I honestly present my reflections surrounding workplace diversity, I hope to influence others to look closer and rethink their attitude towards the people around them. After doing some analysis, I now firmly believe that the fundamental principle to successfully managing cultural diversity starts with three key ideas. These ideas are not new, they are as old as time. Read on and know what they are.

In an attempt to describe the impacts related to the three key ideas, I have presented specific ordinary situations that could increase the reader's awareness. It is wise to recognize that if we do not understand the cultural universe and the diversity involved therein, even a small gap to the communication style, decision, and action we take can lead to misunderstanding and division. It is imperative that organizations find a way to prevent this from happening.

8.2.   Risk, Multiculturalism, and Pluralism

If we look in the past, multiculturalism has a long and wide history in Canada. The government of Canada adopted the idea during the 1970s and 1980s (Kobayashi, 1993). A journal called Place/Culture/Representation talked about the same subject (Duncan & Duncan, 1993). From that time onwards, various religious and cultural influences flourished in our society, from the family to the workplace and even into the building blocks of Canadian politics. They all now consist of people from a multitude of racial, religious, and cultural backgrounds.

Multiculturalism was an open invitation to cultural pluralism, a state where smaller groups within a larger society maintain their unique cultural identities. This means that the wider culture accepts the values and practices of a distinct cultural group, provided they do not violate any governing laws and values. Note that "cultural pluralism" is often confused with multiculturalism. Yes, the attributes are very similar, except for one evident distinction-"multiculturalism lacks the requirement for a dominant culture" (Wikipedia, Cultural Pluralism, 2013). In the midst of these diversities are the risks and questions that we all have to answer and manage every day.

How would you handle the following situations?

- Your project failed
- Someone refused to shake hands with you after being introduced
- A new acquaintance started to ask too many personal questions
- Someone jumped the queue
- Someone near your cubicle talked too loud
- Your office-mate asked you not to talk too loud
- Your female co-worker embraced you in front of your wife at an office party

Have you encountered any of the above situations? Probably more than fifty percent of you did. You would most likely feel bad if one of them happened to

166

you. You start asking questions to yourself but your questions remained unanswered.

The Canadian workplace is highly diversified. Your boss, your co-workers, and your colleagues heavily influence your success at work. Refusing to admit that such situations exist is a mistake. Denying the issues will get you nowhere. The truth is, (whether you admit it or not), there are times and occasions where you just cannot seem to get your message across and vice versa. The other parties apparently do not appreciate what you are bringing to the table. You often wonder what is wrong with them.

One of these days, you will wonder why one office-mate suddenly reacts negatively to something you say while the other keeps smiling. You will be surprised when a group of people does not agree with what you are saying just after two sentences. Relationships turn more personal rather than professional. Frustration comes creeping into your life, with you practically giving up the quest to understand. In extreme cases, you might already be in the midst of a conflict, spending negative energy, fighting and fending off adversaries, and trying to get even. The vicious cycle of conflict has started and there is no end to the stress. You conclude that your work relationship with your boss, direct report, colleague, or stakeholder is no longer important. It is not necessary to fix anything. The project you are managing is going south due to silent bickering or has already failed, so why bother? It is now a serious situation because the worse is about to come; you are going to start doubting yourself.

We know what it is like to become a victim of perception. You will not like it. They will not like it. Nobody will! It is for these reasons that I want you to have the opportunity to learn and try to get a good handle on these challenges. Nobody can do this perfectly, but we all have to start somewhere. We need to be aware, for without a good understanding and appreciation of another person's external and internal cultural dimensions, we can get lost, creating conflicts instead of harmony in the process.

In an article by John Hooker (2008), Tepper School of Business at Carnegie Mellon University, Intercultural Business Communication, he states, "the key to cross-cultural business is to understand one's business partners well enough to make cultural adjustments... A practical rule of thumb is that business transactions should favor the cultural norms of the social infrastructure on which they primarily rely."

The emphasis Hooker alludes to in his write-up is that business should not be seen as a self-contained activity that can disregard all other culture, but instead viewed with a sincere respect to the culture that provides the business. Since no one can really please everyone, this philosophy is very practical and makes perfect sense!

Cultural differences are one of the top fifteen reasons for project failure according to Symonds. Although it was the bottom position on the list, the threat posed by improperly managing cultural differences can easily land in the top five. Regardless, she is one of the many present day thinkers who believe that this concern has to be considered seriously by organizations, because it is real. She says, "… even on simple, straightforward projects there are many areas that can cause the sorts of problems that can eventually manifest themselves in failure. Add to the many possible causes of failure any level of complexity and problems can rapidly escalate into disasters (Symonds, 2011)."

Managing Cultural Diversity in Technical Professions (Laroche, 2003) is an excellent book that offers insightful observation on a subject that most of us take for granted. Used as a textbook and reference book in courses offered by several Canadian universities, including the University of Calgary, it provides guidance on the complex attitudes and behaviors of other human beings. On the back cover, Laroche highlights the facts that "1) …most technical professionals do not recognize the impact of cultural differences in the workplace and 2) cross-cultural issues lead to significant under-utilization of talent negatively affecting productivity."

As you read and appreciate some of the situations in this book, the clarity that eluded you in the past draws nearer. A closer view of what actually transpired is now available to consciously, and even unconsciously, understand. You will appreciate what really contributed to the conflict. A person who goes out there in the workplace without understanding the cultural universe, and the diversity that surrounds him or her, will be in for a big surprise or a good share of heartache.

8.3.   Case 1: Nho Klu

Not more than a decade ago, Nho Klu (not his real name) was sitting in the office of John Didnotsee to complete the annual appraisal. He exerted all his best efforts, hoping for a promotion to a manager's role. He felt that he had all the reason to expect advancement because he had exceeded all his goals and objectives.

After some small preliminary talk, the two went through Nho's goals. There were a lot of nice praises and commendation, after which; John finally said, "Nho, you know what? You are good at what your do, but although you are the best technical person in this group, you could never be a manager. You will not be a manager."

Nho Klu was shocked at his leader's concluding statement. He had always thought that he was doing excellently. He confidently felt that he had the knowledge, the education, the skills, and the experience needed to succeed. He was a respected senior engineering manager for almost 15 years, with several direct reports, in his country of origin. The unexpectedness of the statement hurt his feelings.

Trained in a hierarchical culture with large power distance, Nho controlled himself. He respectfully responded to John's shocking conclusion by citing his accomplishments and his other qualifications. Unfortunately, it did not change John's perception, and in the coming days and months thereafter, their relationship soured and finally eroded. John's opinion of Nho remained unchanged. Adding more damage to Nho's reputation, John spread his perception to the other managers. Another six months from that fateful meeting, Nho decided that since he could no longer grow, he would resign.

Nho spoke about that incident recently, and he has this to say:

"My family immigrated to Canada in 2003 and was into my second year when I got employed in that engineering, procurement and construction (EPC) company where I eventually reported to John. When John talked, I was all ears. By not being vocal against some of his methods, I thought that was showing respect and loyalty. Although, I sometimes felt he does not have any idea about the task, I kept my mouth shut. He was the leader and I trusted him to do things correctly. I have never done anything unless I have his blessing. What kind of leader was he that after I gave my best approving-yes-attitude and support, that was how he repaid me? I have no idea!"

"I've attended so many meetings and interactions in my working life before Canada. They were all good experiences. My word as a manager is almost sacred. All direct reports follow exactly what I ask of them. The right behavior summons respect for the one who has a higher designation or authority. I am not allowed to say anything unless I was asked to give an opinion. I have no great appreciation for people who talks a lot. I see them talking for the sake of talking, to get attention and be visible only. I give recognition based on what was actually delivered against a goal. Teamwork is important and no one should ever claim the group's accomplishment as oneself. When someone hops offices and talk, that's how they take the credit solely for themselves!"

"I always consider that too much talking as a waste of time. This kind of thinking was the problem. As you can imagine, my leader thought I was not qualified to be promoted, and I thought my Leader was not qualified to be my leader. It was such a bad combination."

"Fortunately, the company I am with now has embarked into a program called Understanding Diversity in the Workplace. Everyone in the organization completed a prescribed mandatory cultural re-education. After my training, I saw to it that I make significant adjustments to my way of thinking and positive changes start to happen."

8.4.   Case 2: Puro Mali

Puro Mali (not his real name) was one of the company's project reviewers and auditors. He had just completed his review of the project. He gave the project two high findings for: 1) not submitting the required project documents on time and 2) submitting a project schedule that fell below the company's minimum quality standard. High finding points to high priority items requiring mandatory resolution. It means that the project has deviated from plan, standards, and best practices by being incomplete or non-compliance. Failure to address the finding satisfactorily will adversely affect the direction and subsequent result of the project, adding considerable risk to cost and schedule. The category of the findings can be concerning financial, social, safety, environmental, health, reputation, strategic, and others.

Within the day, Puro received an e-mail from the project manager Don Notagree, with copies to all the department's bigwigs.

Don's e-mail:

"I do not agree with the position you have taken. High findings are unjust as they assume that the project team has blatantly ignored the fact that we are required to prepare the requested information. In addition, to assume that the team did not generate or have information that is more current is rather short sighted. At a minimum, the initial findings should be "TBD" (to be determined) while your review continues."

Puro was very unhappy with the e-mail. He felt slighted by the personal, strong, and accusatory tone of the message. He made sure to reply promptly, copying the same bigwigs.

Puro's e-mail:

"The deadline for the submission of findings had passed. Your group submitted nothing and as a result, the project got a high finding. I am not trying to insinuate that you and your team are irresponsible. Please do not make it personal by attacking me like this. We can always talk between ourselves before you issue a broadcasted e-mail. The high rating is in accordance with the review guidelines. There was nothing shortsighted about it. I hope that this brings you some understanding. If you like, we can meet face to face, have a cup of coffee, and resolve this disagreement on neutral grounds."

In spite of Puro's apparently cool-headed approach, a cold war had started. This was now a strained work relationship, and upper management did not even know about it.

He also discovered, during a follow-up meeting, that the words and phrases he used in the same report had elicited some negative reactions from Don and the other two members of his team. They complained that the wording was too harsh.

Puro was not expecting that kind of feedback. In his view, the words and phrases that he used were all perfectly normal. Why did they see it that way?

"It cannot be this way," he thought.

He has a Master's degree in business communication in his country of origin. The intention of the review process is to identify room for improvement, and bridge gaps to help the project. It was not his purpose to create a gap. He thought, "*#!% ... there's something wrong with these people. Why are they extremely sensitive?"

I captured the words and phrases that Puro used on the list below.

- "The quality of the project schedule is **questionable**. It was below the minimum standard of quality."
- "The project **should follow** the governing procedure and **must see to it** that…"
- "…schedule resource loading was **incorrect**."
- "There were **mistakes** in …"

Groping for answer and seeking a peaceful co-existence, Puro unhappily agreed to change his wording, resulting in the following:

- "The quality of the project schedule could be improved as it is below the minimum standard of quality."
- "The project is requested to review the governing procedure and to check …"
- "…schedule resource loading did not match the baseline estimate."
- "There were some misalignments in …"

8.5.   My View

Whether you are the Chief Executive Officer (CEO) of your company, the janitor or cleaner under contract, or a jobless person on the street, I am sure you want some respect. An intelligent person wants to be heard and a chance to be understood and validated. The American writer Max Ehrmann (1872–1945) Desiderata, which he wrote in 1927 underlined this principle in the first few lines of the famous prose poem.

"Go placidly amid the noise and haste, and remember what peace there may be in silence.

As far as possible without surrender, be on good terms with all persons.

Speak your truth quietly and clearly; and listen to others, even the dull, and the ignorant; they too have their story.

Avoid loud and aggressive persons. They are vexations to the spirit."

TIP "If you compare yourself with others, you may become vain and bitter; for always there will be greater and lesser persons than yourself."

I, for one, find the ideals of yesterday more and more unsuitable to our current complex society. As such, it is imperative that organizations train and prepare all their employees not only to manage others, but also to manage themselves in a culturally diversified workplace. We all have to open our eyes wider, as it is crystal-clear that mismanaging cultural differences will adversely affect even a strong, skillful, and qualified workforce.

The challenges brought about by cultural differences like nationality, region, education, language, family values, political and professional affiliation, exposures, training, expectations, communication styles, philosophies, roles, positions, responsibility, unspoken languages, and many other potential differences produce the common office interactions and relationships we are seeing today in the workplace. It is very interesting how new Canadians (newcomers to Canada) cope at work compared to their Canadian-trained counterparts in various settings. In that aspect, communication being a two-way street, we can conclude that it will affect Canadian trained professionals to the same extent. The degree of understanding can improve only if one takes enough time to look through each other's lenses. Seeing another person's perspective with an open mind will influence the success and failures of any endeavor.

Culture affects work behavior, attitude, relationships, productivity, objectives, and more. One of the common tasks that Human Resource Department (HRD) faces is to find the right talent and successfully assigning him/her to the right role.

In spite of this, why was there no serious program to run a culture education program in many large companies? Yes, many large organizations have not given enough attention to the management of threat and opportunities. They failed to see the valuable investments that can improve organizational management of cultural differences.

Human Resource Departments (HRD) of these companies have not seriously taken the initiative of arranging and coordinating the training of their employees on the subject. Instead, they chose to ignore the issues related thereto. What these companies did not consider is that the issues of today can easily generate the risks of tomorrow. It is better to address this proactively than to relegate the responsibility to the Canadian government's multicultural bureaus.

If we review Case 1 and Case 2, we will notice a glaring mismatch in the communication style of the characters. The most basic natural behavior that each one of them brought to the work environment reflected their styles.

The problem was that they did not match each other's style. It goes to show that the key to better understanding depends equally on all involved. Nho, John, Puro, Don, managers, and colleagues should have an open mind to avoid quickly succumbing to personal perceptions based solely on their own cultural lenses.

Nho came from a background where informal office talks are considered a waste of time, a mere rambling discussion about things that will not contribute to work objectives, where everyone was required to focus on business productivity through strict time management.

He carried this training in the Canadian workplace. He avoided what he perceived as idle talks around the water coolers or in the hallway. He avoided what he thought might be construed as wasting time. They labeled Nho as weird and anti-social. They referred to him as a team-slayer instead of a team player.

With the pressure mounting, Nho eventually resigned.

Even now, Nho still refuses to accept that he should have made the necessary adjustments. He feels that he did nothing wrong. He did his job well and was passionate about accomplishing work objectives, but completely unaware of any prevailing social norms which he should have followed, at least for his own sake.

If the others had some understanding about managing diversity, the outcome would have been more on the positive side. They would have provided Nho some leeway and helpful insights.

The idea of hierarchical culture is tied closely to the power distance dimension (PDI) forwarded by Geert Hofstede. A visit to the Mind Tools website in 2012 provides the reader a starting plain look at what Hofstede calls the "Five Dimensions of National Culture". A revisit to the same website recently has added one more dimension to the group. Suffice it to say, without delving into details, these general dimensional attributes is a good tool in managing and distinguishing one nationality from another.

"The cultural dimensions represent independent preferences for one state of affairs over another that distinguishes countries (rather than individuals) from each other. The country scores on the dimensions are relative, as we are all human and simultaneously we are all unique. In other words, culture can be only used meaningfully by comparison (Hofstede, 2015)."

PDI according to Hofstede articulates the effects of the more powerful members of a society to the less powerful. The degree of respect and fear is an accepted form of measure in the eyes of common observer. The other dimensions are individualism (IDV), masculinity/femininity (MAS), uncertainty avoidance (UAI), and long-term orientation (LTO).

He describes the general tendencies in groups of people, not the individuals within those groups. You can review the scores by country, or compare Canada with other countries to see how the various cultural dimensions that Hofstede identified in his website, The Hofstede Center, play out globally. The higher the score, the higher the tendency towards such national attribute.

Pay particular attention to the countries that the people you deal daily come from. The proper explanation of each dimension is in this same website (MindTools, 2013). IDV is a measure of a person's belief in one's self and his freedom to choose and achieve what he wants. He believes that no one has his best interest except himself. IDV's extreme is selfishness.

In light of these scores, think about some interactions you have had with people in other countries. Figure 78 and Figure 79 compares Canada and other countries on various cultural dimensions; i.e. Canada-Venezuela-India, and Canada-Philippines-UK.

With this information in the back of your mind, your future conversation or forthcoming associations with anyone can now make more sense, thanks to this newly found insight.

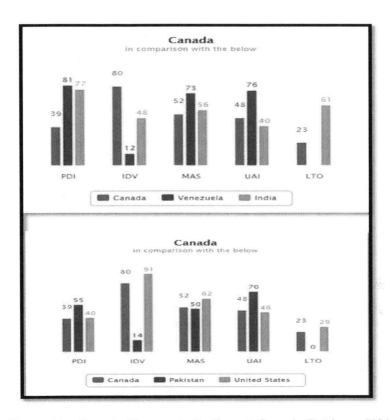

Figure 78 - Canada-Venezuela-India and Canada-Pakistan-USA

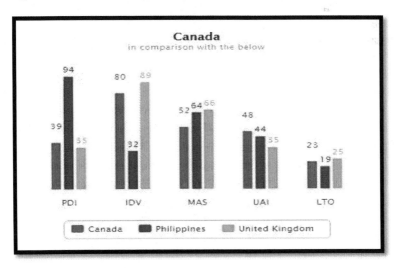

Figure 79 - Canada-Philippines-UK

Nho and Puro's predicament is quite similar in many ways because both boils back to communication norms. While Nho respected hierarchy, Puro valued the standards and procedures that were in place. He was honest, candid, direct, and task-focused. Unfortunately, he gave his opinions raw, without regards to the typical political cushioning. He was oblivious to the strained relationship created at the opposite ends, due to his cultural make-up.

In a similar way, Don and his two project members would have not reacted the way they did if only they understood Puro's cultural make-up. The issue that came up was work related and should have been dealt with more effectively on a professional level. The disagreement was aggravated when it started to circle around personality.

TIP The inner workings of giving feedback to another person follow a ruled-range of feedback reception.

The reception to what one says is either positive or negative depending upon the individual's cultural feedback scale regardless of intent. Examples of the feedback scale between different nationalities mentioned in the book titled Managing Cultural Diversity in Technical Profession (Laroche, 2003) prove keys to understanding.

Knowing that the feedback scale of each individual varies considerably from country to country, or culture to culture, lets one conclude that one source of cultural misunderstandings is feedback misinterpretation. Look at Figure 80 and graphically correlate the feedback concept discussed by Laroche.

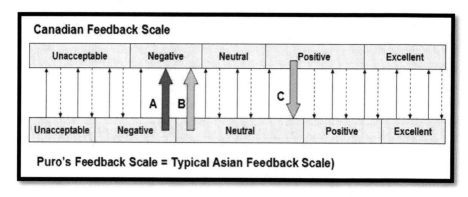

Figure 80 - Feedback Scale Concept

When Puro made that slightly negative comment (A) to his Canadian counterpart, the feedback interpretation was harsh criticism. It prompted an unexpected reaction. He also delivered what was to be a neutral commentary (B) and yet, his comment was taken negatively. Two people belonging to different cultural groups should expect these kinds of feedback scale differences.

The studies I did on the combinations of fundamental communication theories, guidelines, and processes, as well as their corresponding practical applications, show that Case 1 is a case of a "task-focused" versus a "person-focused" communication style. Donna Stringer and Patricia Cassidy wrote about it in their write ups titled "52-Activities for Improving Cross-Cultural Communications" (2009). The authors stated that the "Communication styles and patterns differ vastly among people from different cultures" with every culture having their own "communication style norm."

When these specific styles mix with others, stereotypes begin, and sometime inaccurate perceptions arise. This culture manual can be applied globally wherever your business interests are (Rush, 2011). The issue that has to be resolved in the majority of places is not singly about work competence, but is also about teamwork and good work relationships. In conclusion, we will achieve good relationships only through mutual, thoughtful understanding, appreciation, and acceptance.

I have mentioned in various project management professional discussions what I fondly call a "cultural universe." This universe is the totality of everything that has to do with culture and all of its attributes and dimensional elements. The zooming in and the zooming out of each one of us is the reason why we see each other differently. It is the rationale why we understand others the way we do.

This is the reason why people have different perspectives. A person who dislikes another person because of cultural differences is not actually biased. While it is true that, in their individual perspective, they perceive another differently, they are not biased, but ignorant.

The real problem is that we all tend to see one another through our own lenses, and make unfair decisions through them.

Culture is multi-faceted from the start. This was why another person's (or another group's) culture can be seen as a threat and/or an opportunity (note the "and/or") by another.

It is for the same reason that, regardless of how much we try and control ourselves, the ways we perceive somebody else's culture heavily depends on whether our respective individual (or group) objectives are aligned to that person's objectives. I refer this to as relativity applied to culture. Each individual player within the cultural universe will see things differently compared to another, who may see exactly the opposite. It will be either good or bad, depending on his/her involvement with the goal at stake.

Now, if we can become an independent observer in a different plane of this cultural universe and open our mind, we will see different cultures' multiple facets from different angles. If one zooms in, he/she will perceive culture as either "negative, positive or neutral," but if one zooms out, he/she will see all attributes.

As soon as this happens, we can begin to attain a level of understanding that most of us never thought possible. We can see the different perspectives that eluded us before and finally realize that the good and the bad attributes depend on where the observer lies in this cultural universe. You know now that the reason you feel perfectly fine and unaffected is that you have no stake at play.

Is this a state of neutrality? How does one define being neutral? Perhaps, one becomes neutral when the total quantitative interest values brought about by cultural aggregates and combinations, in terms of a specific objective, cancel out. Otherwise, it is normally very difficult to see things this clearly. It is quite clear that culture is not absolute, but relative.

With globalization comes an increased interaction between people of different countries and an increase in the need to deal with cultural differences. A project manager needs to understand his or her own culture and the cultures of the other project stakeholders. The key to success in international business is the sincere desire to integrate into a new and different culture (Ranf, 2010).

We all know that you do not have to go to China just to encounter a taste of Chinese culture, or to the Philippines to understand the Filipino culture. They come to you at work before you know it.

In order to be successful in Canada, Chinese or Filipino immigrants should adapt to the accepted and prevailing Canadian culture. It is difficult but not impossible for Canadians to adapt to an imported culture such as theirs. Since adapting to another culture is difficult, the only way to go is to bear the differences through tolerance and acceptance.

TIP Tolerance in turn, gives rise to pluralism. Tolerance is a nice big word in Canada, except that tolerance without understanding is empty. With proper orientation on Canada's diversity, we can remove this uneasiness from the workplace.

Only someone endowed with super-awareness can fully appreciate and benefit from the totality of this cultural universe and the risk it brings. A conscious effort from all is required if one is to not become prey to cognitive and personal biases. Be aware that biases tend to come out almost unconsciously due to some inherent cultural designs of a person.

This is why it is better to think twice (or more) before saying or doing something. An adage describes it this way, "It is better to say nothing with everyone thinking I am stupid, than opening my mouth and confirming it."

We should all learn to hold back our judgment and avoid stereotyping people. Then and only then, we can one move to the realm of acceptance.

I like the recent entry in a Linkedin post very much where a contributor describes the difference between "tolerance" and "acceptance" precisely in the context of organizational culture.

> She said, "Tolerance suggests that there is one, dominant and accepted way of being by which all other ways of being are judged or measured. Ways of being that differ from dominant way are tolerated and allowed to be present but not allowed to shape into something bigger nor change the environment (Chuda, A., 2015)."

> "Acceptance on the other hand, allows for deeper integration of difference into institutional structures and ways of being. Culture that is accepted means allowing the culture to shape, influence, and possibly control the organizational ways of being (ibid)."

There are three key ideas that can help one navigate through the ever-changing Canadian workplace.

These are: 1) Do not judge a book by its cover, 2) A person perceive others based on his personal goals, and 3) Developing pragmatic competence.

The principal idea is universal and applies to other workplaces. It is the idea of awareness and acceptance.

If one is aware of what is happening around him, he will be successful not only in Canada but also in several different places in the world. If we learn to accept a person as a whole, there is no need for tolerance. Tolerance is not as good as acceptance because it accompanied by resistance. The presence of resistance creates heat that tends to make seemingly good relationships artificial.

8.6. Do not Judge a Book by its Cover

Figure 81 - Do not Judge Books by Their Covers

Every text that I have read about the proper management of a multi-cultural workforce has emphasized that one must neither judge nor make any quick conclusion about anyone on the basis of just what one sees, hears, or feels through one's personal lenses.

The world would be a lot better if each individual uses the other's or group's lenses, with an objective to understand better from their end and to increase one's awareness of the existing similarities and differences between people.

Only when we take into consideration what the other person sees that we begin to see a new and wider perspective. It is through an improved appreciation of culture can we start to formulate our own guiding theories, tools, and methodologies.

Key Idea # 1 is "Do not judge a book by its cover" is an old adage. It is not something new, for it existed hundreds of years before the time of motivational theorist such as Maslow, McGregor, Herzberg, Arthur, and other more modern experts on managing multiculturalism such as Lionel Laroche, Shapiro, Thompson, and many more.

The iceberg representation of culture is another way of presenting this old saying. It makes a lot of sense because it visually represents the same old key idea above. The exposed portion of an iceberg is only about ten percent of its entire volume so do not judge an iceberg by looking at its tip.

This statement is a philosophy, not just a guide. It is a critical reminder that prompts us to be more conscious of a person's behavior.

It underlines complexity more than meets our immediate observation.

To quote Lionel Laroche, "Parts of culture are visible, whereas others are deeply submerged." (2003, Lionel Laroche on Managing Cultural Diversity in Technical Profession- Exhibit 1.2, page 4).

The external dimensions of an individual includes all external appearances and information, marital status, country, religion, work experience, company, education, income, and other factors, while the internal dimensions consists of race, gender, nationality, sexual orientation, age, etc. (Gardenswartz & Rowe, 2003).

TIP Our degree of understanding depends on how we zoom in and zoom out our viewpoint.

The truth of the matter is this. People are easy prey to outward appearance. Another person is quickly assessed based on one's norms of beauty, social status, profession, gender, and others.

It should not be a surprise because physical appearance is something publicly displayed. No intimacy. Direct contact is not necessary. It is almost like appraising merchandise through a glass pane display.

It comes without attachment or time investment.

Do we want to see one perspective only? Do we want to see the whole? A person's attitude hinges on one's overall understanding of others, coupled with the desire to understand truly.

To comprehend, the overall approach must be holistic!

8.7. A Person Perceives Others Based on His Personal Goals

I remember very well what my father said thirty-nine years ago, while I was visiting his work place as a young boy in the Governor's Office, Province of Batangas, Philippines. He was the Provincial Administrator-in-charge of socio-political affairs at that time (1976).

TIP He aptly said, "There's no greater interest than self-interest." Self-interest is the driving force of every person.

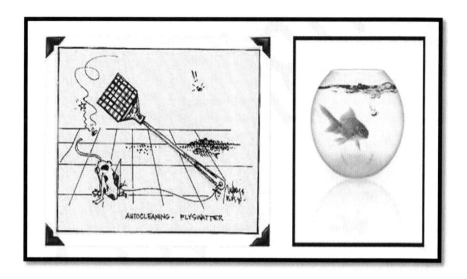

Figure 82 - The Fly and the Auto-cleaning Fly Swatter

Figure 83 - The Fish Appreciates Only the Bowl it Lives in

My dad articulated that the statement is about goals, objectives, missions, and visions. Some are grander and some are simpler. Instead of saying, "there's no greater goal than personal goal," he chose the word "interest" to sum it all. Of course, as can be expected of most teenagers, what I heard went from one ear and out the other. I only began to realize the wisdom of his statement years later.

The message he conveyed is something philosophical and deep-rooted. Interest drives people to do what they do. Tatay, as we fondly call him, had since passed away in 2006 but his simple statement has lived in our memory because we found what he said is true.

It is so true that we have not found anything that will disprove its application. It is so far, without exception.

TIP All of us have interest. Everyone pursue a goal. Nobody does something without a purpose. All humans have a goal.

Even the person who just floats around the city's sidewalks has a purpose. He might not even know his grand design but he has a goal, even if it is just a short goal at a time. Doing nothing is also an objective. In a business enterprise, the summary objective of all stakeholders becomes the organization's objectives.

Just think about it. If I decide to go out for a walk tomorrow, I must be going somewhere. I might say when you ask me that I am going nowhere but at any point in time, I will be somewhere. In so doing, I have a purpose. After all, what is the value of doing something for nothing? Ergo, we measure our success by how close we come to our objectives.

The frog, the flies, and the fly swatter exist relative to each other. Each one has a purpose. Maybe, the swatter kills the fly that the frog cannot catch. The flies either avoid the swatter, escape to die according to its lifespan, or end up gobbled by the frog (Figure 82). Any which way the story ends, each has a place and a role. They all touch one another.

We are all part of a great relationship network that has no end where each one has a purpose. We primarily perceive other people based on our personal goals. A person who supports our individual objectives will most likely receive automatic acceptance from us, and vice versa. We may realize that we have to work a lot harder to be impartial and appreciative of others, yet we always fall into that same trap repeatedly. Our biases become clear now.

The risks or uncertainties brought about by many influencing factors are always associated with our end goals, our interest.

What people do or don't do will influence the results. The fish in the bowl illustration describes the origin of this bias.

An engineer who has twenty years of experience in a Canadian manufacturing workplace will find it difficult, if not shock if suddenly transferred to a Japanese's or a Saudi Arabian's workplace. This is why a cultural orientation of the new workplace is called for before such deployment takes place.

A senior manager of a big EPC company who suddenly exclaimed that he smells a dead rat after an Asian engineer heated up his specially prepared exotic dish in the microwave oven indicates to all that he lacks exposure. He is unable to hold his view before blurting out his judgment as he has not experience the smell or taste of such dish.

So, what does it tell us? It tells us that the fish appreciates only the bowl it lives in (Figure 83).

People looks at things that are not familiar with fear, suspicion, and sometimes disgust, much like the senior manager in the story.

A teacher in Business Communication for Internationally Trained Professionals correctly pointed out, "..., it is complex indeed! We may not "like" someone whom we feel is thwarting our goals, but at the same time, their behavior may help us reflect, re-examine, and maybe even redefine or readjust our goals and objectives so they are less opportunistic and more holistic. In this case, the person we initially see as our barrier turns out to be our benefactor."

I believe that it is all in the character of the individuals. You might have a great leader, great motivator, but if the employee is not perceptive, or is not interested, no matter what the manager does, he cannot influence the employee. He will fail in what he is trying to achieve.

There is the opposite case, where a manager might not motivate the employees enough; however the employee is self-motivated, self-propelled, and will achieve great results, even without motivation from the manager.

I know these are extreme examples, but I do strongly believe that it is all based on personality. It depends on how each person perceives the other's actions.

As you have noticed, we are back to the core of our subject matter; i.e. a person perceives another person according to his personal interest.

8.8. Pragmatic Competence

Pragmatic competence is the knowledge of the linguistic resources available in a given language for realizing particular illocutions, knowledge of the sequential aspects of speech acts, and finally, knowledge of the appropriate contextual use of the particular language's linguistic resources.

Although the exact nature of the relationship is still unknown, and requires further research, preliminary evidence indicates there is a close link in the development of pragmatic and grammatical competence (Barron, 2003). It is the ability to use language in a contextually appropriate fashion. Pragmatic competence is a fundamental aspect of a more general communicative competence (Nordquist, 2013).

Undoubtedly, pragmatic competence is cultural intelligence (CQ). To have one is to promote good interpersonal relationship in an organization (Langton, 2013). CQ is an individual thing. An organizational culture does not mean it has cultural intelligence. In fact, the CQ of one leader among hundreds can sometime falsely reflect the culture of the whole organization.

It is a pity when that happens because it introduces reputational risk to the business.

In many ways, by having CQ, a person will say the right thing at the right time. He knows how to handle conflicts and disputes, thereby promoting harmony in the workplace. CQ suggests that individuals vary in how they deal with other cultures. CQ helps in determining whether a person's behavior is representative of all members of a group or just that person.

Figure 84 - Words Play, What do People Say in the Desert?

TIP In order for us to be effective in managing other people, the cultural map that we should use, must be tailored according to those we are want to influence.

Culture affects work behavior, attitude, relationship, productivity, objectives, and more. In fact, one of the frustrations that Human Resource Department (HRD) faces is being able to get the right talent and successfully assigning him/her to right role. Getting the right fit reduces business risks. In spite of this, why was there no serious program to run a culture education program in many large companies?

It is unfortunate that until now, many organizations had not given enough attention to the threat & opportunities brought about by diversity. It is all talk.

Improving cultural competence is the starting point of understanding cultural differences. Mitigating or enhance risks begins with awareness, followed by identification of cultural risks. Correct response and management of cultural differences follow close behind.

The HRDs of these companies should take on the initiative of arranging and coordinating the training of its employees on the subject instead of ignoring the issues related thereto.

It is better than relegating the responsibility to the Canadian government's

185

multi-cultural bureaus.

If the other person is less hierarchical, we should tend to be the same. If he/she is more direct, we have to be similarly direct. As our relationships in the work environment grow and form, we have more than ample time to make conscious adjustments.

We then find ourselves improving in our cultural competency from this conscious competence to unconscious competence.

There are challenges for sure, but our newfound knowledge and understanding of culture, its general indicators, elements, approaches, and management techniques should move us forward. I believe that by seeking to understand first, we can be better managers and team players.

A well-planned orientation should educate internationally trained and Canadian-trained professionals on how to understand the rich cultural diversities that surround them. It is not surprising that such orientation becomes a real revelation to many employees.

All businesses should assign qualified resources to improve the pragmatic competence of its employees. It would be a big step forward if major organizations support a business case recommending all employees to go through a mandatory study and orientation of people's culture.

Would it not interest and excite you to get a program like that going if you are the CEO, an upper management person, or a director of your company?

Chapter 9

Project Integration

9.1. Introduction to Project Integration

The challenge many project managers are now facing is how to reconcile their own understanding of what the word "integration" really means in project management. It is the acceptance that a project team has to comprehend the integrative requirements of the project in a holistic way for one to identify and highlight the critical elements needed for success. It entails the integration of people/resources, standards, procedures, work instructions, methodologies, and tools. It requires risk-based management maturity.

The measure of maturity emanates directly from the leadership. The drive to reach that certain maturity point comes from the people running the organization. It goes to show that people are the foundational strength of a business enterprise.

Pulling the project portfolio together has pre-requisites in order to achieve full integration. One of them is making sure that the sub-elements are themselves complete. The temptation of going ahead with the project despite a deficient plan, an incomplete scope, engineering holds, and high uncertainty is always present. Project managers must be prudent before making a decision by understanding that integration only works when all components are acceptably ready.

This chapter shall attempt to share some stories that can reinforce that integrative project management concept, while demonstrating the importance of a good quality plan in pursuit of an effective risk-based project execution.

9.2. Causes of Project Failure

According to UK Bull Survey (1998), the top three causes of an IT/IS project failure are communication breakdown, lack of planning, and poor quality control. The Canadian KPMG Survey (1997), on the other hand, identified poor project planning, weak business case, and lack of top management support as their three top reasons. Chaos Report (1995) enumerated incomplete requirements, lack of user involvement, lack of resources, unrealistic expectations, lack of management support, changing requirements, and lack of planning as their seven top drivers (IT-Cortex, 2013).

The UK Bull Survey was the result of about 203 telephone interviews of IT leads within the top 100 corporations, using negative consequence criteria focused on missed deadlines, budget overrun, poor communications, and the inability to meet project requirements. The positive consequence criteria, on the other hand, focused on meeting milestones, maintaining quality, and meeting budget. The Chaos report used the inputs 365 IT managers, using cost overruns, delays, and content deficiencies as its negative consequence focus of concern.

9.3.   Example of Failed Construction Projects

The list never ends, but for this chapter, I would like to concentrate on projects in Canada, the country I call my own. Here are some of them, in no particular order.

Figure 85 - Direction of Success and Failure

- The Pickering Nuclear Generating Station (Wikipedia, 2013) reportedly had a cost overrun from $780 million (2002) to $2.5 billion (2005), ending with only two reactors in service instead of four. It shows costs 221% above target.
- The Montreal Olympic Stadium (Payne, M., 2006, and Wikipedia, 2013) had a cost overrun from $310 million (1970) to a debt of $1 billion (1976), with a final cost settlement of $ 2 billion (2006),

effectively accounting for about 545% cost overrun. On top of this dismal end-result was a poor quality structure.

- The Long Lake Project (Journal of Commerce, 2008) had a cost overrun amounting from $2 billion (2004) to $6.1 billion (2008), going about 205% over-budgets. Contributing to this result were serious schedule delays and unmet oil production rate target.
- The Aecon, Firebag 3 Project (Reuters, 2011) recounted a cost overrun totaling up to $59 million, due to schedule delay and too many changes. The lesson learned was that their fixed-price contract with Suncor Energy was not suitable for a large and complex project.

9.4.   Project Cost Management Plan

A good cost management plan starts with a good estimate followed by manageable cost breakdown, preferably down to the work package level. Establishing a plan leads to a cost and schedule baseline. The baseline provides the project its target, which will permit the measurement of progress and performance. Note that progress and performance measurement (monitoring and control), keeps cost and time components under check. It keeps risk at bay.

TIP The management of cost and schedule can only be effective through proper process documentation.

Establishing a cost baseline lets the project know its target to measure performance. Measurement, monitoring, and control keep cost at bay, permitting the project team to manage cost through risk management.

9.5.   Project Schedule Management Plan

The sound schedule uses the fast-track project philosophy applied to all activities. The project manager must make sure the schedule aligns with the project execution plan and strategy. The plan must precisely describe the criteria from which the schedule was developed. Document all criteria, including assumptions and current facts. It is recommended that schedule durations are built using modal (most likely), median (P50 midpoint), or mean (average) values but tallied to the estimate.

Look at the report in Figure 86 and ask yourself what is wrong with it. Sorry to scare you, but the report sure is scary. The man in the picture is the project manager, who is probably asking how and why such misalignments happen. He is also scrambling to find a solution.

191

If the project team plans to integrate components, then all stakeholders should work the plan.

The report below underlines the breakdown between construction and module yard schedules. It shows a lack of project integration. Modules worked on dates that do not satisfy the schedule of module setting.

Delays to the schedule resulted in the reshuffling of priorities. Adjusting to all these changes is stressful, challenging, and in some cases impossible.

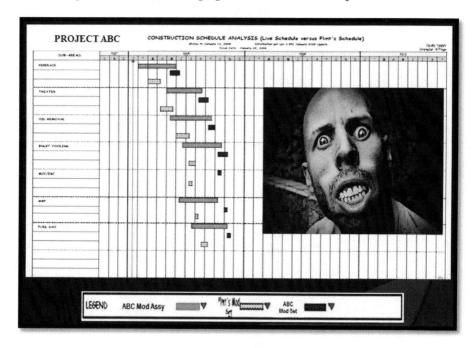

Figure 86 - Schedule Analysis Showing Misalignments

Do you know why this failure happened? It's because the project manager and the team did not recognize the proven saying that a disjointed plan equals a disjointed schedule.

The sad part about this true-to-life story is that it was due to a wrong scheduling tool version. The version that the contractor uses was different from what the module group was using. Although it would have been an easy thing to fix, the project manager did not lift a finger to address the situation.

It sacrifices the logical links of thousands of activities in favor of Excel spreadsheet milestone monitoring. The results were massive module delays disrupting the installation of many work packages.

How can a structure stand the load and the pressure if its components are misaligned and loosely fastened?

The answer is simple. If the structural links are weak, then it fails on its weakest link.

Missing members indicates fault that translates to weakness. If there are missing scopes in the plan, then there are bound to be missing activities in the schedule.

Missing activities mean that the right critical path will be difficult to calculate if not impossible.

This syllogism, referring to the integration requirement, is a critical question that everyone in the project should ask and properly address.

9.6. Integrative Planning and Scheduling Process

The schedule remains preliminary in Design Basis Memorandum (DBM) stage or before Gate 2 (Figure 87). This is the stage when project execution and supporting documents are not yet final, baselined, or approved for execution.

The schedule should not pass the DBM checkpoint unless the engineering resource-loaded schedule undergoes a series of interactive planning review sessions.

An integrated DBM schedule should be a mandatory project requirement (Frago, Preliminary Project Execution Plan (Schedule & Cost), 2013).

An integrated execution schedule should be a mandatory project requirement. It is good practice to issue the approved schedule before issuing the approved project management plan (or project execution plan).

As long as there is one major plan component not yet completed in the iron triangle of cost, schedule, and scope (quality), the review findings should indicate high risk. An incomplete element is probably worse than having none.

It is a given! If the project has no schedule, it will not proceed with execution, as there is nothing to execute. If an incomplete, half-baked schedule is available, the project is tempted to go ahead in spite of identified deficiencies.

If the chunk of work is substantial and becomes part of the critical path, then the problem starts.

They might say, "We will keep on tab of the situation, and add the missing scope later."

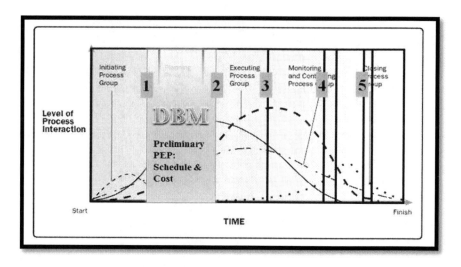

Figure 87 - Design-base Memorandum (DBM)

9.7. Project Implementation Framework

Projects work best with an implementation framework. While PMBOK models the project implementation framework by process and knowledge areas, many companies use stages (phases) and focus management areas such as business, project, engineering, procurement, and construction, as shown in the example implementation model (see Figure 88).

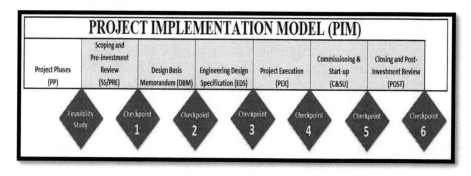

Figure 88 - Project Implementation Framework

There are hundreds of framework variations available on the net or in books and literature. Any company can adopt their own strategic implementation model. When placed closely together for comparison, the concept, philosophies, and strategies do not depart greatly from each other. Most of them have parallels and equivalent.

Another example I accidentally bumped into while surfing the net was the project implementation framework of the Government of South Australia.

The 5-Steps Framework and Project Implementation Process is a generic policy that applies to all types of prescribed construction projects. It guides specifically procurement and construction (Australia, 2011).

Other type of project implementation model abounds. There were bunches and bunches of them. At random, I picked one that caught my attention. It was the 7FE Project Framework under the Management by Process website.

The author claimed that their project implementation framework is appropriate to all organizations, and that it will suit all circumstances while recognizing the challenge that each organization is not the same.

7FE management by process shows phases called pad, understand, innovate, develop, people, implement, and realize value leading to sustainable performance (Jeston, 2013).

9.8.   Project Processes and Phases

All management processes are integral to the project. Nothing can stand by itself. Otherwise, they become ineffective, if not useless.

The phases where these processes occur most times overlap throughout the project. They are incremental deliverables. The exchange of information throughout the project lifecycle is a continuing collaboration resulting in what is termed by project professionals as rolling wave planning.

It is important that the project constantly work together in partnership throughout the different phases and stages until completion.

Although PMBOK has removed the preliminary project execution plan in its process list, it remains with many organizations. Projects feel safe when they retain the word "preliminary" during the early course of project development.

Preliminary documentation is one of the key deliverables during the design basis memorandum stage (DBM Phase). These same documentations will be carried forward and further developed to the next stage. Project management calls them EDS quality documents.

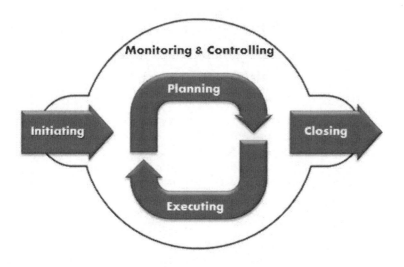

Figure 89 - Continuous Collaboration Plan-Do-Check-Act Process

 Stages or phases divide the project life cycle.

It clearly shows the window of process group interaction, as the chart below depicts. The earlier the company is able to make a sound decision as to whether to proceed or not, the better the prospects of success.

It is for this reason that the DBM stage is of special interest to the project team think tanks.

The DBM stage is an important stage (Figure 90). It gives the stakeholders the first real practical opportunity to take an early peek into the future and see whether the project is a GO or NO-GO. Reviewing Section 3.10 will give more light to this particular phase.

The ability to influence the project's final deliverables without adverse cost impact is highest at the start of the project, and it decreases as time goes by, (as the project progresses towards completion).

On the other hand, making changes and correcting errors typically increases considerably as the project approaches completion.

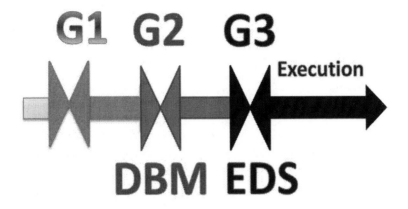

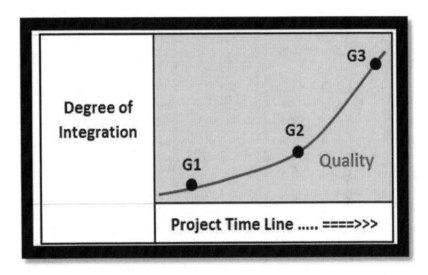

Figure 90 – Integration, Quality, and Phase Interaction Chart

In all these, quality plays a major role. As the saying goes, it is better to do it right the first time. A growing shared belief and strategy of many companies is to make the right decision as early as the initiating, scoping, and DBM stage. With that in mind, many companies have changed focus from Gate 3 (EDS) to Gate 2 (DBM) and even Gate 1 (initiating and scoping) as the point of serious reckoning.

This is a good idea if the project already has most of the information. The problem is right there. They usually do not have enough information to go by. The danger of pursuing such an ambitious philosophy is falling into the trap of making guesses, and making assessments dictated mostly by assumptions.

Remember, the completeness and quality of data is of the utmost importance. It is irreplaceable. Bad data is worse than no data. Little data should be taken in as if the project has no data.

With no data, there is every reason to be cautious, and stop the project. Projects will automatically gravitate to a more rational decision of not proceeding to the next phase.

The more dangerous situation is when there is bad or wrong data, causing the project to proceed but eventually end in failure. Avoid forcing the project to make a final go or no-go decision during Gate 2 DBM unless there is enough information to base this decision on.

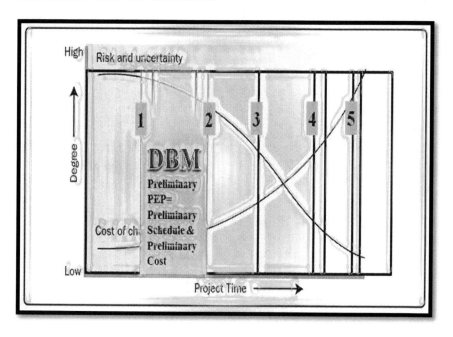

Figure 91 - Risk and Cost of Change over Time

Chapter 10

Key Risk Indicator (KRI)

10.1. Introduction to Key Risk Indicators

The key risk indicator (KRI) is the gap between actuals and a benchmark. In this sense, the key risk indicator is not a benchmark, but if the gap itself becomes the reference point, then it becomes a benchmark.

KRI is the measurement we would like to compare our plan. For example, when the duration of the current schedule compared to a successful and previously completed schedule, the difference in duration between the two becomes the point of assessment. The difference compared to a KRI assists in making decision. Many risk practitioners had said that the bigger the gaps compared to the project benchmarks, would potentially generate the bigger and higher risks.

Standards and benchmarks are yardsticks that exist because a group of people, associations, lawmaking body, a community, or culture agreed to have one and use it as a comparison for future work.

TIP A standard forms a box to confine processes, systems, responsibilities, and relevant others. It represents the boundaries of doing things using established methods and guidelines.

Standard is like a box. This box limits what it can contain. It does not allow some items. It permits only what should be. It sets the boundaries. The lines we see in the parking lot, for one, are a good metaphor for boundaries.

If we stick within that boundary in parking our vehicle, there is less risk of getting a dent. If we go over the line boundary, the probability of damage rises. In the same manner, in the world of project management, such situations permit the risk manager to put together his key risk indicators by looking at the gaps before him.

These gaps represent the project's departure from the agreed-to measurements (the aforementioned benchmarks or standards). Whether these base measurements reflect the best practice in the industry is another story. It is contentious as usual when the subject of what is best comes up.

Simply put, identifying the boundaries give one more than ample KRI information. As for the parking lot, the gap or the lines can be our KRI. It cannot be clearer than that.

Note that to avoid contentions; the project manager should get stakeholder's buy-in. Get a formal agreement as to what benchmarks governs. If an in-house benchmark standard exists, use it. Departure from the agreed-to benchmarks should automatically raise a flag.

The gaps with the benchmark can be the project's KRIs, and they are very critical to formulating and creating an effective project execution plan. Crossing a limit or a physical marker can also serve as a KRI.

The baseline schedule is a type of benchmark. If the latest update to the schedule resulted in the final date sliding four weeks forward in time, that delay is a time gap. It represents a valuable key risk indicator (KRI) that affects the project.

The project can qualify the issue, quantify the impact, and activate a response plan. Gaps derived from actual comparison against accepted standards or benchmarks are themselves, KRIs. Comparison is not limited against a singular value or a line, like the parking lot boundary. Comparison can be against multiple values or a range of values.

We can compare variance against another variance; e.g. current tolerance versus benchmarked tolerance, current date variance versus a baseline variance, and others.

10.2. Defining KRI

The definition offered by Wikipedia was by far the nearest to my own understanding of the term. The definition might not be from any governing body, but it is quite appealing because it is the simplest, and avoids introducing any complicated premises.

KRI is a measure used in management to indicate how risky an activity is. This means it is a result of quantification. KRI is an indicator of the possibility of future adverse impact. KRI give us an early warning to identify potential events that may harm the continuity of the activity or project (Wikipedia, Key

Risk Indicators, 2014).

A paper published by Scarlat and Chirita on KRI is one among many that supports what I found in Wikipedia. Here is what it says:

> "A risk indicator provides a forward direction, and information about risk, which may or may not exist and is used as a warning system for future actions. With a KRI it can be monitored a specific risk and can be undertaken mitigation actions. KRI is metrics used to provide an early warning sign for increased exposure of risk in different aspects of the enterprise."

An indicator is a key indicator if it serves a very important statement (Jonathan Davies, Mike Finlay, Tara McLenaghen, Duncan Wilson, 2006). Key risk indicators are "statistics or measurements that can provide a perspective into a company's risk position, tend to be revised periodically (monthly or quarterly) to alert the company about the changes that may indicate risks" (Les Coleman, 2009).

Key risk indicators are metrics used by management to show how risky an activity or investment project are (E.Scarlat, 2012).

These definitions are enough to formulate the KRI concept in any construction risk organization in making risk-based decisions.

It is clear and logical that there should be a reference measurement that serves as a reckoning point to quantify critical gaps or key risk indicators (KRIs).

10.3. The Difference between KPI and KRI

There was some argument recently as to whether a KRI really exists. KRI is a measure used in management to indicate how risky an activity is. A KRI is an indicator of the possibility of future adverse or beneficial impact. KRI gives us early warnings to identify potential events that may harm the continuity of activities. KRI is a mainstay of operational risk analysis.

Key risk indicators are metrics capable of showing that the organization is subject risks. It helps calculates the probability of being subject to risks that exceed defined risk appetite (Wikipedia, Key Risk Indicators, 2014).

One day, I punched the terms "KRI" and "key risk indicator" into the Google search engine. There were 3.3 million hits. This result is an indicator that the terms are already in the mix. There is high probability that the terms are now quite common, an indication of better understanding. It sufficiently proves that this is now a subject of interest.

A key performance indicator (KPI) is a measure of how well something is being done.

We cannot really compare KRI and KPI because they are not on the same footing. Each one is looking at a different timeline. KRI is a warning indicator of what may be (future) while KPI is an assessment indicator of what has happened (past).

The former identifies, qualifies, and quantifies risk while the latter identifies, qualifies, and quantifies performance. One is not a subset of the other.

The preceding paragraphs about KRI will not satisfy every management professional out there, but they can at least be the start of a good intelligent conversation.

10.4. Examples of Key Risk Indicators

One popular and widely known key risk indicator in project risk management is the distribution chart and tornado chart generated by the schedule quantitative risk analysis process. They show the overall probability of achieving the schedule, and the relevant schedule drivers associated with each key deliverable, while looking at an established schedule baseline and agreed-to company/project risk standards.

They provide warning bells to all if the overall probability of the schedule completing was, say, less than P10 or even less than P1. The amount of schedule contingency compared to the estimate will influence some of the corresponding actions generated. The cruciality, criticality, duration sensitivity reports, and other similar quantified values are all KRIs.

What else would they be? The challenge for a risk professional is translating all these into an actions or response plans. These indicators are all future looking.

Risk-based management is what we all do every day. Some real life examples can best explain what it is.

Here are two examples common to all of us at one time or another in our lives.

Let us say that the goal is to find a parking spot for Joe's high-end car in a crowded mall parking area. The parking spots have proper labels and markings. Joe drove around for what seems like forever until he found one near the entrance of the mall.

Ooopps! Hold on! Through the snow-covered pavement, he sees something painted blue. He concludes that it must be a sign. The spot being near the entrance signifies the possibility that the spot is for disabled customers.

> He stopped thinking, "if that's a blue marking then it probably is a no parking zone." He did not park there and continued searching.

Later on during the day, a car did park on the very same spot. After just a little while, the park security tows the car. Joe was happy because it would have been his vehicle. If he had chosen to ignore the KRI, then he would have been quite sorry.

As he continues to go around and find another spot, he notices one spot available between two big pick-up trucks. Looking at the yellow paint marking the potential spot, he sees that one of the truck tires crosses it while the other truck has come very close to the other yellow line.

> He thought, "I can get my car in, but it will be in a tight spot. These are risk indicators as well. Any thinking person will not park there and risk getting his vehicle damaged."

Risk indicators look at the future. It gives the observer some kind of foresight to predict the risks that might happen. Assessment of the probability results to a prediction of high risk.

Being patient, Joe decided to wait and find another vacant space. Joe exercised risk-based management.

This very same logic holds true with any one of our daily activity, real projects, regardless of size and cost.

KRI exists as excellent point of reference in daily decision-making. KRIs are applicable in all types of risk-based management, whether operational, construction-related, personal, project, logistic, risk, personnel, and many others.

Chapter 11

P50 Risk-based Baseline Schedule

11.1.   Introduction to P50 Risk-based Baseline

In any management endeavor, time is a precious commodity. It is so valuable that it is only wise to use it with respect. Individuals and organizations can plan all they want but the schedule becomes the focal point comes execution. It is impossible to accomplish all activities on time if the schedule is poorly developed. While a bad schedule will most likely fail, a good schedule will succeed. The quality of the schedule translates easily to the end quality and cost of the project. A project manager is foolish to expect a timely delivery of a bad schedule. A bad schedule will result in budget overruns, and poor quality facilities, products/services. A poorly prepared schedule will not stay to expectation. Enhancing success is possible by creating a P50 Risk-based, sound, and achievable baseline schedule.

Two terms need introduction, i.e. deterministic schedule, and probabilistic schedule. A deterministic schedule is a schedule based on a single point estimate. It is a closed network schedule that the project team developed, reviewed, and approved for risk analysis. It is the accepted project schedule before undergoing quantitative risk analysis (QRA). This schedule assumes certainty that durations and dates will work out exactly as planned. A probabilistic schedule is a closed network schedule that resulted after a deterministic schedule undergoes Quantitative Risk Analysis (QRA). All activity durations have calculated probability distribution after quantification. The variant forms of the word probabilistic, is probability or/and likelihood. These words are widely used in oral or written form (Bacani, 1979). The empirical or relative frequency definition of the word probability is more attuned to the tossing a coin.

In scheduling terms, when outcomes of overrun and underrun are equally likely to occur, then the schedule has 50% chance of success and a 50% chance of failure. This is the midpoint in a resulting normal curve indicating statistical mean or average. The mean is the expected value, the point of balance that most of the same or similar activities will have as duration. The duration data is from work history and project experience. P50 is the fundamental criteria or basics of developing a good schedule. It is the statistical confidence level of the corresponding date value in the schedule.

The P50 schedule duration is not aggressive. It is also not too lax. The central limit theorem supports the idea of a P50 as a point of reckoning that has more chance of occurring. In probability theory, the central limit theorem (CLT) states that, given certain conditions, the arithmetic mean of a sufficiently large number of iterates of independent random variables, each with a well-defined expected value and well-defined variance, will be approximately normally distributed, regardless of the underlying distribution (Rice, 1995). A cumulative distribution can show more clearly the range of values that can realistically arise and the likelihood of exceeding any value in the range (Grey & company, Tutorial\Project Range Analysis, 2007).

Therefore, as the project becomes larger, the number of activities (referring to the same level of details) increases.

TIP When data population increases, despite the randomness of available variables, the end-result is normal distribution.

It is with this concept in mind that a P50 risk-based baseline holds a possible solution against the possibility of overrun. Preventing unachievable schedule is quite possible. In order to develop the P50 baseline, each of the activity making up the sub-projects has to be at a P50. Each of the sub-projects making up the projects portfolio has to be at a P50 as well.

Instructions before the concluding section of this book describe in details how to create a P50 schedule. Adjusting the probability of each sub-project schedule is simple. Changing final activity dates to reflect the P50 date is equally easy. In the past, identifying the right dates and duration to increase achievability is just a wish. This time it is different. The tool is available to convert all project activities to a P50 or any other probability value.

11.2. Good Quality Schedule

The pre-requisite of a P50 Risk-based baseline schedule is a good quantitative risk analysis. Good schedule quality results in good quantification. The quality of input data drives the correctness, accuracy, completeness, and usefulness of the schedule.

The rule is simple, garbage in-garbage out or GIGO. Quality of system output depends on the quality of system input (Jill Butler, 2010).

It is a golden rule, one of the principal reasons why risk qualification comes first before risk quantification. Good inputs beget good outputs. Quality is the foundation of a believable result.

TIP Organizations have to select the schedule quality criteria to compare with. This benchmark is a measuring stick of all deterministic schedules before they are risk analyzed.

Three fundamental schedule qualities are integrated, complete, and aligned. Approved quality benchmarks are minimum schedule qualities that if properly satisfied, effectively support a reliable schedule quantitative risk analysis. Achieving the minimum schedule quality, in effect, address and successfully mitigate high inherent schedule risks. Sticking to approved schedule quality standard prevents and reduced risks. It helps achieve project objectives.

Cost and time pressures are greater than ever before in a project set up. Target dates and durations of project schedules remain uncertain. Even schedules put together on years knowhow, years of experience, and best practice cannot always accurately predict the future.

There is no absolute guarantee to the behavior of a present day projects. Schedule certainty is in doubt every time a project ignores quality.

One should remember that it is a major risk driver. It can also be a risk source. Probability estimate that includes schedule quality in the equation deserves praise. Quantified schedule risks without respect for quality value compounds errors over time to give management a false assessment of the outcome. As risk managers often say, uncertainty builds on uncertainty (Safran, 2014).

The methods and tools in the field of schedule risk quantification had immensely improved. Subject matter experts have better understanding of schedule and risks since the first Monte Carlo black box of yesteryears.

The process of schedule quantitative risk analysis has slowly gained client sponsorship as a more objective tool. Using risk analysis tool as effective aids to management decisions has gained momentum. These tools are project vehicles to expedite analytic results.

TIP Fundamental concept: Use the right tool to the tool right.

The concept of using the right tools to the tool rights maximizes benefits. A hammer is for driving down nails to fasten two wooden members together. Basic to successfully deriving the best result is to understand and appreciate the tool (hammer) right (driving down nails). The inherent right of a hammer is to drive down a nail into a wooden frame not to screw a nail into it. What do you think will happen if one uses the hammer to drive a screw or tighten a bolt?

Qualitative and quantitative risks become mainstays in modern day management framework. The approach is accepted best practice in many industries. The qualitative, quantitative, and analytic processes have become part of project assessments prior to any gate approvals. Qualitative and quantitative risks are of prime importance during project execution, and at any point of interest, throughout the project life cycle.

There are several tools available. In this book, we use OPRA. It t does not mean it is the only one that can do the job. Irrespective of the tools used, the important thing to consider is the tool right. Make sure that the tool can do the work properly.

11.3. Integrated Schedule

One of the first quality items to check is schedule integration.

There is a world of difference between integrated and not integrated. Good integration results in intuitive, connected, or linked schedule. It will translate to excellent management of time, cost, and risk. Other benefits are accurate critical path calculation, sound quantitative schedule risk assessment, good communication, positive effect on productivity, flexibility, and increased achievability. The project will potentially increase the chances of meeting its most important objectives. The opposite of integration brings forth many problems and issues with the schedule becoming counter-intuitive, disconnected, and disjointed.

Small size sustaining and capital projects of up to US$ 50 Million dollars might not experience the challenge of integration unless they became too complex. Medium to mega-projects of One hundred ($100 M) Million US dollars to greater than one ($1 B) Billion US dollars have big hurdles to make by sheer size that translate to costs, volume of commodities, and large number of different resources. The size issue is a hurdle because even the sub-projects of a mega-project are quite significant. Sub-project accounting for several hundred million up to more than a billion dollar is common. The only solution to big sub-projects is to divide them again into manageable work areas or sub-sub projects. Dividing the schedule into smaller pieces does not mean the pieces should remain disconnected. On the contrary, the more they need to integrate. If they are poorly integrated, chances of project failure increase. Integration helps align achievability of each sub-project, making the interphase point more reliable.

Developing an integrated mega-project schedule needs to be approached with some serious planning. Dividing the project is a good strategy. It is acceptable and recommended in all kinds industry. Slicing to smaller pieces is easy. It is bringing the slice together to form the whole that is challenging. How can each slice logically communicate and work together according to plan? That is the question to answer. It is an alignment challenge too daunting for many large projects.

Due to its size, a mega-project can end up compromising or sacrificing the integration quality of the schedule. After dividing into smaller work chunks, the project tends to develop each one separately. They even eventually reside in different scheduling database. When this happens, key dates and probabilities of each major sub-project become misaligned. The set-up creates constraints that in turn create path convergence.

The problem is quite visible when one observes sub-project activities. Equipment arrival dates are not supporting required at site dates (RAS). Module transport does not support the schedule module set dates. Turnover dates of one area do not support the start date of other areas.

There might be efforts to align requirements and deliverables using a common key interface table but such a table is taxing, prone to error, takes a lot of time to update, and has a reporting turnaround delay that can adversely affect effective actions from being executed on a timely basis. Such portfolio schedule is not properly integrated.

When sub-project schedules with different, wide, and varying range of certainty on activities are pulled together to form one big schedule, another potential problem comes up. They end up blocking each other. Critical disconnects are formed in both vertical and horizontal logics. This is why projects need to address uncertainty gaps and misalignments.

11.4. Complete Schedule

It is untrue that a plan looks at a much bigger scope compared to the scope of the resulting schedule. Planning and scheduling are from a single cloth. They are very much connected.

There is only one total scope in every project. The planned scope, baseline scope, or target scope are expected to have the same scope as their schedule counterpart. The planned scope must be in alignment to the scheduled scope. Scope of one cannot be greater. Continuous collaboration sees to it that is how it is throughout the project timeline.

If part of the planned scope is missing, the schedule is not complete. Scope alignment should be part of the main review checklist for each gate, especially the gate leading to project execution. Establishing the scope helps prevent scope creep and missing scope. It also prevents confusion, issue, risk, and additional cost resulting from doing activities not part of the plan. An incomplete schedule will not produce the right P50 Risk-based baseline schedule because any result does not represent the real thing. It does not represent everything.

11.5. Aligned Schedule

An integrated schedule deserves an integrated plan. Project schedule should align to the execution plan. One such plan is the construction execution plan (CEP) that contains the path of construction. The CEP outlines sequential work strategy across the geographical division of the project plot. A good schedule follows the plan. If the schedule is resource-loaded, the loaded resources should align with the latest baseline estimate. It follows that an execution baseline schedule aligns with the approved execution estimate. If the total number of direct hours in the estimate is 5 Million work hours, the loaded work hours in the schedule must be the same. The distribution of hours per work package must line up on a one to one work package correspondence between estimate and schedule. The gate or baseline estimate shall be the same as the gate or baseline schedule respectively.

TIP
The level of schedule accuracy is reflective of the all the available information at the time of the review.

It cannot be overemphasized the need for the schedule to align with the following key documents: Basis of Schedule (BOS), Project Management Plan (or Project Execution Plan), Engineering Management Plan, Procurement Plan, Contracting Plan, Construction Execution Plan, Commissioning and Start-up Management Plan, etc. The bottom line expectation is that a schedule be capable of supporting the required decision-making process of the project. The schedule shall follow the quality criteria formulated and agreed to by all stakeholders. The business can utilize any tool available as long as it can do the job. A review checklist is a great way to manage, keep track and control schedule quality.

Variances between the two set of values can become a threat to project objectives. It generates wrong projection on workforce requirements and delivery dates. It will affect the accuracy of camp requirements, logistics, earned value calculation, risk quantification, and progress reporting. Large discrepancies between the approved estimate and resource- loaded values indicate scope issues.

TIP If the schedule contains more hours than the estimate, it points to excess scope. If the estimate has more hours compared to what is in the schedule, it signifies missing scope.

If not, there is probably a quantity error in the schedule or in the estimate table. In view of the potential consequences, it is prudent to always check and ensure schedule alignment. This is the fundamental idea when one works the plan. It is a good feeling to have an aligned schedule that addresses future problems.

11.6. The Risk of Competing Probabilities

A relatively large project portfolio divided into smaller work chunks called sub-projects makes work more manageable. It can have two, or more practicable smaller pieces. The sub-projects are broken further down to work package level readying them for execution. Each sub-project is usually developed semi-independently based on critical interface milestones. These key deliverables are the reckoning points in synchronizing and aligning sub-projects to the overall plan.

The independent or semi-independent creation of each schedule most often results in misalignments on several date objectives. Even with an MS Excel file interphase monitoring, the varying uncertainty of schedule deliverables makes control difficult.

Competing probabilities are bad for the project. There is a need to improve full control, attainable only through a fully integrated project portfolio. An integrated schedule facilitates the creation of a P50 Risk-based baseline schedule.

The activity of installing an equipment foundation that has to complete on a definite date so a large pressure vessel can be set is a good example. If foundation installation has a completion certainty of P10, then it has a very high probability of failing. In fact, completing it on its deterministic finish date is next to impossible. It is unachievable.

If the activity fails, equipment setting and other subsequent activities are bound to fail as well.

Failure comes even if their stand-alone certainties are much higher than P10.

213

By P10, nine out of ten activities of that same duration and resources will fail to deliver.

If foundation activity ends up delayed, the next activity that has a probability of a P60, or even P100 value will most likely succumb to the delay incurred. It will force successor activities to push their planned dates to later dates.

One must learn to recognize and accept that whenever the probability of an activity is too low, the target is unachievable.

Nobody should agree to an unrealistic schedule even one with a fat contingency. Being overly optimistic or overly aggressive is not a good idea. It is uneconomical and it is foolhardy to carry out.

The story of two friends who have agreed to meet at a certain time to deliver something is a good illustration (Figure 92). One person has to undergo a complex maneuver to reach the meeting point and the other a considerably simple trip.

Even if each person has the same point to point distance from the destination, it would be intellectual deceit to expect the two would come generally around the same time with the same certainty. It represents real-life scenario that needs to be addressed.

The duration it takes for each one to be there given the same degree of effort will be different. If the two activities represented by the two individuals are interdependent, one will delay the others.

When more effort is exerted by one facing more obstacles, the additional energy will push the other elements out, like cost and quality, with a tendency to create additional supporting activities.

If one activity depends on the other resource to be there before doing the next task, then the successor activity has to wait for the other resource to arrive, however long it takes.

Anything that affects or influences the preceding activities affect the succeeding ones. If A influences B, and B influences C; it is clear that A influences C and so on.

There is a big possibility of overall delay despite one hundred percent certainty of one person to deliver on time. This example supports the recommendation of an aligned P50 Risk-based baseline.

Figure 92 - Meeting a Friend: Illustrating Uncertainty

11.7. The Risk of Planning Fallacy

Developing an unachievable schedule is more frequent than one would tend to think. More and more managers continue to target schedules that results in delay and overrun. They tend to refuse to heed the warning brought about by too much optimism. They see aggressive as positive, something that reflects a sought-after management style. Unfortunately, unachievable schedule equals project failure. It represents a schedule that is unrealistic. Making a baseline based on an unachievable schedule can invite disaster.

Planning fallacy is an interesting cognitive bias. It occurs when people envision that everything will go according to plan. They assume that no delay, no negative surprises, no big issue, and no problem will happen. If something comes up, they believe that they have the resources to handle the event quickly. It is like daydreaming when one tends to imagine that everything is just where they should be.

Predicting how much duration to complete an activity is not simply picking a number resulting from a straightforward calculation. The chance of setting in motion optimistic bias (misjudging the time needed) is quite common.

215

Miscalculation occurs despite the subject matter expert's knowledge of past undertakings of highly similar projects (Roger Buehler, 1994).

The bias produces unachievable, over-aggressive schedules. The tendency to predict completion times optimistically than the actual time needed to complete the tasks is a serious problem.

The schedule baseline subjected to quantification generates a synchronized P50 to counter this risk. It is the application of the P50 profile across the project portfolio. The adjustment not only improves interdependent relationships between activities but also provides a way to distribute contingency.

11.8.   The Risk of Schedule Misalignment

It is schedule misalignment when the schedule substantially deviates from the project plan and strategy. Misalignment is also visible when the work-hours resource loading of the schedule varies significantly with that of the corresponding approved quantity estimate. A schedule that has more scope than the plan is another example of misalignment.

A schedule scope less than the plan gives strong sign of misalignment. Other indication of misalignment are when schedule uses wrong baseline, schedule uses wrong assumptions and constraints, schedule has different calendars than what was approved, schedule does not follow path of construction, schedule dates different from execution documents, and others. All the aforementioned affect the delivery of overall portfolio's end goals. The problem leads to poor schedule management and control. It can affect productivity, and communication. Achievability suffers. Misalignment affects critical path and the QRA calculation.

The danger of assumptions is worth mentioning. A decision maker who assumes that he has all the essential information is asking for trouble. It dangerous to assume that communication loop is complete and understood. It is wiser to check if in doubt. Each member of the team especially the manager should have a questioning attitude. Assumptions can create wrong perceptions. It is bound to form conflict with stakeholders due to unrealized expectations.

Root causes of misaligned schedule is traced to lack of project management knowledge and skills, ineffective communication, no communication, too much communication, personal biases, assumptions, mistakes, lack of commitment, perception, miscommunication, self-interest, contract structure, organizational strategy, and many others. If misalignments are considerable, the project encounters problems that derail goals. It affects the project's chances of successful completion. It promotes bickering at all fronts related to schedule.

216

TIP To address this risk, the proposed schedule baseline must achieve the minimum quality required.

Organization should have a quality scoring approach. Whatever agreed to criteria shall represent the minimum quality set forth. The effectiveness of quality review relies on the reviewer's understanding of the criteria and inner workings of the tool. It includes consideration of schedule clarity, and maturity of schedule information presented.

Each organization must put in place a standard of quality before generating the P50. Application of the P50 across the project portfolio not only improves interdependent relationships of activities, but also has the capacity to distribute contingency evenly.

11.9. Sample Situation: Project ABCDEFG

Sub-project A has an interface end date of P10 (Figure 95), while sub-project B has a target end date with a calculated probability of P30 (Figure 96). Sub-project C, D, E, F and G schedules have deterministic probabilities of P40, P45, P55, P60, and P70 respectively.

Since dates and probability estimates are themselves a function of each other, the project team will see the problem as soon as the team start to execute the plan. What is being highlighted here is obvious: the certainty of each silo schedule is not aligned, with one nearly impossible to achieve, one unlikely to be achieved, one more likely achievable, and so on up to achievable.

As explained in the story of the two friends who agreed to meet at a certain time, this schedule setup is destined to be a pain. Going forward, this demonstration will be limited to the first two connected sub-projects, A and B, instead of tackling the whole portfolio ABCDEFG, to facilitate better understanding.

Observing the two is more than enough to convey the importance of a realistic schedule. We will look at A and B as if they comprise the whole project ABCDEFG portfolio.

11.10. Silo Approach in Scheduling

Shown below are the roll up summaries of sub-projects A and B, developed semi-independently based on agreed-to key milestone interfaces.

For the sake of simplicity, we will discuss only two of these seven sub-projects using assumed dates and durations designed to convey the general idea of the risks of unachievable schedules and of integrating silo schedules with a wide range of uncertainties.

As this is a simplified example, do not be surprised that A and B have only 100 days duration each. The important thing here is the ability to demonstrate that uncertainty of one sub-project has a cascade effect to its successors.

Figure 93 shows that sub-project A starts on May 21, 2013, with 100 days duration, and has a deterministic end date of October 7, 2013.

The calculated probability value is P10. Sub-project B starts right after sub-project A finishes. It has 100 days duration, and a planned end date of February 24, 2014, with a calculated 30% probability or P30.

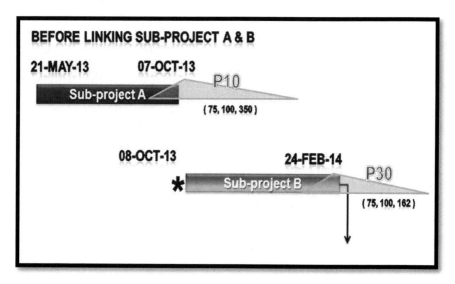

Figure 93 - Two Sub-projects with Different Finish Date Probabilities

The schedules of sub-project A and sub-project B appear fine except for the nagging question of how the unachievable P10 Sub-project A schedule support the successor B's P30 date.

The former has a very low probability of P10, and the latter, a higher probability of P30. Figure 95 and Figure 96 show the individual probability distribution profiles for A and B.

The effect of the lower certainty schedule on the higher certainty schedule becomes evident after linking the two schedules.

11.11. Linking and Integrating Sub-projects

As soon as the scheduler connect sub-project A (P10) to sub-project B, the certainty of B changes to P20.

When the probability of A is adjusted to P30, intending to support B, the latter's deliverable date decreased from P30 to P5, making the date of February 24, 2014 even less achievable (Figure 94).

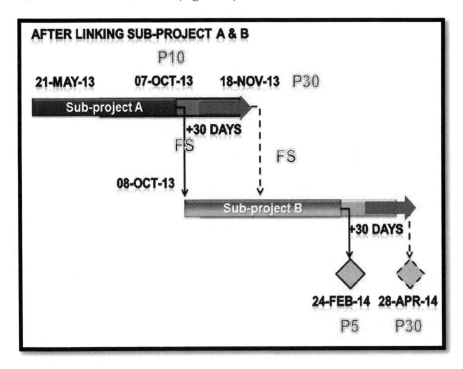

Figure 94 - Summary Bars of A and B (Linked and no Constraint)

Figure 95 shows that sub-project A has a deterministic finish date of October 7, 2013, with 10% probability of happening. This chart represents the distribution profile of sub-project A before linking it to sub-project B.

It is not under the influence of any driving activities. It has a start date that is driven by the data date. The first activity sitting on the data date in the cascades of activities, is like having a "Start On" or "Start On or after" on that activity. The only available expansion is to the right of the network.

This declares that the probability of starting sub-project A depends on the data date or the start constraint date.

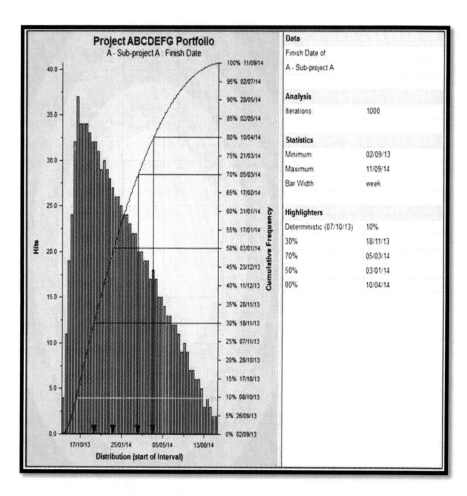

Figure 95 - Probability Distribution of A before Integration

Figure 96 shows that sub-project B has a deterministic finish date of February 24, 2014, with 30% probability of happening. This chart represents the distribution profile of sub-project B before connection from sub-project A.

A start constraint on B declares that the probability of starting sub-project B on the date is 100%, an unrealistic assumption that often times becomes a project's burden.

It is unrealistic once full integration takes place and the constraint released.

To integrate B to A, release the constraint in sub-project B and calculate (F9). Let the schedule flow freely and check the critical path.

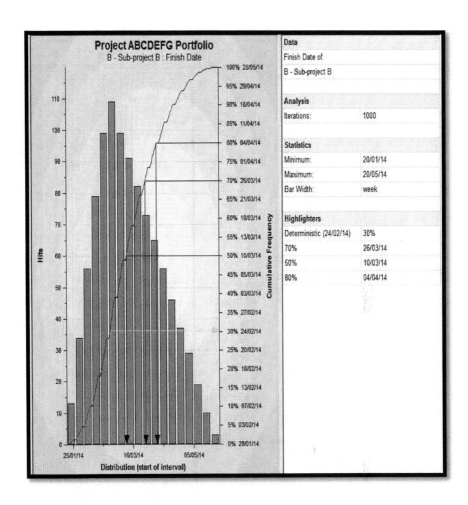

Figure 96 - Probability Distribution of B before Integration

Figure 97 shows a deterministic finish date of February 24, 2014 at P20 after releasing B's constraint and linking sub-project A (P10) to sub-project B (P30) with no prior adjustment to the deterministic dates of either one.

Since we are looking at A and B as the overall project portfolio, we can conclude that the probability of completing B has suffered.

While previously the whole portfolio's chance of completing on February 24, 2014 was 30%, it is now merely 20% after integration and quantification. Because sub-project B holds the project's last deliverable in this simple example, the whole project became less achievable, if not entirely unachievable due to A.

There is, therefore, a strong motivation to align the certainties of each sub-project, from upstream to downstream.

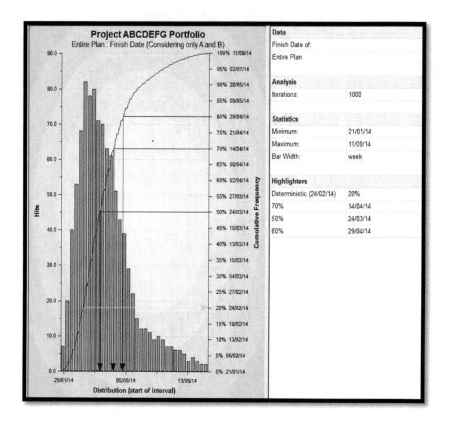

Figure 97 - Probability Distribution of Portfolio AB after Integration

What if the project wishes to change the duration of sub-project A to support sub-project B's higher certainty value of P30? This scenario is to adjust sub-project A such that it becomes more achievable than the original P10 deterministic finish date of 07-Oct-2013.

In this case, the project pushed A's deterministic finish date of 07-Oct-2013 to 18-Nov-2013, improving P10 to P30 and aligning A to the P30 sub-project B schedule (Figure 94 and Figure 98), an accepted possible delay of ~30 days added to the original deterministic duration.

By doing this, the tight (P10) sub-project A schedule was given 30 day of breathing room to become 30% certain, supporting and aligning itself to sub-project B's certainty target of P30 and making the schedule more achievable.

222

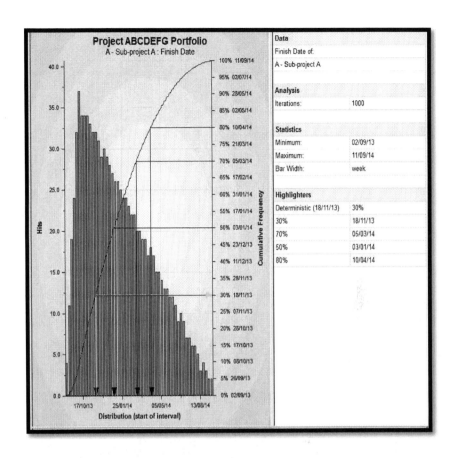

Figure 98 - Sub-project A Showing 30% Probability

Realizing the impact of misaligned certainties in the portfolio, the project proceeded to make adjustments such that A aligns to the target P30 probability estimate of sub-project B.

The duration of sub-project A was adjusted to a P30 date without change in resource loading. It seems fine at first glance but it is not because changing the date means having a later finish date.

This later date pushes sub-project B start date out, which in turn pushes the finish date as well. In the end, this simplistic solution is not as attractive after all.

Read on and together, we will try to come up with a recommendation.

11.12. Linking the Adjusted Schedule to another Sub-project

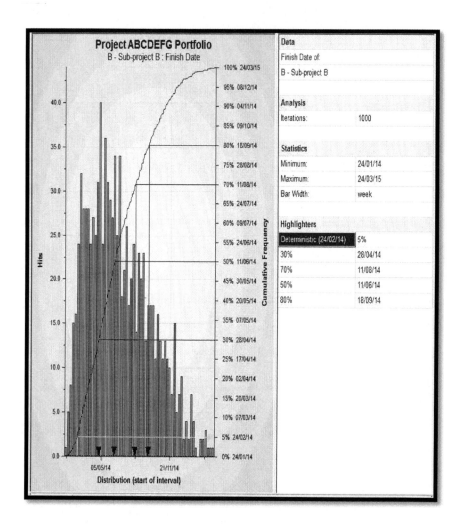

Figure 99 - Sub-project B P30 Reduced to P5 after Linking

The probability distribution above in Figure 99 shows the deterministic finish date of sub-project B's original date of February 24, 2014 going down to just 5% probable. The same date was P30 before integration (*FS* linking).

The adjusted sub-project A's deterministic schedule pushed sub-project B to the right by as much as 30 days. In order to improve the unachievable P10 sub-project A schedule, the project team has decided to push it to the right, moving the successor P30 sub-project B schedule forward by the same amount of time.

Regardless of the overall risk appetite of the organization, any portfolio, or program schedule developed individually without respect to final integration is an out-of-step scheduling approach. It is bound to prevent the project from being successful, primarily due to this kind of misalignment. This is the likely outcome when integrating silo schedules with deterministic finish dates with different certainties.

11.13. Creating a P50 Risk-based Baseline

Developing a schedule needs to be approached with success in mind. Dividing the project or portfolio into smaller manageable pieces called sub-projects is a good principle, a strategy acceptable and recommended in various industries (Section 11.3 has associated information).

However, as the number of activity grows in the schedule, completeness, integration, and alignment challenges becomes the next hurdle. Key dates ends up not supporting each other. Probability of one activity finishing on time cancels out by the lower probability of another activity. This happens when sub-projects are not integrated and project portfolio fails to form a cohesive whole.

Disjointed schedule prevents the calculation of the correct critical path. The project that is able to develop a high quality, complete, integrated, and aligned schedule sets itself up for success.

Part of the alignment process available is the use of P50 dates on all activities across the project portfolio. The purpose of synchronizing the probability to P50 is to increase achievability.

The details on how to generate the P50 Risk-based Baseline using Oracle Primavera Risk Analysis tool is described here in this section. Quantifying Project AB to a probabilistic distribution equal to P50 followed at the end.

Both sub-projects and all underlying activities have a uniform P50 certainty of achieving objectives. A P50 Risk-based baseline schedule becomes the more logical benchmark.

The following sections provide detailed steps/guide to the creation of a P50 Risk-based baseline schedule.

11.14. Upload the Deterministic Schedule to OPRA.

Import the baseline XER to Oracle Primavera Risk Analysis (OPRA). Group and sort all activities; e.g. by discipline, or by work breakdown structure (WBS). Check summary view if the dates are correct compared to the schedule before import.

The three-point estimate should be correctly loaded into respective activity. All imported start and finish dates must have negligible variance.

Make sure to do the import process correctly with all relevant settings between the two tools properly aligned. Chapter 6 was especially dedicated to the OPRA import process in this book. Review sections 6.1 to 6.6 to get a refresher.

This simple process is where many self-professed risk analysts and experts fail. It is time to solidify your reputation as a risk specialist, if this is part of your knowledge gap. Do not let the issue of simple import process puts the translation of ranged values in question.

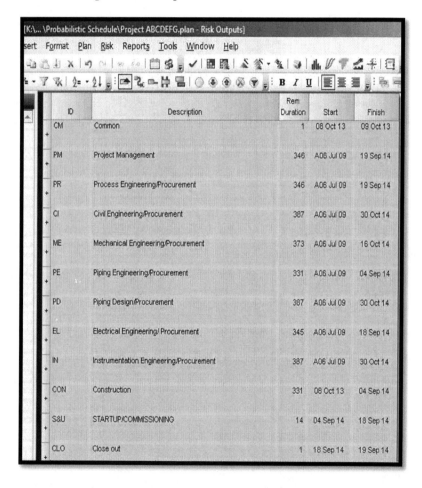

Figure 100 - Activity Window Showing Deterministic Schedule (*OPRA*)

11.15. "Risk" Pull Down Menu and "Risk Percentiles"

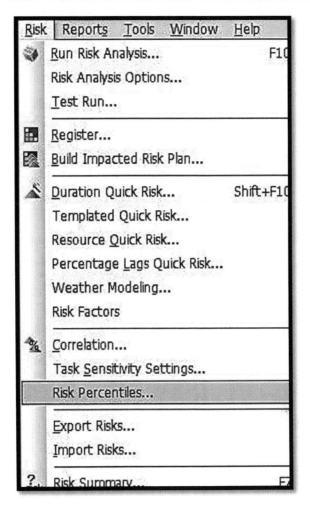

Figure 101 - Risk Percentiles Menu

11.16. Input and Set the Target Percentiles

Clicking the "Risk Percentiles" button has opened a table dialogue window. Change the percentiles setting to what the project wants to generate. The project can produce any percentiles such as P50, P60, P70, and others.

In this case, the project wants to generate the P50 Risk-based baseline schedule. To do so, set the field to 50 start and 50 finish dates.

If there are other values there, overwrite it with 50.

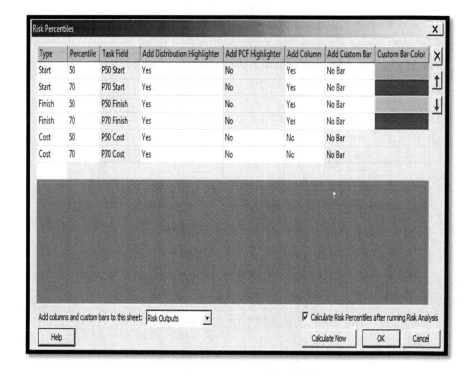

Figure 102 - Risk Percentiles Window

11.17. Set the Risk Analysis Options .

Select "Risk Analysis Option" and modify values according to what the project wants.

For schedule risk analysis alone, make sure to click on Calculate Risk Percentiles, Calculate Duration Sensitivity, and Save Resource Data. All cost related button can be left unchecked.

The other buttons are relevant only when performing an integrated cost and schedule risk analysis.

The cost portion was not included in this section.

Select "Use Default for all new plans" if you want to use the same setting for all future risk analysis. Click OK and proceed to the next step.

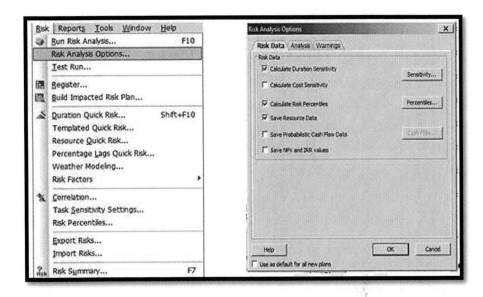

Figure 103 - Risk Analysis Options Dialogue Box

11.18. Click the Dice Icon and Run Risk Analysis

Run "Risk Analysis" by pressing the dice icon or pressing F10. Pressing this button is the first step to start the iteration/calculation process.

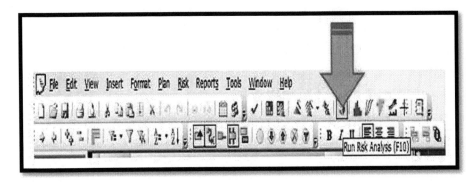

Figure 104 - Run Risk Analysis

11.19. Run the Analysis

Choose 1000 iteration as a minimum and click "Analyze" button. It is okay to increase iteration to more than 1000. The difference in terms of time it takes to complete the calculation is negligible.

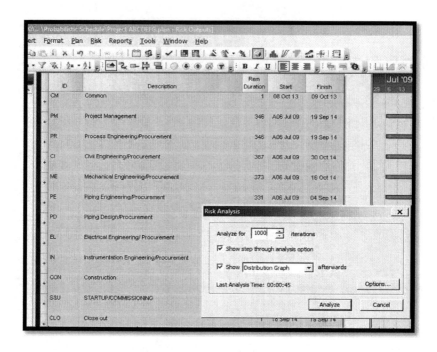

Figure 105 - Risk Analysis Dialogue Box

11.20. Completing the Risk Analysis Calculation

Press on "Complete" (red arrow) to start calculation. The iteration status box shows the progress of simulation.

It should take only a few seconds or several seconds for a bigger file. Errors and warnings messages will come up if any. Address and fix them as needed.

Warnings will not necessarily stop calculation but can affect the accuracy of the result if not corrected. They point to certain activity attributes that does not seem to make sense.

Only ignore them for good and sensible reasons.

Otherwise, they contribute to unreliable results. Some are valid and some are not logical. Correct the warnings that are not making sense. Examine closely and correct all error messages.

The simulation will not commence unless those are fixed.

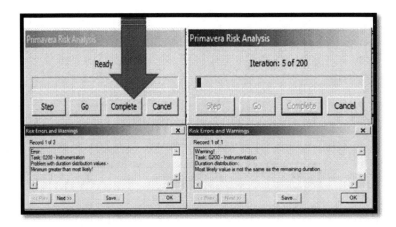

Figure 106 - Iteration Indicator, Risk Errors, and Warnings

11.21. Generate a probability distribution graph

Distribution graph generation signals percentile generation. Figure 107 displays the overall distribution graph of Project ABCDEFG.

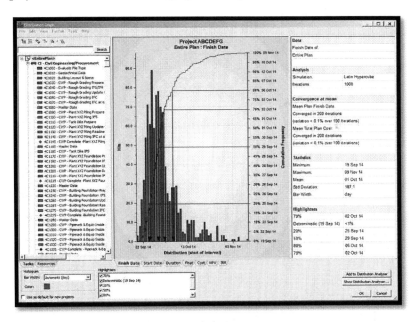

Figure 107 - Distribution Graph Window

11.22. View the Probability Distribution Graph Datasheet

The distribution graph below shows a P70 Finish Date = 02 Oct 14, P50 Finish Date = 29 Sep 14 and P<1% Deterministic Date = 19 Sep 14. Note that the deterministic date of this schedule is unachievable.

After confirming the state of certainty of the deterministic schedule, the project has everything needed to generate the P50 probabilistic schedule as benchmark information.

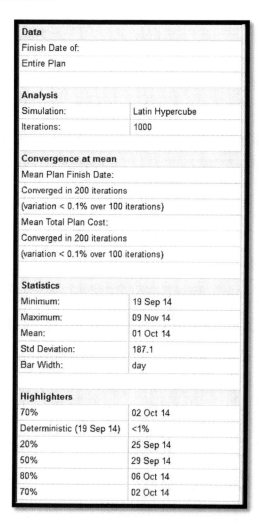

Data	
Finish Date of:	
Entire Plan	
Analysis	
Simulation:	Latin Hypercube
Iterations:	1000
Convergence at mean	
Mean Plan Finish Date:	
Converged in 200 iterations	
(variation < 0.1% over 100 iterations)	
Mean Total Plan Cost:	
Converged in 200 iterations	
(variation < 0.1% over 100 iterations)	
Statistics	
Minimum:	19 Sep 14
Maximum:	09 Nov 14
Mean:	01 Oct 14
Std Deviation:	187.1
Bar Width:	day
Highlighters	
70%	02 Oct 14
Deterministic (19 Sep 14)	<1%
20%	25 Sep 14
50%	29 Sep 14
80%	06 Oct 14
70%	02 Oct 14

Figure 108 - Probability Distribution Datasheet

11.23. Formatting

In order to see the P50 dates activities on the OPRA Gantt chart window, customize the bars by clicking on the "Format" pull down menu and select Custom Task Bars.

Customize the task bars by selecting whatever colors the project wants to differentiate the P50 activity bars versus deterministic, P70, and other percentile bars.

After changing the value on the Custom Task Bars window, click OK.

It will bring back the Activity and Gantt Window.

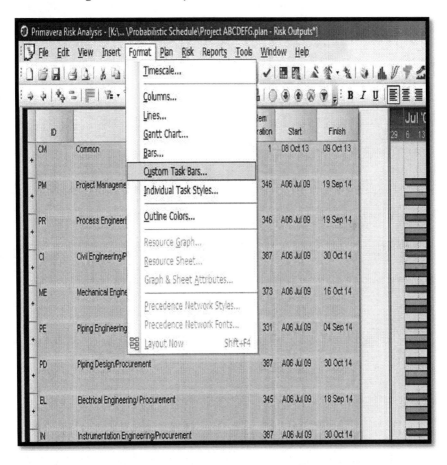

Figure 109 - Bars Formatting Window

11.24. Customize Task Bars on the Formatting Window

Customize the task bars as shown in Figure 110. Choose whatever colors you want to differentiate the P50 activities from deterministic and other percentiles such as P70.

If you want to choose other percentiles, just add them.

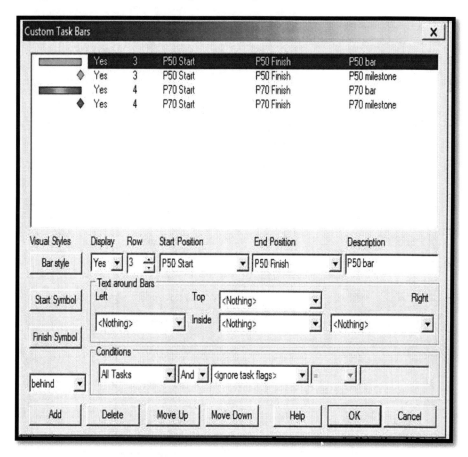

Figure 110 - Customize Task Bars on the Formatting Window

11.25. Check Customized Bars on Gantt Window

The deterministic, P50, and P70 bars will display on the Gantt window.

The columns representing the P50 Start and P50 Finish date will also be

234

displayed.

If not displayed, point the mouse on the header band and right click. The P50 start and finish columns is there to add.

Other probability start and finish (Px) column like the P70, P80, and others are also available for selection.

Add them as required.

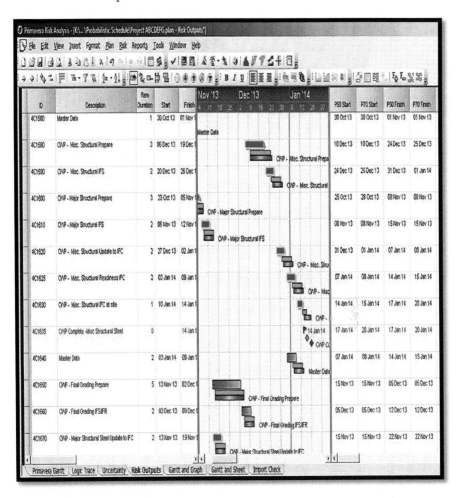

Figure 111 - Gantt Chart Showing P50, P70 and Deterministic Bars

11.26. Export the PLAN File as XER

The plan file containing the P50 risk-based baseline is now ready for export to the Primavera Project Management (P6) database. This schedule created in OPRA has to find its way into the main Primavera scheduling tool. To do this, export the plan file as an XER file to an accessible directory.

Do not make the destination folder too deep and the file name too long. The more shallow the directory, the better. Do not exceed three tiers. The file and folder destination name must be short.

Try to make it less than 15 characters. If this does not work, check with the IS/IT support the default limitation of the network workspace.

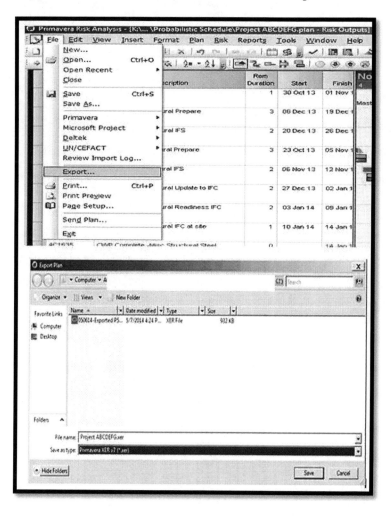

Figure 112 - OPRA Exporting Window

11.27. Import the XER to Primavera Scheduling Database

Open the Primavera scheduling tool and import Project AB XER file into one of its EPS node.

Importing procedure is available in the P6 HELP menu. Import the Project AB XER file into one of the EPS node.

A progress box comes up when import is in progress.

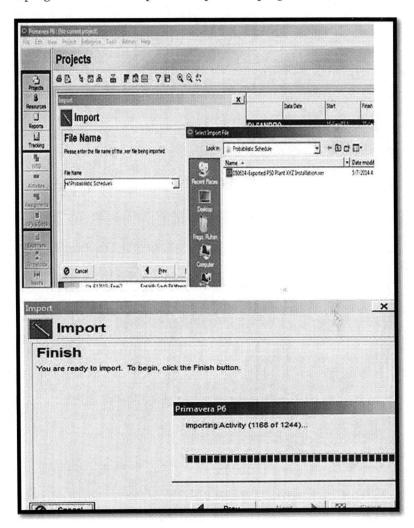

Figure 113 - Primavera (P6) Import Window

11.28. Format Bars and Assign Columns to P50 Dates

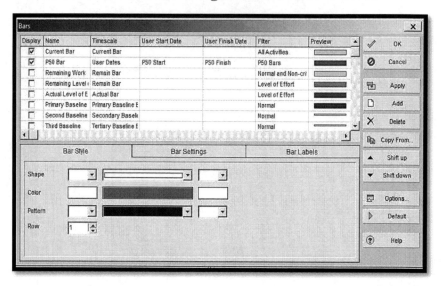

Figure 114 - Format Gantt Bars Dialogue Window

Figure 115 - Assigning the Probabilistic P50 Dates Columns

11.29. P50 Conclusion

Using a poor quality schedule is bad enough, but having deliverables with unsupportive probabilities can make key dates and even the overall project schedule unachievable. This fatal combination is a sure formula to project failure. The project should use available tools to avoid this scenario!

As proven in the simulated test project ABCDEFG, differences between silo schedules, or disconnected schedule activities in a big project, will create issues unless their calculated certainties align closely.

It is logical that the success of a large portfolio with individually developed projects can vastly improve after aligning the certainty of each silo. The case in point is well documented here, starting with sub-project A targeting a deterministic date that has low 10% probability.

Despite a simplistic model and the minimal duration assumptions we used, linking A to successor B successfully demonstrated the significant effect of misaligned certainties. Silo B's 30% probability of achieving the target date is reduced to 5% when linked to A, suddenly making its deterministic date unachievable (Figure 94 and Figure 99).

TIP   The lesson is clear that two independent variables connected to each other by a logical relationship can affect the dependent and overall result either positively or negatively.

If the predecessor has a greater certainty than the successor, the unconstrained successor will improve its previous certainty value, keeping the same deterministic target date.

If the predecessor has a lesser certainty than the successor, the unconstrained successor will decrease its previous certainty value.

This method is useful for any project, regardless of size. I recommend the following exercise:

- Develop, create, and use a P50 risk-based baseline.
- Use P50 as a scheduling benchmark.
- Develop and create a probabilistic schedule with specific certainty values.
- Align silo schedules by generating a common probability value.
- Complete an in-depth review of deterministic schedule activities and deliverables versus their mode, mean, and median values.

The project can also generate other percentiles such as P60, P70, P80, and others. It is not limited to just P50. The ultimate decision as to what standard probability value is used might depend largely on the risk appetite and risk tolerance of the sponsoring organizations. The business will make the choice.

While the previous statement is true, the P50 risk-based baseline schedule derived from the probabilistic quantification espoused in here is more acceptable, economical, and less stressful as a reckoning benchmark to use.

It offers a much better comparative point, while the project fine-tunes the final baseline execution schedule.

Yes, one can choose a tight or loose schedule depending on sound business acumen.

If your organization has not thought of this yet, maybe it is about time to review your project portfolios such that they line up properly.

Make sure that the silo schedules do not compete or contradict each other's time   commitment.

Chapter 12

Mega-projects Schedule Integration

12.1. Introduction to Mega-projects Schedule Integration

Effectively managing the overall and overarching schedule of a super mega-project portfolio has always been a challenge to all project managers. In spite of having divided the project into smaller pieces or sub-projects, the size issue remains because each supposedly smaller project is still quite sizeable, perhaps several hundred million, to a billion dollars or more each.

In this section, I have experimented on a theoretical mega-project portfolio using a pilot model that I have divided into five major sub-projects, each one of them approximately $1 billion to $2.5 billion. Primavera Enterprise Project Portfolio Management Release 7 was the tool of choice in this study. The use of the term silo instead of sub-project in this chapter merely highlights the usual work management division existing between subs.

12.2. Sample Mega-project Model

The project controls group received instruction to develop an integrated schedule of a mega-construction project with a portfolio amounting to $10 billion. The project portfolio has five major sub-projects or silos. These portfolio sub-projects are Project A, Project B, Project C, Project D, and Project E. Each silo manages a $1 billion to $2.5 billion budget. Area schedule was defined and broken down to the work package level. The number of activities in each of the five schedules range from 7,000 to 10,000. Total number of activities in the entire project portfolio is about 43,000 activities. All five sub-projects are EPC sub-projects that was further divided into phase components. The scheduling tool chosen by the organization is Primavera Release 7.

12.3. Risk-based Issues

Full integration using hard linking between areas is the main issue in this schedule integration initiative. It is quite daunting, and the Project Controls (PC) group tasked to carry it through is unsure about the proper approach. Half of the company planning and scheduling subject matter experts oppose it. They argue that Primavera (F9) calculation of the critical path needs all the linked schedules opened. The 43,000-activity schedule is just too large to maintain good control. On the other hand, everyone knows that without those inter-project links (IPL), accurate critical path identification is not going to happen.

The project would like to use a key interface milestone (KIM) table outside of Primavera to manage the overall project portfolio. I have big reservations using a separate KIM table as a tool to consolidate date information. Using a separate application seems like managing the overall schedule using two versions of the truth. It is a dangerous proposition.

12.4. Objectives

- To come up with a workable alternative to the most common KIM schedule management method of using a flat file from a separate application
- To come up with a method that preserve the critical path calculation and identification
- To propose a method that does not require opening the whole project portfolio at the same time to do the scheduling calculation
- To simplify the management of the overall schedule though the use of a KIM schedule without losing that essential inter-project relationships or being limited by the project portfolio's sheer size
- To propose a workable method that will support accurate, quick date analysis and timely decision making
- To do away the time-consuming collection of data by offering a common work environment and promoting "what you see is what you get" information quality

12.5. KIM Criteria

KIM is an acronym for key interface milestone. The noun adjective "key" describes the importance of this schedule milestone. The word "interface" describes the purpose such milestones, or its role as an interphase point. An interface milestone helps the project recognize, monitor, assess, and manage current schedule versus time commitment.

Time commitments are essential reckoning points that are more often than not, tied closely to the contract. The variance between the baseline interface date and the current schedule date drives the project's decision.

A Mega-Project such as the one we have as an example can easily have 100 to 200 KIMs, and maybe even more. There should be a central integration team facilitating the identification of these milestones based on an agreed-to definition of KIM. A common understanding is imperative in order for the concept of KIM management to succeed. Define KIM first before identification starts.

Listed below are the proposed criteria for judging when to use KIM.

- Can be part of a horizontal or vertical logic
- Lies on the critical path between sub-projects
- Lies on the critical path between phases
- Lies on the critical path between major work packages
- Activities point of convergence
- Activities point of divergence
- A transition key milestone between phases
- Contractually pertinent milestones such as those required for progress billing
- Special request from controlling stakeholders
- Milestones ushering sensitive activities subject to public or government scrutiny
- Milestones that are deemed important by the silo management for good reason
- Milestones that will serve as key risk indicators
- Milestones that will serve as performance indicators
- Milestones that provide a better handle to forecasting

12.6. KIM Mapping

Figure 116 is a high-level map of key interface milestones with respect to each silo. The project team should take a good look at their multi-billion dollar project and understand how the sub-projects are related. In this way, the team will better understand how the deliverables of one feed another, how many there are, and their impacts to the overall project portfolio.

The green arrows demonstrate that the relationships between sub-projects can be both unidirectional (singular dependency) and bi-directional, with mutual dependency or a two-sided interface as seen in Figure 117. When a silo is dependent on other sub-projects but the other sub-projects are independent from it, it is singular dependency. When one or more sub-projects depend on each other to complete each of their sub-projects, it is mutual dependency.

TIP KIM mapping provides a high level understanding of the relationship that crosses sub-project boundaries. It will dictate how the calculation cascades as described in later sections.

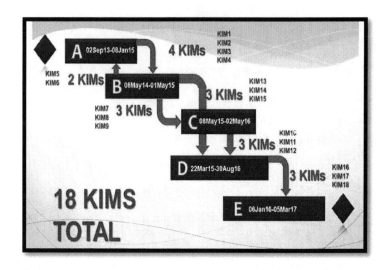

Figure 116 - High Level KIM Mapping

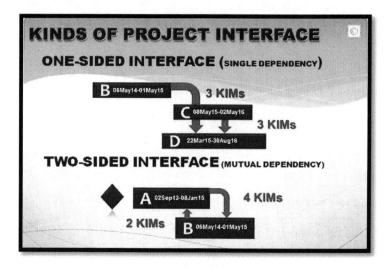

Figure 117 - Sub-projects (Silos) Relationships Chart

12.7. Portfolio Strategy

The strategy is to create and build the enterprise project structure of each sub-project in the same scheduling database. Looking at the overall portfolio is like looking at one project. They are integrated and at the same time, able to maintain their grouping (Figure 118). Each project in the portfolio is a sub-project of the overall project. The yellow demarcation line between each sub-project illustrates a boundary that the green arrows cross. Any tie line that crosses the boundary is an inter-project link. To make it clear, the word tie, link, relationship, and logical relationship are scheduling jargons that mean practically the same. If you are new to project management, then your vocabulary has grown.

⚠️ The subject mega-project integration set-up will work only, and only all sub-projects of the project portfolio lies in the same scheduling database.

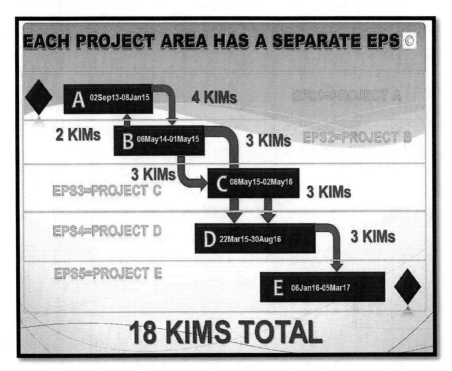

Figure 118 - Primavera Database EPS Schematic

12.8. Interface Milestone Schedule

Create a separate enterprise project structure node (EPS node) assigned to the overall milestone schedule (MS). Add a project with a project ID easily recognizable as the overall milestone schedule. In this example, the Project ID is KIM Schedule and the EPS node is coded MS (Figure 120).

Open the empty schedule and add all the approved KIM activities (see below). The first detailed exercise then followed and that is to type in the list of key interphase milestone into the schedule shown in Figure 119. Once all the agreed-to MS are in, this step is finished.

Layout: Admin01=Classic View | Filter: All Act

Activity ID	Activity Name	WBS
Overall Milestones Schedule		
KIM01	Key Interface Milestone 1	MS Schedule
KIM02	Key Interface Milestone 2	MS Schedule
KIM03	Key Interface Milestone 3	MS Schedule
KIM04	Key Interface Milestone 4	MS Schedule
KIM05	Key Interface Milestone 5	MS Schedule
KIM06	Key Interface Milestone 6	MS Schedule
KIM07	Key Interface Milestone 7	MS Schedule
KIM08	Key Interface Milestone 8	MS Schedule
KIM09	Key Interface Milestone 9	MS Schedule
KIM10	Key Interface Milestone 10	MS Schedule
KIM11	Key Interface Milestone 11	MS Schedule
KIM12	Key Interface Milestone 12	MS Schedule
KIM13	Key Interface Milestone 13	MS Schedule
KIM14	Key Interface Milestone 14	MS Schedule
KIM15	Key Interface Milestone 15	MS Schedule
KIM16	Key Interface Milestone 16	MS Schedule
KIM17	Key Interface Milestone 17	MS Schedule
KIM18	Key Interface Milestone 18	MS Schedule

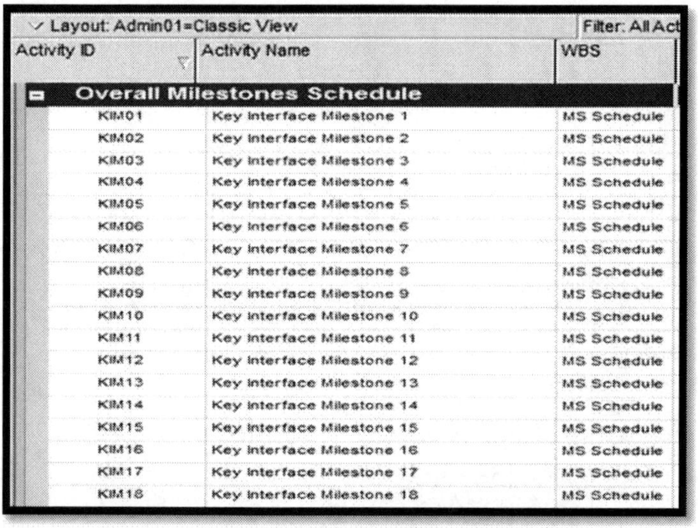

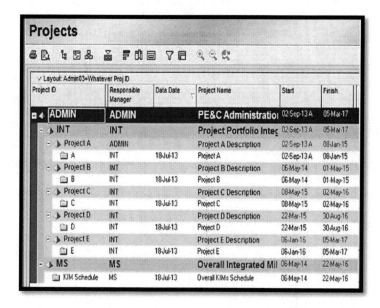

Figure 119 - Key Interphase Milestone Schedule

Projects

Layout: Admin03=Whatever Proj ID

Project ID	Responsible Manager	Data Date	Project Name	Start	Finish
ADMIN	ADMIN		PE&C Administratio	02-Sep-13 A	05-Mar-17
INT	INT		Project Portfolio Inte	02-Sep-13 A	05-Mar-17
Project A	ADMIN		Project A Description	02-Sep-13 A	08-Jan-15
A	INT	18-Jul-13	Project A	02-Sep-13 A	08-Jan-15
Project B	INT		Project B Description	06-May-14	01-May-15
B	INT	18-Jul-13	Project B	06-May-14	01-May-15
Project C	INT		Project C Description	08-May-15	02-May-16
C	INT	18-Jul-13	Project C	08-May-15	02-May-16
Project D	INT		Project D Description	22-Mar-15	30-Aug-16
D	INT	18-Jul-13	Project D	22-Mar-15	30-Aug-16
Project E	INT		Project E Description	06-Jan-16	05-Mar-17
E	INT	18-Jul-13	Project E	06-Jan-16	05-Mar-17
MS	MS		Overall Integrated Mil	06-May-14	22-May-16
KIM Schedule	MS	18-Jul-13	Overall KIMs Schedule	06-May-14	22-May-16

Figure 120 - KIM Schedule in a Separate EPS Node

12.9. Setting up EPS Folders of Sub-projects

It is necessary to develop and finalize the execution schedule down to the work package level. A work package level is commonly termed as a Level 3 in construction projects.

Each of the five major sub-projects will be located into separate EPS nodes, each containing an EPC/CSU schedule (Figure 118).

EPC is an acronym for engineering, procurement, and construction phases.

CSU is an acronym for commissioning and start-up phase.

After creating the key interphase milestone schedule containing all the KIMs in a separate EPS (Figure 120), the sub-project schedules come next.

A sub-project can be the deliverer or/and a requestor.

A deliverer points to the sub-project that has the responsibility to complete an activity or activities to the other sub-projects according to the time commitments involved.

The deliverer and the requestor share a common milestone in the KIM schedule for each of the deliverable.

Once the scheduler ties the pertinent activities in each sub-project and the KIM schedule, a baseline is set, execution commence, then monitoring and control starts.

12.10. Upload the Sub-projects

Load the sub-project schedules into the assigned EPS node using direct upload or assigning codes.

Create, maintain, and assign the sub-projects level 3 BL and the KIM schedule BL.

Do this while in the "Maintain Baselines" (Figure 121) and "Assign Baseline" (Figure 122) dialogue box of Primavera scheduling tool.

Upon stakeholder sign-off and approval, publish the KIMs baseline schedule. Use the KIM schedule to monitor and control the project. Create the overall key interphase milestone schedule. Create the portfolio baseline.

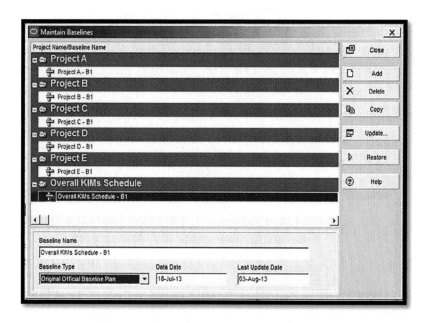

Figure 121 - Sub-projects and KIM Baselines (Maintain Baselines)

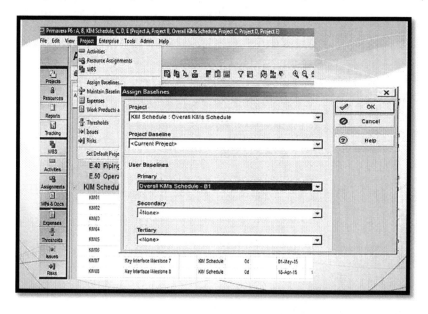

Figure 122 - KIM Baseline

12.11. Ensure Sub-projects Supports KIM Schedule

Make sure that the KIM schedule lines up with the approved project portfolio baseline before the first update.

It means that each sub-project fully supports the KIM dates. Do this alignment check before freezing the KIM schedule as a baseline.

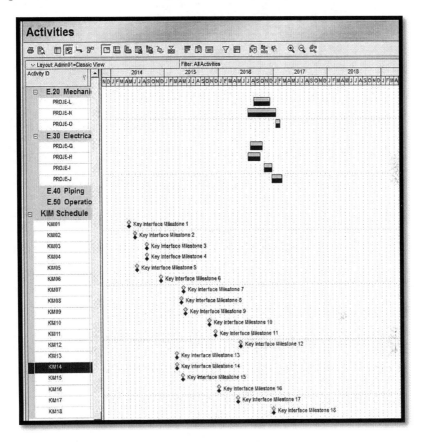

Figure 123 - Align KIM BL to Portfolio Baseline

12.12. Move the Data Date on the Schedule (all Sub-projects)

Change the data date of each sub-project as shown by the succeeding illustrations below and calculate. The example shows that the project updates the original data date of July 18, 2013 to September 20, 2013 starting with Project A (Figure 124).

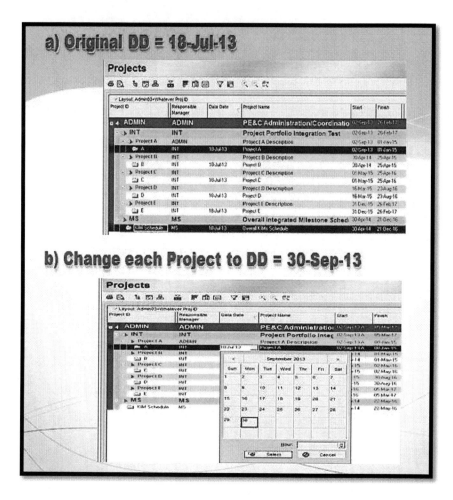

Figure 124 - Update Data Date Starting with Project A

The "Fill Down" feature in Primavera facilitates the entry of the new date to the other projects or sub-projects.

Pointing the cursor on the first date field while pressing the "Shift" key and dragging the pointer to the last field at the bottom highlights the target sub-projects requiring update.

Right-click and press "Fill Down" to change the data date of each sub-project (Figure 125).

As can be seen, the project had successfully updated the original data date of

July 18, 2013 to September 20, 2013 starting with Project A.

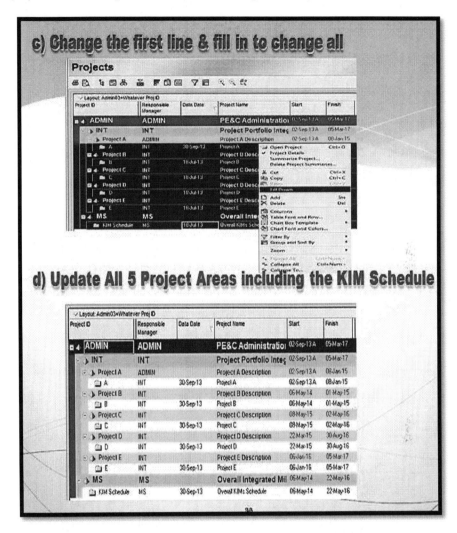

Figure 125 - Updating the Data Date Using "Fill Down"

12.13. Update Project A (Silo A) and the KIM Schedule.

Update each of the sub-projects together with the KIM Schedule starting with the primary sub-project that drives the downstream. Take the sequence of update from the high-level KIM map.

Do the calculation twice for sub-projects that have mutual dependency (see Section 12.6). In this example, the update starts with Sub-project A.

253

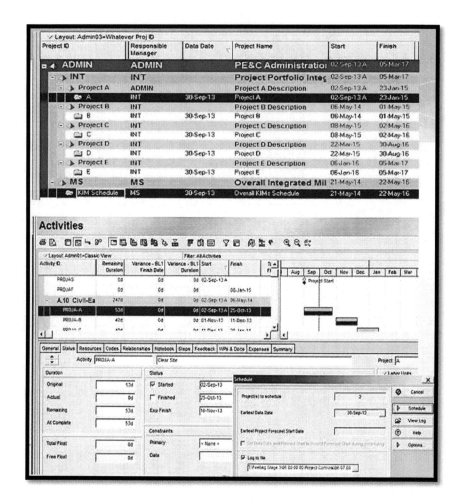

Figure 126 - Project A and KIM Schedule Update

12.14. Open and Update Project B (Silo B) and the KIM Schedule

Open both the KIM schedule and Project B. As before, go to the activity window and press F9 to calculate. Take the sequence of update from the high-level KIM map. Do the calculation twice for sub-projects that have mutual dependency (see Section 12.6).

In this example, the second update involves Project B.

254

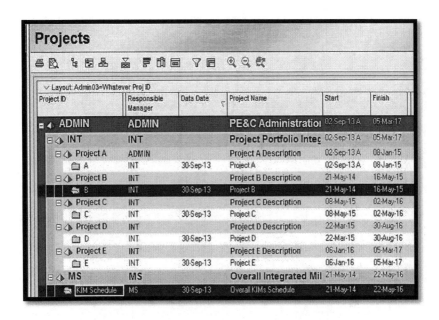

Figure 127 - Project B and KIM Schedule Update

12.15. Open and Update Project C and the KIM Schedule

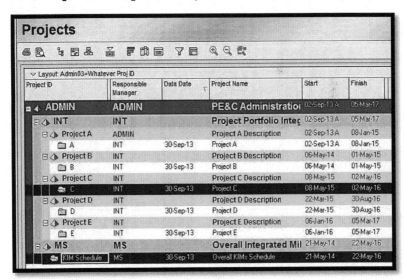

Figure 128 - Project C and KIM Schedule Update

12.16. Open and Update Project D and the KIM Schedule

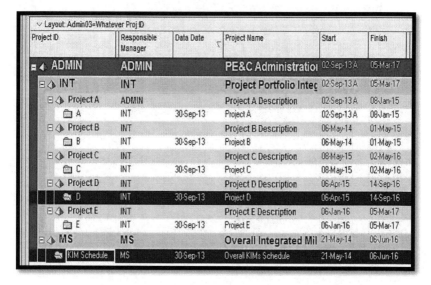

Figure 129 - Project D and KIM Schedule Update

12.17. Open and Update Project E and the KIM Schedule

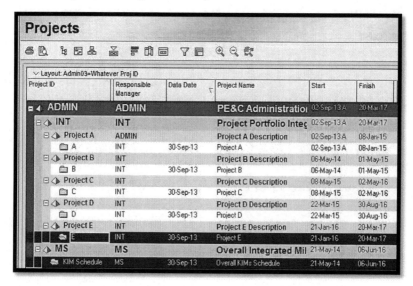

Figure 130 - Project E and KIM Schedule Update

12.18. Open and Run KIM Schedule Variance Report.

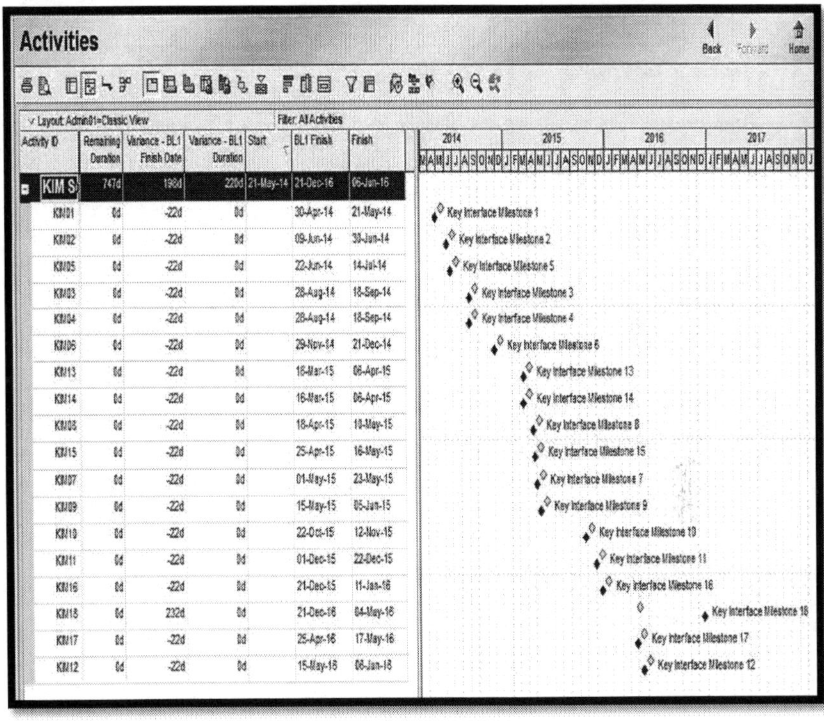

Figure 131 - KIM Variance versus Baseline

12.19. Open Each Project and Run Variance Report

Open and calculate (F9) each project. Run an analysis without opening the KIM schedule.

With the KIM milestones now acting as external links, the constrained effects will produce a critical path within each of the project schedules.

The date variances will now serve as a good decision tool. It will show the critical path, traceable to upstream activities unable to support the interface KIM dates.

The calculation works because the updated KIM schedule constrains the sub-projects.

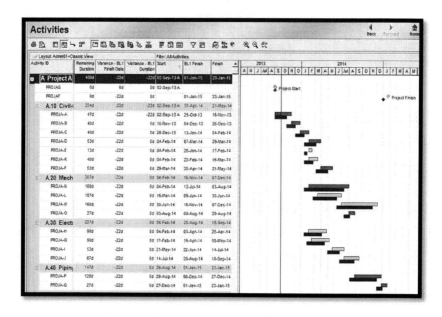

Figure 132 - Project A Schedule Variance Analysis

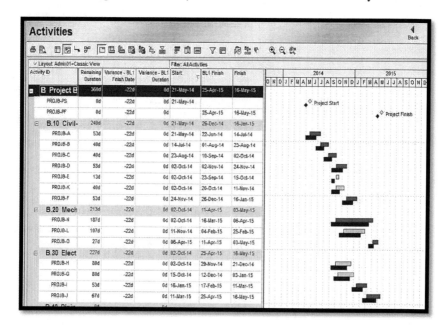

Figure 133 - Project B Schedule Variance Analysis

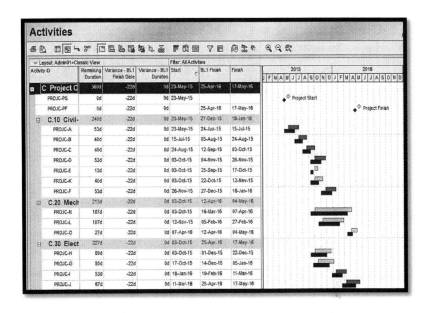

Figure 134 - Project C Schedule Variance Analysis

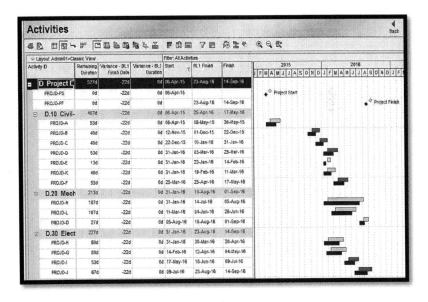

Figure 135 - Project D Schedule Variance Analysis

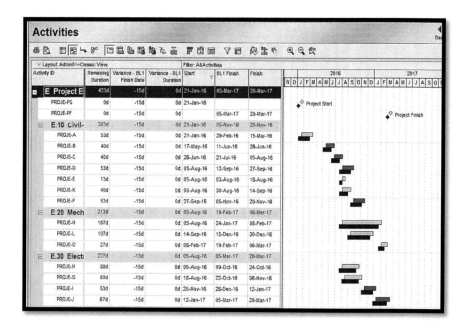

Figure 136 - Project E Schedule Variance Analysis

12.20. Conclusion

The chapter has presented a workable alternative to managing extremely big project portfolio through key interface milestone schedule. A singular version of the truth stays, as the project makes sure that logics are preserved.

It is an excellent way of retaining the capability to identify the portfolio critical path. The project has managed to stay away from using multiple applications, including the temptation of reverting to using a flat file.

This method solved the schedule calculation challenge posed by a huge schedule because we can now calculate in cascade, one at a time, without opening the whole project portfolio.

It is not necessary to open all the sub-projects at the same time. Management of the overall portfolio schedule though the use of a KIM schedule without losing that essential inter-project relationships or being limited by the project portfolio's sheer size becomes a reality.

The chapter introduces a workable method that supports an accurate, quick date analysis, and timely decision making. The time-consuming collection of data is no longer an issue because a common work environment is now available.

Chapter 13

Risk Assessments and Treatments

13.1.   Introduction to Risk Assessments and Treatments

Risk assessment is the process of assessing identified risk, and extracting data about its probability and consequence to business objectives. If the risks are borne out of some known hazards, the assessment focuses around it. Assessment of the risks includes finding all available ways to remove or control the hazard. In many ways, the hazard presents itself as an issue (see Sections 7.10 to 7.13). A business must address the issue to prevent new risks emanating from it.

The response to prevent, avoid, transfer, mitigate, enhance, promote, retain, and exploit risks is known as risk treatment. Risk responses are timely decisions describing the strategy and specific approach to each risk. Treatment to threats increases the probability of achieving common objectives or decreasing the impact of the consequence just in case the negative risk does happen.

 The best response plan comes after risk assessment.

In this Chapter, we will discuss a school district operation case, looking through the eyes of various stakeholders, mainly those representing the business. The topic touches risk identification and control techniques like avoidance, modification of likelihood or consequence, risk transfer and retention among others. Supplementing the subject are ways of reducing claim liability through loss control.

13.2.   Case Study - School District Bus Operation

The risk management professional for an urban school district is considering the feasibility of applying various risk control techniques to the district's liability exposures arising from the operation of the school busses the district now owns. Identifying, assessing, prioritizing, treating, and controlling operational risks will ensure that the district can successfully meet its objectives. To simplify this case study, we have selected some high-risk items from a list of many. In this way, the new risk practitioners can understand better, without further in-depth clarification.

Section 13.3 lists all the identified risks and illustrates the use of four different risk control techniques that the district could apply to its liability exposures arising out of the operations of the school busses it now owns, including the enhancement and exploitation of any identified opportunity. The school district said that it is going to continue operating its own busses.

For each of the following loss control objectives, we will describe at least one action plan for the school district that can reasonably reduce the frequency or severity of liability claims for injuries to students on these busses.

Several groups have a stake in the success or failure of the bussing program. Knowing who your stakeholders are is important, and the process begins by developing healthy relationships with them. Stakeholders help decide on issues from the beginning, during planning, execution, and operation of the bussing program (Figure 139). They should understand how the project functions, including the program scope, milestones, and goals. We have grouped the stakeholders according to power/influence and interest, as shown in Figure 137.

A proper risk assessment requires proper consideration of human factors, procedures, routes, local geography, climate, and the management liability connected thereto.

One has to understand that operation of the school buses follows operation and safety procedures utilized, controlled, and monitored by people. Busses might be traversing mountainous road, deserted highway, dirt tracks, unpaved roads, highways, or freeways. School bus fleet faces traffic and is bound to interact with other vehicles at a wide range of speeds.

This is not mentioning weather risk factors such as rain, floods, snow, sleet, blizzards, fog, freezing rain, and ice.

We have covered as much ground as necessary, including Strength, Weakness, Opportunity, Threat (SWOT) table (Figure 138), the stakeholder's map (Figure 139), and the power-interest grid (Figure 137) to certain extent. This case study is intentionally limited to pure risk but does not intend to answer every threat or liability there is, for they are many and the nuances brought by different risk factors have wide and varying ranges.

It is imperative that the readers understand the risk assessment framework to which the operation of the district busses hinges heavily on.

13.3. Identified Risks

    A. Road accident resulting in injury to student, staff, bus driver, third party, or other driver

    B. Mechanical breakdown on highway or normal road

    C. Student, bus driver, or staff becomes ill or injured

    D. Health risk – Diesel exhaust from school bus (NRDC, 2001 and WebMD, 2014)

    E. Exposure of students to sex offenders, drug pushers, and other criminals

    F. Losses due to weather related events such as blizzards, heavy snow, windstorms, and floods

13.4. Risk Avoidance

District to stop bus service altogether and let parents and students arrange their own individual private transport. In this way, the school will not be responsible for anything, effectively avoiding Risks A to F. Converting district busses to gas or green/electric busses (treatment for risk D). Conduct pre-departure checklist on the weather. If not in good state, do not allow the bus to leave. Administrator can cancel the trip and reschedule when it is safe to go (treatment for risk F).

13.5. Modify Likelihood or Impact of Risk

Ensure qualified and licensed bus drivers (treatment for risks A, B, and F). Students and driver must always fasten seatbelts while bus is running (treatment for risks A, C, and F). Rule that no passenger should move around when the bus is running (treatment for risks A, C, and F). Arrange toilet stops on longer route travel (treatment for risk C). Avoid distracted driving (Treatment for risks A, B, and F).

On normal roads, keep students in the bus while waiting for bus repair (treatment for risks A, B, and C). On the highway, move the students to a safe location, away from oncoming traffic (treatment for risks A, B, and C).

Ensure regular bus maintenance (treatment for risk B, D, and F). Conduct a pre-departure checklist on the bus and driver. If not in good state, do not allow the bus to leave. Cancel the trip and schedule another bus (treatment for Risks A, B, C, D, E and F). Check attendance before each departure (treatment for Risks C, E, and F).

Regular inspection to ensure that emission levels are well within government health standards – Converting district busses to gas or green electric busses (treatment for risk D). Develop contracts containing clauses such as waivers, hold-harmless, exculpatory agreements, or some form of unilateral notices (treatment for risks A, B, C, D, and E).

Start first Aid training (treatment for risks A, C, and D). Employ security guards as driver (treatment for risks E). Activate ID card check and buddy system (treatment for risks E).

13.6. Risk Transfer

All passengers and drivers must have appropriate and mandatory insurance coverage. Outsource bussing service to a private contractor (treatment for risk A, B, C, D, and E). Bring students to a common, short, convenient, and well-secured location where their parents or guardians can pick them up (treatment for risks E).

13.7. Risk Retention

Creation of an in-house contingency fund that will be doubled each year intended to cover whatever claims come up (treatment for risk A, B, C, D, and E). Develop full complement of resources for bus maintenance and towing outfit (treatment for risk B). Develop a fully resourced medical emergency outfit (treatment for risks C and D).

13.8. Loss Control Objectives

Remove or limit the district's obligations to others. The district can use express contract as defense against claim. It can summon contract clauses such as waivers, hold-harmless, exculpatory agreements, and comparative negligence defense so that liability and responsibility are shared.

Other methods of limiting direct obligation are through negotiation, arbitration, or conciliation, especially if using favorable the jurisdiction clause (Elliott, Risk Assessment and Treatment, 2012).

Prevent invasions of the district's legally protected interests. Using the legal privilege (Jones, 2012) defense will allow the school district and its staff the right to refuse disclosure of confidential information that might undermine the organization on matters of claims.

Getting an injunction against the claimant is a remedy to prevent them and others from acting against the district's legally protected interests.

The simplest way to protect physical properties is to install no entry signs, hazard posts, and no trespassing notices around the legally protected interests.

Copyright, patent, and trade secret registration will protect the district's intellectual properties just in case they become targets of claims (Canada, 2014).

Prevent harm to those who handle the district's legally protected interests. Use closed circuit television (CCTV), security personnel, and physical barriers such as security fences, and fail-safe door locks to safeguard those who handle the district's interests.

Using assumption of risk defense can be effective because the blame does not fall solely onto the district's shoulders.

The last clear chance doctrine defense against negligence will shield the district from harm by avoiding responsibility.

Control all forms of legal action that may be brought against the district. Use the immunity defense, pointing to certain specific instances where the school district has shield from liability (Elliott, Risk Assessment and Treatment, 2012).

13.9. Additional Action Plan

It is good practice to develop stakeholders register, similar to that in Figure 137, but with more details. This register should be included in the bussing operation and communication plan.

The register is a simple table with the specific stakeholder's name, contact details, requirements, and classification. It is a living document that needs to be updated (and it will be updated many times) as the stakeholder-specific information changes.

After identifying the stakeholders, the responsible program manager spearheading this initiative has to find out their individual expectations and create a strategy to manage those.

All this information should be in the register.

The list classifies stakeholders according to their power, influence, and interest. Grouping them enables the risk manager to manage expectations effectively (Frago, R., 2013).

Using a SWOT structured analysis to evaluate the strengths, weaknesses, opportunities, and threats involved in the district bus operation should be required, and revisited on a periodic basis (Wikipedia, Wikipedia-SWOT Analysis, 2013).

Good risk preparation upstream prevents many liabilities downstream. See Figure 138 for SWOT guiding questionnaire (Palomino, 2013).

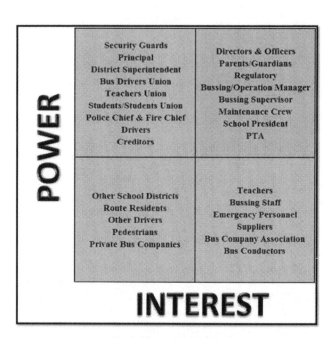

Guiding Principle

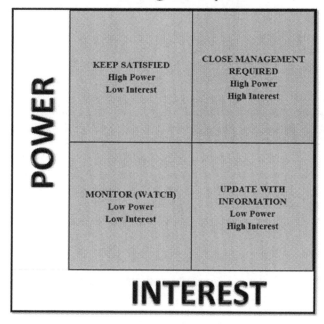

Figure 137 - Stakeholders Power and Interest Grid

STRENGTHS	WEAKNESSES
1) List of strengths (strong points) 2) List of improved items compared to previous work 3) List of unique attributes 4) List of available useful resources 5) Third party perspective of your organization's strengths 6) Strong reputation-specific list	1) List of weaknesses (flaws and possible source of errors) 2) List what areas lags compared to competitors 3) Identify vague processes 4) Identify weakest links in the process 5) List of items needing improvement 6) Third party perspective of your organization's weakness 7) Weak reputation-specifics list
OPPORTUNITIES	**THREATS**
1) List all positive trends and conditions 2) List all available positive breaks 3) Keep tab of current events that increases probabilities 4) List all issues that might create favorable conditions	1) List all negative trends and conditions 2) List all available negative breaks 3) Keep tab of current events that decreases probabilities 4) List all issues that increases bad consequence

Figure 138 - SWOT Table

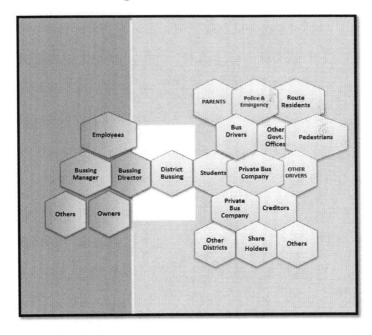

Figure 139 - Stakeholder's Map

Chapter 14

Root Cause Analysis (RCA)

14.1. Introduction to Root Cause Analysis

Root cause analysis (RCA) digs from the general into the underlying causes of the event under inspection. If a project fails, the risk-based manager analyzes what caused the failure in order to avoid the same failure in a future similar project. If a machine failure results in a life threatening accident, identifying the predominant cause that led to the accident uses RCA. By breaking the chain of cause and effect anywhere between the bottom indenture levels and the top levels, a business avoids major future losses, and possibly reduces present liability.

 RCA is both a process and an approach.

The analysis to determine the root causes and effects examines the driving relationships leading to the main issue. This approach must line up with the plan and strategy of the company. The effort to do RCA depends upon the degree of complexity an issue has. If the relationship network involved is so large, the method used in investigation boils down to discerning the patterns of effects in the system.

There is reportedly a growing interest across various industries on the subject of big data. Every time I hear about it, I am compounded by a nagging question of how big "big data" is. Is it fundamentally because of the volume of information or the big impact that effective use of stored data brings? Is it so big that information resides in a data warehouse so indescribably large, so large that it is limitless and infinite? I have touched the term big data to remind the reader that everything in this world is connected in some ways.

I see the root cause network like a grand schedule with multiple ends. Identifying an end issue is like targeting an end deliverable, a final consequence is traceable using its critical path. The root cause drives succeeding sub-causes. It eventually leads to the final consequence via its critical path. RCA is applicable to any form of investigation. How deep one should go is fit for purpose and requires good judgment. The rationale behind the effort must make sense.

Tracing to the very bottom might not be practical. The stop nodes should be deep enough and something the business can control or modify.

An accident investigation utilizes the Fault Tree Analysis (FTA) and Failure Mode and Effects Analysis (FMEA) approach in this chapter applied to a business called WOW Taxi.

When investigating an accident where there are unavailable information, fault assessment should undergo several simulations entertaining all what-ifs to identify probabilities.

At the end, the investigator analyst chooses the more plausible cause by virtue of it having the highest certainty.

14.2. Case Study - WOW Taxi Company

In this chapter, we will embark into the field of root cause analysis as a risk-based management tool. Various techniques are available. These techniques have wide-ranging applications in industry:

They include Failure Mode and Effects Analysis (FMEA), Fault Tree Analysis (FTA), and Fishbone Analysis or Ishikawa (using the 5-Whys and more questioning approach), to name a few.

A real major risk that a transport company needs to consider in depth is an accident happening to one of its many units. The risk of an accident brings unwanted consequence, such as physical injuries to drivers, passengers, or pedestrians. There are also penalties imposed by regulatory bodies, court litigations, property damage, and several other derivative losses to prepare for. Of course, the more pronounced aspects are those that involve health and safety, or threat to life, followed immediately by property and direct financial losses.

Transport companies like WOW Taxi are out there moving, transporting, and providing the services they are to do. The whole system is comprised of moving vehicles, drivers/operators, passengers, pedestrians, road conditions, other vehicles, and accidents, which are dynamic elements that bring about hazards and generate risks.

The more complex the process, the more changes involved, and the greater the probability of risk.

Using root cause analysis techniques, let us investigate an accident in the city of Calgary involving a WOW Taxicab rollover and build an FTA chart to show findings. The accident is real but occurred in another city, but to preserve anonymity of those involved, we assumed it happened in Calgary as is now indicated.

14.3. Accident data

The first step to RCA is the collection of data, but not just any data. In order to avoid remodeling and unnecessary repetition of the process, one must ensure the quality of information is sound.

It is best to get the information from site inspection and official reports and statements. Crosscheck the stories from bystanders and witnesses close to the time of the event even if they appear to be very near the truth.

Working information that will facilitate results is available from the following. However, they would need validation.

- Official reports (police, witnesses, and those directly involved in the accident)
- Blogs and threads
- News reports (video webcasts, TV, news, or the internet).
- Injury lawyer's website
- Government website
- Transportation regulatory website such as the Federal Motor Carrier Safety Administration (FMCSA)
- Various statistical studies published via the internet.

For our example, read the short hypothetical news clip below:

Date: January 25, 2014, Calgary, Alberta

An alleged drunken cab driver and his teenage passenger were rushed to Foot Hills Hospital early this cold morning after the taxi they were riding rolled over multiple times (Figure 140). The accident happened in the intersection of 36th Street and 17th Avenue.

The crash occurred at about 2:35 a.m.

John Not Him, 53, the driver, said that the brake failed. Witnesses and police said Mr. Not Him appeared intoxicated. John claimed he was not drunk. He got several fractures and broken bones.

The seventeen-year old female passenger thrown from the vehicle suffered serious life-threatening injuries. Investigation revealed that neither the driver nor the passenger in the taxi was wearing seatbelts.

The taxi was westbound of 17th Avenue when it hit a barrier, running into a pole and cutting the vehicle in half before it then rolled two or three times, ending in the middle of the road. The damage to the vehicle was heavy.

A charge of driving while intoxicated is expected.

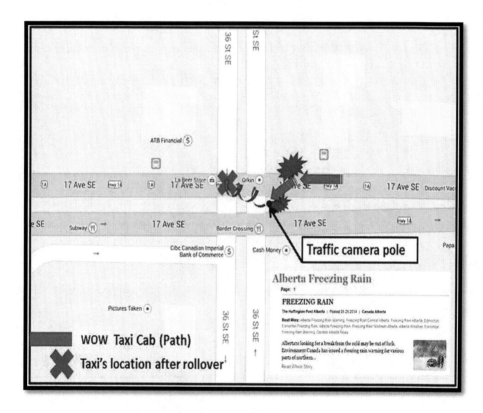

Figure 140 - Accident Plot Reconstruction

14.4. Causal Factor Charting

This is the second step to RCA. The risk-based manager starts his analysis of the chain of specific events from what is obvious and known to be true, going backward and forward to zero in on the underlying causes (Figure 141).

He traces the cause and effect chain from the more specific to the general event. It is important to spend enough time around the critical point. In this case, the collision juncture is a critical point of reckoning of all underlying causes. Each of the causal factor in the root cause map helps to determine the real root cause.

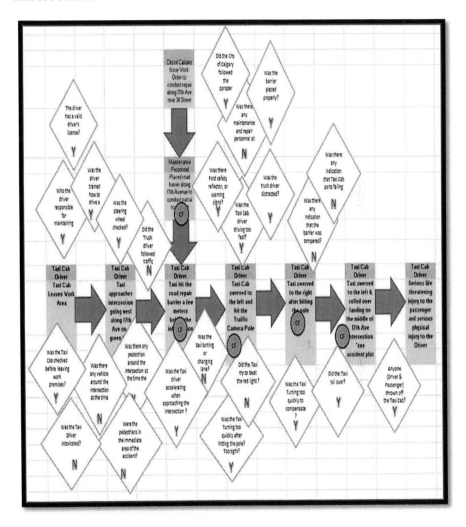

Figure 141 - Causal Factor Chart

14.5. Fault Tree Analysis (FTA)

Fault tree analysis is a tool used to determine the underlying causes of risk events. It uses a deductive method of seeing from the general to the specific, identifying potential accidents, and predicting the most likely system failures

(Elliott, Risk Assessment and Treatment, 2012).

FTA identifies different ways of breaking the fault tree and prevents future events of a similar, even if not exactly the same, nature from happening. Addressing the root cause breaks the chain of events that lead to the final unwanted event or failure.

Note that FTA can take many iterations depending upon the latest inputs and their individual probability.

The analyst can do as many as he needs. The number of iteration is tied closely to how the known facts has changed. As more information is gathered, information that is more complete is fed into the model.

Each iteration is a what-if scenario of the connected network of events. It provides various angles to the fault tree that eventually thresh out the real culprit.

FTA is useful in forecasting a future event and in investigating a past incident. This method is useful for project management professionals trying to anticipate future critical risk events. Identifying driving root causes is tantamount to identifying key risk indicators. It is a useful aid to improving foresight.

Let us take one of the Boolean logics (.AND.) branches on the diagram below; e.g. branch 14 and 15. Boolean logic are simple words operators (AND, OR, NOT or AND NOT) used as combinations to perform a search, or calculation to come up with more useful outcomes.

The concept originated from a nineteen English philosopher George Boole works on logical calculus.

Boolean algebra has since come into wide spread use as an analysis tool (Hohberger, 1971).

The same idea is what we are using in the succeeding examples.

$P13 = P14 \times P15 = 0.90 \times 0.75 = 0.675$

Now, let us one of the (.OR.) branches on the diagram; e.g. branch 13 and 18.

$P6 = (P13 + P18) - (P13 \times P18) = 0.93 - 0.17 = 0.75625$

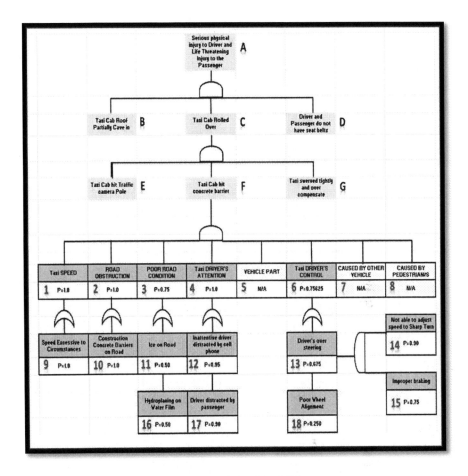

Figure 142 - Fault Tree

14.6. Conclusion

Although it initially appeared, from data gathered, that an intoxicated taxi driver was the cause of the accident, an in-depth follow-up assessment says otherwise.

The breathalyzer test taken right after the accident showed normal reading. It effectively eliminated that angle. There is no sign of brake failure, as indicated by road markings, mechanical linkage, electronic records, part wears or failure, or other evidence.

A reconstructive analysis of the event using FTA points to a distracted driver as the primary cause of the accident, as it has the highest calculated probability among the underlying causes.

It is also evident that distracted driving and excessive speed with respect to the road conditions becomes the trigger combination that led to the accident.

The rollover happened when the taxi driver tried to avoid the camera pole after hitting the concrete barrier.

The over-compensated steering resulted in two tight turns, causing the taxi's center of gravity to shift, finally resulting in a rollover. The excessive speed also contributed to the driver losing control of the cab.

14.7. Recommendations

- Improve safety awareness using videos to expose drivers to the situations leading to rollovers. It should be part of Commercial Taxi Driver License programs.
- Simulation can allow WOW Taxi drivers to experience the results of rollover, inducing errors without the consequences.
- The city of Calgary should make barrier-warning signs bigger. Include flashing lights and post lower speed limits at that intersection when construction has not yet completed.
- Introduce a higher penalty for drivers and passengers not wearing seatbelts.
- Introduce a stiff penalty for drivers using hand-held cell phones.
- Renew continuing education and skill training on taxi defensive driving every year. WOW Taxi shall support all training renewal to improve driving safety.
- All taxi drivers should be extra cautious when approaching intersections and should keep speed appropriate to driving conditions.
- Strip the license (for a considerable time) of Taxi drivers who are persistent traffic violators.
- Install stronger rollover bars on all WOW taxis.
- WOW Taxi should get higher insurance coverage.
- Introduce electronic monitoring of vehicle speed, hand-held devices, and seat belt use.
- Introduce a point system. For instance, reward safe taxi drivers through special bonuses.
- Acquire litigation coverage through the Taxi Association.
- Acquire psychological experts to represent WOW Taxi in dealing with victim's traumatic experiences to maintain a reputation as a caring carrier.

Chapter 15

Road to Operational Excellence

15.1. Introduction to Operational Excellence

Operational excellence (OE) is simply a business state of continuously achieving its top business objectives. It can be a five-point or ten-point objectives usually highlighted as top-level statements of what the company values. Achieving an accident and injury-free workplace is a common statement. Declaration of social, ethical, health, environmental, reliability, and cultural vision follow right next. Operational excellence is doing the right thing, the right way, at the right time always.

Miracles do not bring excellence to the business. It is not through magic that an enterprise prospers. The effort it takes to excel on something is deliberate. Sustaining the excellence is the bigger challenge.

The case study that follows is about a company, whose identity we have changed with another name for the sake of confidentiality. In the course of our chapter discussion, we will call this company SFF Group. Any resemblance to any organization or person, existing, living, or dead respectively, is purely coincidental.

15.2. SFF Group Strategic Plan, Design, and Execution

SFF is one of the leading engineering and construction groups in the world, a major player in the ownership of infrastructure headquartered in Montreal, Quebec. It has offices in over forty countries worldwide.

The risk-based manager's mandate is to come up with a plan, design, and execution strategy on how to maintain SFF's exceptionally high standards of environmental protection, health, safety, ethics, and regulatory compliance, in addition to keeping its envied top competitive position in the world, and increasing revenues in a challenging and competitive global market.

The group has to revive great leadership that stimulates organizational quality and leads to operational excellence. They are committed to delivering quality projects on budget and on schedule to the complete satisfaction of their clients.

However, the last employee survey taken reveals lack of engagement across the organization in Canada and a growing skepticism about the leadership team's ability to sustain market share. Stakeholders doubt that the company can continue to grow the business internationally. The study shall inspect, assess, and address the group's current issues and potential risks.

The result of this case study shall be the SFF roadmap to organizational and operational excellence (OE). The top management mandate is for the risk-based manager to come up with a plan, design, and execution strategy on three major levels of the organization while satisfying the written objectives.

15.3. Objectives

- To help top management promptly plan, design, and implement a strategy to build a sustainable, high performance culture
- To propose ways of enhancing leadership capabilities, improving teamwork, and increasing collaboration across the business establishment
- To assist management in enhancing the manager's engagement level
- To ensure alignment with the rest of the organization, worldwide
- To approach this case study differently, as if one is reading an interesting story intended to spark a whole but separate set of ideas, customized for SFF's use and for the future reference of other organizations.

15.4. Strategic Plan in Various Levels of Organization

The result of this case study shall be the SFF roadmap to organizational and operational excellence (OE). The top management mandate is for the risk-based manager to come up with a strategic plan, design, and execution strategy on three major levels of the organization while satisfying the written objectives. We have to identify benchmark information first before strategic planning takes place.

This is to enable SFF to compare whether or not there are significant improvements after applying the adopted strategies.

TIP

A benchmark is an accepted standard data point of reference, a value to compare against another measurement. If the organization does not know where it came from, it is improbable that it will be effective in knowing where it is going. It is similar to the heuristic that if one does not know where he is going; it does not matter where he goes (read Section 17.4 and reflect).

The effective way to address the growing doubt and skepticism about the leadership team's ability to sustain market share and grow the business internationally, and the apparent lack of engagement across the organization in Canada, is to establish a baseline performance measurement first as a take-off point.

Doing otherwise, the organization has no concrete proof in the future that it did improve, leading SFF to nowhere.

15.5. Increasing Leadership Effectiveness

How can the managers increase leadership effectiveness? There is no doubt that cultural intelligence, also known as CQ, or cultural IQ (Langton, 2013) is a critical qualification of managers to achieve good interpersonal relationships in an organization.

It is the risk driver governing many endeavors because CQ is an individual thing. Success and failure hinges on CQ.

TIP An organization, although considered a distinct entity with own personality, does not have that CQ, but one leader among hundreds can sometimes falsely reflect the cultural IQ of the whole organization. It is a pity when this results in negative perceptions.

Cultural intelligence also referred to as "pragmatic competence" in management circles. It is the "knowledge of the linguistic resources available in a given language for realizing particular illocutions, knowledge of the sequential aspects of speech acts, and finally, knowledge of the appropriate contextual use of the particular language's linguistic resources" (Nordquist, 2013).

For more clarity, please read Section 8.1 to 8.8.

In many ways, by having pragmatic competence or CQ, a person will say the right thing at the right time, successfully avoiding conflicts and disputes, thereby promoting harmony in the workplace.

Resistance will fade if managers communicate this way. Employees become motivated and enthused.

The management leadership must understand the employee's needs down to the personal level if need be. They should have the authority, the budget, and the accountability to address these needs. Managers must build on the idea of the leadership putting into practice the things they preach, sending a clear signal to employees that these values are truly important to them and to the organization.

Integrity reinforces trust. Trust cements respect. Respect results in an almost venerable leadership. SFF managers should focus on this core value to grow trust and professional ethics, because such quality goes beyond just education, knowledge, expertise, and soft skills.

Integrity equates to truth and honesty. Management should be straight, never relying on subterfuge nor feeding employees with half-truths or half-lies (Figure 84).

We know that all things change, but not the truth. Truth does not change and never deviates. The truth can be hard to take and is as pointed as an arrow, but the long-term benefits are undeniable. Organizational changes based on the truth will succeed. It prevents confusion, inefficiency, low productivity, ineffectiveness, mistrust, misunderstanding, and adverse situations.

Engagement should start with the managers. When a manager walks the talks, it exhibits truthfulness, and his direct reports will respect him. There is only one version of the truth. Adhering to this principle will guide SFF management to its goal.

Some years back, one psychology student said that humans are naturally mimicking organisms. Knowing this makes us realize that it is a kink in the armor of resistance to leadership.

Once respect is there, the employees will imitate the leader and follow. They will mimic him. Employees are therefore motivated to follow his/her lead and trust in his/her values.

He/she should be open and approachable, on tab with the daily rigors of the team, showing sincere interest in his/her employees. Small things like this can fuel motivation. I see recognition as a non-monetary reward that can go a long way. It is empathy in the highest order.

A manager shall make sure that his goal is cascaded clearly to his employees. Such goals should be according to a specified organizational structure of goal setting.

Goals must be SMART (an acronym for specific, measurable, achievable, results-oriented, and time-bound). SMART goals eliminate confusion and mistrust.

Organizational culture driving the employee's behaviors and attitudes should be something that comes from a good business sense. The vision, mission, goals, and values set forth by the organization are the inspirations that will lead toward success in the midst of the sea of change.

They represent the company's culture that everyone has bought in. As I always say, "a common organizational goal means a strong organization culture."

Therefore, addressing the culture aspect should be the first phase of the change, before any other successful change can take place.

Aligning the cultural norms of the organization is the highest priority, for it will govern the other possibilities.

Managers who enjoy mentoring and bringing the best out of their direct reports will find great pleasure in knowing that they are viewed as good leaders.

Leaders develop followers. Managers implement the vision and strategy provided by leaders, and organizations need strong leadership and strong management for optimal effectiveness (Langton, 2013).

15.6. Motivating and Empowering Employees

How can management motivate and empower employees to improve decision making, while increasing performance and efficiency?

If management people are to influence and empower employees, they have to have a connection. They have to have the ethical stature, responsibility, and authority to empower.

Someone who has no power cannot hope to empower anyone. Managers have to validate and quantify their own power to proceed with empowering others.

Connections are made through politics and political maneuverings, whether they are done directly or indirectly to establish relationships (Figure 143).

Relationships must exist between the manager (power source) and the employee (person influenced) before motivation and empowerment can take place.

Without such a relationship, the power level is zero.

Figure 143 - Power Runs through Relationship Lines

Have you noticed how emotionally invested people are in something they really care about?

Their reactions are understandable because they are connected. Relationship lines exist between them.

SFF managers can influence their direct reports by connecting through empathy.

TIP The undeniable proof one has to consider is this: a person who wants to influence another is also under the influence of that person.

The reality of it all and I say this to anyone, "Influence is being exerted on him by the person he is trying to influence."

Influence between individuals is mutual and bi-directional.

If he wants your vote, it means he needs you. You have influenced him to be interested in you. Scratch his back and he will scratch yours.

At that instant, you have influenced him too, so he tries his best to influence you. You can now have your say about what needs done because he needs you.

You have power over him while both of you play the same political game.

This is as true in real political arenas that shape our country's future as in the work place. The word politics is becoming "PLOT-ticks" more and more. There is always a plot in mind and it ticks continuously.

People learned that in order to get what they want, and be successful; they have to focus their strategies on the person who can help them achieve their objectives.

To manage and influence them well, we have to appeal to their personal interest. It only works best if it is a two way street.

 To influence, one has to be influenced.

The majority of Canadian companies still follow the traditional pyramid organizational hierarchy (Figure 144), where management is at the top and the employees are at the bottom.

Figure 144 - Pyramid Organization

Any company could consider replacing the pyramid organizational structure to empower employees and to increase their commitment.

Some companies have done it already by choice.

Others made the change in response to trying times (down turns) such as the 2014/2015 crunch in crude oil price affecting national economies.

The embraced solution is to make the organizational structure a lot flatter.

Removing positions perceived as intermediaries or middlemen is the preferred solution.

The inverted pyramid structure (Figure 145) would have more potential to achieve those goals.

An inverted structure demonstrates the importance of employees to company success, whereas the traditional structure is more formal (Althouse, N. et al, 2013).

Figure 145 - Inverted Pyramid Organization

Knowing that they are part of the priority list in the company, the employees will have a feeling of ownership.

Turnover rates will decrease across all operating locations because people are more committed and responsible.

The only layer that will not change, even if you invert the pyramid, is the middle layer representing middle management.

The traditional structure applied to all types of businesses in the past has had generally successful outcomes, but the new structure might be able to offer a better result.

If empowerment is the intent, management will have to remove the middle layer going forward (Figure 146).

If one puts his mind to it, another way of reducing middle managers is to shed the outside top and bottom layers. Letting go the frontlines, make immediate managers the frontlines.

Removing the Vice Presidents, Assistant Vice-President, Assistant to the AVP, and the likes, brings the middle managers to the top, effectively reducing the sandwiched area.

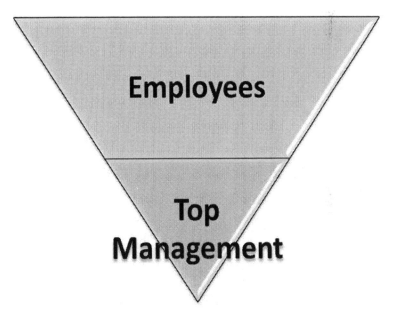

Figure 146 - Modified Inverted Pyramid Organization

The reorganization must be handled with utmost care, as it can cause grave discontentment to top and middle managers who hold their position with great prestige. It is one of the root causes resulting to lost morale on the part of the ranks and files. They quickly see the development as a threat or an obstacle on their individual career path. It will not be easy and the company will have to make the move at the right time, with full participation of those affected from the start, coupled with the right incentives.

On the other hand, the inverted pyramid is something new to many of us because we have not experienced it. Empowerment is the freedom given to the employees or the front-liners to make decisions. Some modern day thinkers now hail the inverted pyramid as the cure-all solution to low productivity and low employee morale, while traditionalists are on close watch because they perceive it as an obstacle.

The theory that by putting more decision-making power into the hands of those closest to the "actions", organizations will become faster, more adaptive, and more effective can be a heartbreaker (Bacal and Associates, 2013). Inverting the organizational pyramid brings with it the notion of empowerment, in the service of better organizations.

The management should reflect this new way of managing, but must exercise caution about accepting a new philosophy hook, line, and sinker. The organization should assess in full whether it is applicable to the business. Giving employees the kind of freedom to decide on what is best without a standard framework in mind could be self-serving and ineffective.

TIP On the contrary, an inverted pyramid structure would work best on businesses or organizations that offer a lot of leeway and do not have detailed processes. If employees can decide for themselves, the structure should not be a pyramid but a flat structure.

Thinking about it, the organizational structure adopted should be something fit for purpose to work. What we have underscored are crucial points and concrete actions to increase leadership value anticipated to stimulate, encourage, and enable.

15.7. Communicating Effectively at Team Level

How can managers communicate more effectively (including cross-cultural communication, face-to-face, virtual with technology, etc.) between departments/units and employees? At the team level, one of the most effective ways to improve cross-cultural communication is to improve the nature of the work environment. The design of a workspace should reflect the type of work a team member is to do, something that will keep him inspired, engaged, productive, and conflict-free.

The company should establish rules on resolving conflict following a framework based on a clear, professional code of ethics and moral values, embedded in an expressed policy of fairness, (such as company rules against sexual harassment, bullying, dishonesty, theft, etc.). If the rules are clear, accepted, and signed by all, there is no misunderstanding if disciplinary consequence need by applied.

One good example of an inspiring and engaging workplace that comes to mind is Google, which successfully adopted a more open workplace concept coupled with a flextime approach in timekeeping. Such a set-up can work for Google, but might fail if implemented in other businesses. SFF should study the possibility of applying a similar but controlled (or perhaps limited) approach to the same Google strategy.

Google also has several outlets for employees to file and resolve issues and solicit feedback, allowing employees to feel empowered in shaping their work environment. Investing in people means learning how to attract and manage trendsetters, encourage engagement, and create a passionate workforce (He, 2013).

Google is a successful company based on their recorded performance, reputation, and the great number of positive reviews I have read in the last few years. SFF has the potential of being on the same level in the future.

Motivating the team members to excel by instilling them to practice their ABC (attitude, behavior, and consequence) the right way is a great approach. A strong and cohesive team demonstrates oneness and maturity. Everyone believes that the whole is as important as the part, for there cannot be a whole without the part.

The pain of the little finger is a pain felt by the whole body. The recognition of one team member is recognition of the whole team. This is the employee's maturity level that management should teach and promote. We are all aware of the advent of the e-leader, e-team, and virtual team taking advantage of present day technologies. There are many successful stories out there.

In spite of that, one might wonder whether they have cooked up the right word. One of the key components of leadership and teamwork is trust. People have to trust their leaders for leadership to be effective. In order to do that, the relationship calls for something more personal, something that requires face-to-face contact.

In the virtual world offered by today's technology, do we think it is possible? Is it enough to see teammates on the monitor and talk to them over the teleconferencing line? Trusting someone over the net can become a risky game. If there is no personal connection, how can one influence another?

Establishing personal connection is a political thing. It is not present or not as strong in a virtual team. How can leadership take place? Did technology also change the requirements to be more personal?

I have experienced working with project virtual teams in several projects, and the curious thing is that I do not recall any clear claims on leadership. The team members know what they need to do. They based work on the work package, the documentation, and the e-mail instructions provided from head office. They received information and I monitored progress. Is that leadership? Is that effective communication?

The realm of information technology and advanced communication, the dividing line that separate those who know and those who do not know have gone blurred, if not completely vanished. The information power base is no longer a strong means of control because everyone has the capacity to know if they work hard enough at gaining knowledge (remember WikiLeaks and the likes). Everyone can be independently knowledgeable and informed. Virtual teams apparently changed the complexion of effective leadership. It also changed the criteria of effective communication.

15.8. Resolving Conflict and Preventing Abuse of Power

How can managers resolve/manage conflicts in the workplace, prevent abuse of power, bullying, and harassment in the workplace?

The biggest blunder that takes place in any organization or situation is perception before engagement. It is not good to make a conclusion even before the first threads of relationship lines are established. Shortsighted opinions destroy the opportunity to be more objective, creating a gap that later on proves too wide to overcome. It makes resolving conflict very difficult.

All of us must remember that perception is different from objective reality. Everyone must exercise prudence when judging others immediately. The probability of being wrong is high and can put one in an embarrassing situation.

When a person is irritated, feels slighted, or is unhappy with someone, the conflict starts. Whining, discontentment, and gossiping become common. You can go around the world, and this tendency knows no cultural demarcation.

It is something every culture has in common because it is more natural than cultural.

It is like cancer and promotes divisiveness in the organization. If you trace the cause of such problem, we will see ourselves looking at the same term over again: "perception."

The best available remedy is increased emotional intelligence, but it is easier said than done. Organizational behavior textbooks mention emotional labor, developing the ability to compartmentalize, with perfect emotional dissonance.

Difficult as it is, sometimes, it is the only answer. Managers should learn how to do this.

As formulated in various textbooks and web publications, there are ways to improve cross-cultural communication. Following their guidelines will improve the manager's chance of success. Here are the ten strategies for effective cross-cultural communication to which I agree to wholeheartedly (Jutta and EMagisterTeam, 2014).

- Be honest (maintain integrity)
- Be flexible (identify real problems and be part of the solution)
- Listen actively.
- Show care and concern, and observe body language
- Respect differences. Identify, recognize, and respect
- Ask questions. Don't assume you know
- Build self-awareness (be proper, watch your etiquette)
- Avoid stereotyping (hold your thoughts and your tongue)
- Distinguish perspectives (walk in the other man's shoes and empathize)
- Think twice (or think ten times, and hold your tongue until you're sure)
- Recognize complexity (know that you don't know everything)

Managers should be aware of what is going on around the workplace and be sensitive to the slightest sign of unrest. Join all in the creation of a more tolerant and fair environment.

15.9. Increasing Engagement at the Organizational Level

How can managers increase employee engagement and overall satisfaction in their job? There is no big difference between approaches at organizational level, and that at the individual level or team level when it comes to motivating employees. Recognizing employees as people with potentials, and deserving respect is an individual thing. The positive effect of recognition will turn to harmony, and productivity enjoyed at the organizational level.

As pointed out in Section 15.5, engagement starts with the managers. When a manager walks the talk, direct reports will be more receptive, giving his words importance. Employees will likely become more engaged and motivated.

Honoring own words strengthen confidence of those who rely on you. Trust cements respect. Respect results in an almost venerable leadership." In this regard, one must remember that trust flows both ways: employer to employee and vice-versa. One earns trust, not given. Such is the nature of trust and trustworthiness.

Engagement starts with everyone in the company having the same end vision cascaded to overall mission, goals, and objectives. Creating or revising the current vision might be required to realign the mission.

In some instances, an important mission can suddenly drive the vision. Visions, missions, goals, and objectives influence all business activities in a cycling top to bottom cascade. They are complementary as well as supplementary.

Many companies forget how valuable engaged employees are because of familiarity with one another and work routine. Some even attribute disengagement to the old adage, "familiarity breeds contempt." According to them, familiarity creates conflicts. It is hard to resolve because many people manage conflict by avoiding the other party. This ends up persisting, and eventually gives rise to disengagement and withdrawal.

A person who talks too much may appear to be engaging but he probably is not. One of my mentors often reminds me that less talk, translates to less mistake. It sums up the first statement. The advice is that managers should exercise prudence when expressing themselves. Remember, "it's not what goes into the mouth that defiles a man, but what comes out of the mouth, this defiles a man (Matthew 15:11.The Bible)."

SFF managers have to watch out for these kinds of issues because they are sometimes very subtle. Conflict can generate hate that eats away from the inside like a worm in an apple. Finding a way to relate successfully with their direct reports plays an enormous part in getting employees to open up, making them more engaged.

Successfully motivating individuals requires identifying their objectives and helping them achieve their needs. Motivation-Hygiene Theory emphasizes the importance of considering motivating factors to promote job satisfaction, rather than focusing solely on hygiene factors, which promote non-dissatisfaction. Some of the motivating factors mentioned and considered are the type of work, opportunity to achieve something, potential for recognition, sense of responsibility, possibility promotion, rewards, self-esteem, and growth (Langton, 2013, p134-136).

15.10. Encouraging Innovation, and Creativity in the Workplace

How can managers encourage innovation and creativity in the workplace? Let us play the devil's advocate here and go against the usual thought patterns. Since globalization started, diversity is the norm, and many organizations are making culture important front, left, right, and center.

It is well been accepted that diversity allows for greater possibilities, more so in the arts and research sciences than in any other endeavors. These two fields live and breathe on innovation and creativity. A world of difference exists between these two fields of endeavors and a manufacturing company that relies heavily on standard product quality with more or less fixed parameters and attributes.

SFF management will have to discover first how to balance innovation and standardization. Noting that projects are temporary endeavors that have a definite beginning and end geared to produce unique products or deliverables (PMI, 2009), they must first conduct a study of the current processes. Those involved in encouraging innovation and creativity should be aware that standardization runs counter to the idea of innovation. It could work for one company but fail for another.

TIP Innovation is the creativity to come up with something new and exciting. This comes with some risks (sometime a lot of risks), so it is best to look at these two qualities with caution. If SFF already has satisfied customers raring for more, why change what is already working? Identification of the gaps and voids will definitely bring focus to the ailing components of the organization.

There, in such spots, great ideas, (innovations), should come into life. Making this clear to employees will guide them as to when to innovate and be creative.

Managers should use the existing company politics to influence people. The final business decision to implement change is a result of politics, so managing the change is also through politics. These influences can encourage or discourage competition and innovation, depending on the nature of the company's political climate.

Employees and managers at a small business must work together to manage company politics and not allow these maneuvers to overshadow the formal hierarchy (Lister, 2014). It is what I call the "hand-holding approach." In a way, it is more like mentorship than politics. Politics and power are the dynamic duo circumventing formal hierarchy in an organization. It is more efficient than any other method of driving motivation and inciting creativity.

An observant employee will be quick to identify that the Administrative Assistant or the Executive Secretary to the CEO of the company has more power than the managers do. He will be quick to see that the manager who spends more time with the CEO is probably more influential than the one who has not seen the CEO's doorway.

The Administrative Assistant can get things done directly if need be, so do not be surprised that Mary, the Admin Assistant, was able to drive change where the designated managers fail. This is the strategy of channeling, or going to the right channel. I have not read this word recently, so I must have made it up.

This is the beauty of understanding the various concepts accompanying organizational behaviors. We do not necessarily have to always echo and be stuck on the terminology to understand. We show our understanding by being able to formulate our own thoughts, customize methodologies, and execute. SFF managers should do the same, collaboratively.

15.11. Changing the Culture of the Organization

How will management change the culture of the organization to transition its employees from disengaged to motivated? Once more, to know where we are going, we need to know where we are. Benchmark information in terms of key performance indicators have to be identified for SFF to appreciate what needs to change and afterwards, to assess the result of the change.

The challenge is effectively carrying out the intended change. Companies should not change anything just for the sake of change. If SFF wants an organizational change like culture change, it is because it wants to strengthen the organization and make them operationally excellent, efficient, and competitive. Of course, if one thinks deeply about it, intention is relative.

The first and foremost reason for making organizational change is for the business to preserve and fortify its own interest. All the other benefits that come with a successful change enjoyed by others are bonuses and windfalls.

If this is the case, why do many people within the same organization resist change? This is because the individual interest runs against the grain of the organization's interest. Employee's reactions to change made in the past are enumerated in various forums, published across the globe. However, we should not stop there, but look at the whole universe of change.

This is the best way to appreciate the systems and sub-systems in which it operates. If we are to formulate some ideas, we need to go higher. Only if we understand that can we come up with a viable solution.

The risks involved in any change process circle around the objectives, goals, and vision of the organization, measured against the critical success factors agreed to by those who drive the change. One thing is crystal-clear in this situation.

Without an objective, there is no risk. Since risk is defined as the effect of uncertainty on objectives (ISO 31000, 2009), and change brings uncertainty, we conclude that without change, there is no risk.

People resist change because of the kind of risk associated with it. If it is a good change (opportunity), they vote yes! If the change brings threat, they vote no! As such, management has to identify the risks of change and manage them using a risk register.

Is there risk without an objective? This is a question embodying the entire constellation of risk. If you have read the earlier section on the story titled The Mouse Trap, you will know the connection.

The story points to what seems to be an unseen, sensitive dependency of succeeding events on an initial non-related situation (the Butterfly Effect). Simple things are sometimes bound to lead to complications. Read Section 1.5 to appreciate more of what risk, objective, and change is all about.

Let us now visualize the logic of motivation and engagement in the highly diversified workplace of SFF. When imagining the schematics, we see relationship lines crisscrossing the workplace (Figure 147).

I call them relationship power lines, or influence lines. The arrow tail indicates the power source and the tip indicates the direction where power eventually resides.

 TIP Without relationship lines, influencing another is impossible.

The greater the number of influence lines going to a person, the greater that person's power is, and vice versa. It shows the dependency of one person on what the other person has. Just like electrical current, the flow of change courses through the path of least resistance.

Managers, therefore, have to find that path of least resistance or, if possible, create one with no resistance.

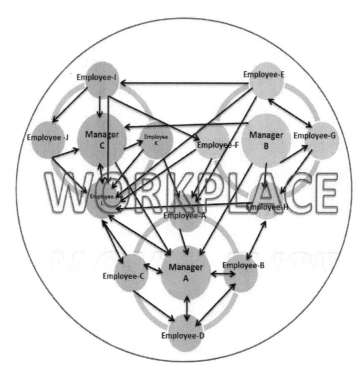

Figure 147 - Relationship Lines are Power Lines

The company should start a program that will increase the appreciation of "relationship-building" between employees in the workplace, focusing on managing cultural diversity. The end goal is to thicken and increase the relationship lines, making the entire organization highly engaged.

SFF management has to inculcate a culture of patience and acceptance for everyone. In order for everyone to feel comfortable in communicating, everyone in the organization must try to be patient and appreciative, to jump participate and enjoy themselves. Wear your smile on your sleeve. A smile is a kind of body language that can conquer nations and lead millions, as proven by our history and the magnificent history of others.

Many of the observations shared in this book were from experiences gleaned while I worked in North Africa for more than seven years. In that place, I rubbed shoulders with a big, diversified workforce originating from all over the world. Various cultural groups worked in that oil field facilities. We had workers from Algeria, Austria, Canada, Croatia, Czech, Egypt, Germany, Indonesia, Iran, Japan, Korea, Malta, Macedonia, Pakistan, Palestine, Philippines, Poland, Serbia, Slovak, Turkey, UK, USA, and several other countries. The large oil field installation is located in the middle of the Sahara desert. Each one has his contracted rotation of service.

Although English is the official language of communication, many of these workers spoke very little of the language. Although they tried, they spoke well below the usual expectation for a professional working in a critical setting such as an oil field facility. It is quite interesting that, despite the language barrier, a form of communication existed, much of it through expression and gesture. Amazingly, things worked out fine. Work relationships were generally good and there was no trouble at all.

A special case was one colleague of ours from Thailand. He was a carpenter who spoke absolutely no English. He was already working there for 10 years when I first met him. Everyone liked him. He was funny, always smiling, making facial jokes, and going about talking in words that were a cross between Arabic and English, with almost indiscernible pronunciation that it came out like a third language.

In spite of this barrier, it was fine to all of us. We ended up understanding what he was saying. He was able to communicate and do his job very well to the company's satisfaction. Verbal communication is important but, to a large degree, the non-verbal type holds more importance and credence in an organizational or social setting such as the one mentioned.

Another strategy that SFF can use is the creation of an employee support system. This would go a long way. It could be set up to receive confidential calls or set up a face-to-face conversation to resolve difficulties in the workplace without fear of reprisal (such as health, family, co-worker, boss, friend, work challenges, coping problem, or others). Organizational change is a business solution.

15.12. Conclusion

We are dealing with potentially making organizational changes, so it is imperative that everyone affected is primed in advance for the upcoming changes. Although each person understands that the only constant thing in this world is change, (making it seems so familiar), many fear the very sound of it.

TIP How an individual or organization deals with change depends on their acceptance level. It is like the physical law of motion regarding constant velocity. When velocity is constant, the acceleration is zero, meaning the change in velocity is zero.

Note the phrase "change is zero." If a person is in this vehicle looking at another vehicle running behind (at the same speed), the other vehicle will appear to be statically in place as if it is not moving.

This is an analogy for one recommended approach for how management should apply upcoming organizational changes.

If the change is small or negligible, it is almost like a zero change. Small change is acceptable. It will generate less resistance. If the item that changes is not the person's point of interest then, to him, nothing has changed.

To him, it is a zero change and nothing has moved. If the point of reference is changing at the same rate as the person's corresponding knowledge, skills, acceptance level, or other attributes keyed to that benchmark before the change, the change becomes less noticeable.

It is zero or negligible change.

If the apparent zero change is in place, the resistance is zero because the perception is that no considerable change has actually taken place.

- "Management should work hard to create an equitable workplace where all employees feel safe, valued, and respected. These are foundational. These are the needs that when satisfied, inspire employees to be effective, and committed. Change is necessary for enterprise survival yet people, managers and employees alike, resist change in one form or another. An awareness of what change is and what it entails, starting from the managers down will improve performances and commitments" (O'Donnell, 1976).

Here are some insightful principles on the subject of change that each manager should know.

- "Change is more acceptable when it is understood than when it is not. Change is more acceptable when it does not threaten security than when it does. Change is more acceptable when those affected have helped create it than when imposed (ibid.p264)."
- Change is more acceptable when it is a result from an application of previously established impersonal principles than when change dictated by a person (ibid.p264)."
- "Change is more acceptable when it follows a series of successful changes than when it follows a series of failures. Change is more acceptable when inaugurated after prior change is assimilated than when installed during confusion of other major change. Change is

more acceptable if it is part of an approved plan than if it is experimental (ibid.p264)."

- Change is more acceptable to people new on the job than to people old on the job. Change is more acceptable to people who share in the benefits of change than to those who do not. Change is more acceptable if the organization has been trained to accept change (ibid.p264)."

There is a feeling of security when the rate of change between the things that change and the change in an individual's perspective are the same rate and in the same direction.

Management has to try its best to communicate the impending change and make the employees part of that change through close collaboration.

Great leadership stimulates organizational quality, and that leads to operational excellence.

Chapter 16

Keys to Organizational Success

16.1. Introduction to Organizational Success

Risk-based management and organizational success go hand in hand. An organization is a group of people who shares the same business end goal. The online Business Dictionary.com describes it as a social unit of people that is structured and managed to meet a need or to pursue collective goals. Success becomes a reality when the business attains its goals and objectives.

This is where risk-based management focusing on people management comes into prominence. If organizations are principally made of people, with all kinds of resources run by people, then managing human risks effectively is of utmost important.

This chapter touches on the Lola Ann Courier Express struggle to improve relationships between management and its mostly South American workforce. Understanding that the cultural make up between two individuals drives the kind of relationship they will have. Try putting this driver into the mix while looking at the organization you belong.

It is laughable for an individual to say he has a good relationship himself. It is clear that it takes at least two persons to create a relationship and more than two persons to create relationships.

The relationship lines (Section 15.6 and 15.11) manifests by each one plugging into the source. Each person is a source to another person.

Poor relationships create risks emanating from the action of people. They might be action by an employee against the interest of the entire business because of his animosity with his manager. It can be the action taken by a leader against his direct report because he felt disrespected. It can be lot of things.

When an employee resigns because he hates his boss, he also feels he hates the company. He thinks the company is guilty of injustice. The company's reputation is at stake. We cannot discount the loss to an organization of a qualified individual. Replacing the employee takes time and productivity loss begins even before the employee resigns. The business sees his waning contribution and his potential contribution in the future. It can be relatively substantial. The longer it takes to find a replacement, the more the gravity of the loss.

Mitigating and preventing the consequence of a bad relationship, go a long way. When one talks about saving a relationship, he is talking about risk-based management.

16.2. Case Study - Lola Ann Courier Express

This case study is about a make-believe company that we will call Lola Ann Courier Express. The names used are fictitious, and any resemblance to any organization or person, living or dead, is purely coincidental.

This study takes a closer look into a unique training program sponsored by Lola Ann Courier Express. The company is one of the world's largest package delivery providers of specialized transportation and logistics services in Canada. The Community Practicum Program (CPP) helps managers to empathize with the employees in order to increase awareness among managers of the challenges that many of their employees face.

This aims to bridge the cultural gap that separates a white manager from a Latin American worker, who might be living just across the border of Ciudad Juarez, Mexico. The internship program hopes to address the problems of Latin American employees who are victims of prejudice and stereotyping by staffs, colleagues, and supervisors.

Steve, a Canadian who was with Lola Ann-USA for ten years, is the new director. He has been on the job for the last 10 months in El Paso, Texas. He says that CPP made him a better director. The CPP takes 50 of the company's most promising executives each summer and brings them to cities around the United States. There, they deal with a variety of problems, from transportation to housing, education, and health care, providing each one with a new perspective.

Just recently, Jose, one of his drivers, asked for two weeks off to help his father who had a heart attack, lost his work due to his condition, and can no longer provide for his family. The company rule says that Jose is not eligible because he has already taken his annual two weeks of vacation.

Steve knows that if he goes by the book, Jose will probably take the days off anyway. He will then have to fire him. Steve chooses to give the driver the time off. It was not a popular decision but he feels he has kept a valuable employee. Had he faced this decision six months earlier, he would have denied Jose. The program changed his thinking process.

Steve said, "My goal was to make the number, and in some cases that meant looking at the bottom line instead of the individual. After CPP, I immediately started reaching out to people in a different way."

Read on and take a closer look at the situation. Reflect on what types of programs you have in your own organization. Check how they compare, and how the programs address the human risk factors in your company. This chapter hopes to give you something new that you can apply to your situation.

16.3. Can We Learn Empathy in a Month?

Do you think individuals can learn empathy from something like a one-month CPP experience?

It is possible. Why would it not be, as long as one seriously pursues his desire to be more empathetic? It is not impossible, especially to a person who has already experienced a broad range of emotions that he can share. Relating to situations through his experiences sparks the necessary connection. Experiencing hardships and difficulties for the first time can provide quick understanding. It probably has a multiplicative effect on a person.

A manager who experienced living with a family who has to travel ten kilometers to the nearest water well will surely appreciate the difficulty. It is experiencing the emotions and feelings that match another person's emotions that will finally grab a manager's attention and comprehension (Wikipedia, Empathy, 2014), (O'Malley, 1999), and (Baird, 2010). Many of us have experienced empathy when we give alms to mendicants. We give while suppressing the logic not to because we are tolerating homelessness.

Any normal person has the capacity to learn. The act of acquiring, altering, or strengthening current knowledge, behaviors, or preferences involves combining different categories of information. However, the progress follows different learning curves for different individuals. Learning cannot occur instantly in a sudden burst of genius. It follows a curve.

Knowing that learning built from an existing knowledge is faster than from what we do not know (Schacter, Psychology-2nd Edition, 2011) makes the potential of learning within a short period quite possible.

TIP One primary factor that will determine how quickly a person learns, other than personality, culture, and education, is interest.

We touched in Section 8.7 that a person perceives others based on his personal goals. Personal interest drives each person to do what he does. Everyone has objective. Note that doing nothing is an objective. Inaction is a decision not to act. Just think about it. If an investor decides not to sell and his stocks go up, he reaps his reward selling it a little later. In the same token, if his stocks plummet, he loses the opportunity to cut his losses.

If we decide to go out tomorrow, we must be going somewhere. We have a purpose. After all, what is the value of doing something for nothing? Ergo, we measure our success on how close we come near our objectives. We primarily perceive other people based on our personal goals. What true statement! A person who supports our individual objectives will most likely receive automatic acceptance from us, and vice versa. We realize that we have to work a lot harder to be impartial and appreciative of others yet we always fall into that same trap over again.

Our biases become clear now. The risk or uncertainties brought about by many influencing factors are always associated with our end goals. What people do and don't do, empathize and not empathize to, sympathize and not sympathize to will all influence the end results (see Section 8.1 to 8.8)." If one has to learn empathy because his life and future career largely depends on it, then the larger the payoff, the more accelerated the learning process would be, all because of his great interest and end goals.

16.4. Job Satisfaction, Performance, and Diversity

How will Steve increase job satisfaction and performance in Lola Ann with its diverse workforce?

Lola Ann Courier Express would like to see increased job satisfaction and performance in its diverse workforce, using the Community Practicum Program as a bridge. The question that management should ask is this: "Has it delivered?" If not, what is the path forward? If yes, how can the company sustain the initiative?

If the program has taken into proper consideration all the stakeholders who have interest in the success and failure of the Community Practicum Program, then triumph is inevitable. Knowing who the stakeholders are is critically important, and the process begins by developing healthy relationships with all of them, especially the most powerful and influential. This is the key to acceptance and satisfaction.

Stakeholders help decide on issues from the beginning, during planning and at execution of the program. They should understand how the project functions, including the program scope, milestones, and goals (Bonner, 2010). They divide into two broad categories, internal and external. Internal stakeholders are owners, shareholders, partners, labor union, program managers, risk managers, senior leaders, staff, and existing employees, which includes Latin Americans. External stakeholders include the locals living in the families and communities of Ciudad Juarez, Mexico, governments, professional associations, customers, special interest groups, and suppliers.

The primary concern of internal stakeholders is how to ensure the program's success. Steve, the supervisors, and the program manager would like to know whether the high level risks identified during the planning phase have come true and if they were effectively managed and addressed.

Did the major and most influential stakeholders realize their goals and expectations?

If performance exceeds all key performance indicators and employees are satisfied, then the program is a success.

Motivation drives satisfaction and performance. Put diversity in the mix and one can easily become befuddled. The company is using CPP to enhance the motivation process by making employees feel that they belong in one big family, where the leaderships understand their needs even on a personal level.

Motivation is a two way process, a two way street where a silent fundamental rule exists. It is not a theory imprisoned by the printed page of our textbook but something real observed in our daily lives. Motivation begets motivation and respect begets respect. It is not just having a good manager or leader. It is also having good direct reports. There is a law of push and pull in the relationship continuum that merits a closer look.

TIP   The kind of relationship tensions and compressions along the relationship lines depends on all involved parties. Managers cannot lead all the time, direct reports have to set the direction sometimes given the cue or without the cue (Frago, R., 2014)." The failure of perfectly good parents trying to motivate their children to study well and excel is a great example. When parents failed to ignite the children's interest, performance suffers.

A case in point: A father forced his son to be an engineer but he has no interest to be one. The son wants to be an IT Specialist and now he is. He has wasted two years struggling to be an engineer but just do not have the drive and the inspiration. Finally, the father financed his college education to be an IT person. He completed it with flying color. Nobody in his right mind should force success because it is not going to happen.

16.5. Can CPP Help Manage Diversity?

How could Lola Ann Courier Express Community Practicum Program (CPP) program help the organization improve its response to diversity?

In order for anyone to be effective, the cultural map that he/she should use to manage another must be according to whom he/she is trying to influence. People learn that in order to get what they want and be successful; they have to focus their strategies on how to make that cultural dance that will help them achieve their objectives.

Pragmatic competence, or what the organizational behavior textbook calls CQ, or cultural intelligence (Langton, 2013), is the key. Section 15.5 underlines it as a leadership quality. CQ is the person's ability to say the right thing at the right time. It helps avoid conflicts and disputes, thereby promoting harmony in the workplace. Go back and review Section 8.8 for more of pragmatic competence or CQ.

Lola Ann's CPP is a serious program that runs a culture education initiative. The company made the right move to encourage its managers to develop pragmatic competence. A successful Community Practicum Program will help Lola Ann Courier Express improve management and employee commitment to a common goal. It will turn managers into leaders by improving the capacity of managers to empathize.

If motivation is a two-way process, so are empathy and commitment. Empathy begets empathy. Commitment begets commitment. There is no cultural boundary to this motherhood statement. As it is applicable to all cultures, one should make full use of it to manage diversity.

One of the greatest motivators for an employee to perform and excel is having a leader or mentor whom he can look up to and respect. They need someone who has integrity, knowledge, and a commitment to do what is right and just. Management expects the same from their employees.

 Integrity reinforces trust.

The program should focus on this core value of growing trust, for it exemplifies professional ethics that go beyond just knowledge, skills, and leadership. Anyone can see through the finely chiseled words of the fake and structured recognition learned from a University or PR course. Such phrases are common these days, but lack sincerity. Too much talk is hollow.

The CPP can improve the knowledge of the Lola Ann managers and leaders, helping them to motivate through their experience living where work root issues emanate. There, they deal with the different types of problems affecting their employees and their families, giving the participants a full understanding and cultivating camaraderie between them.

It opens up an opportunity for informal mentorship where both managers and employees can learn. It bridges knowledge gaps and reduces if not totally prevents the risks of misunderstanding or wrong perception. Timely decisions related to some cultural dimensions are now more effective.

16.6. How Can Steve Ensure Supervisors Motivate Employees?

What can Steve do to make sure his reporting supervisors do a better job of motivating their employees?

Steve should continue with the strategy of the CPP through sustainability training. He could start a formal mentorship program to engage his supervisors and employees, geared to strengthening work relationships. This involves helping the employees achieve their development goals.

If supervisors start to feel Lola Ann Courier Express, through Steve, is giving them full support, it is a strong foundation to start with. The development of other managerial and leadership strengths is possible through consistent cultural orientation. These refresher courses teach managers about Latin American culture.

There is also an opportunity to add studies of other minority cultures existing in the workplace to broaden understanding. As the training courses become more popular, he should roll it out to all levels in the organization. As management-employee relationship improves to the next level, an organizational culture emerges.

A common organizational culture is a bridge to better understanding between all levels in the organization. Steve should get support and cooperation from the board to get it done. There is an expected high probability that all reporting supervisors will grow better at motivating their employees once the company implements the suggestions. It is also a good measure politically speaking.

Applying the "Needs Theories of Motivation" will definitely help spur managers and employees to commit totally. From Maslow's hierarchy (physiological, safety, social, esteem, and self-actualization) which most people are familiar with, to the theory espoused by Clayton Alderfer (ERG), Frederick Herzberg (Motivation-Hygiene two-factor theory), and Maclelland (three needs theory), the company should be able to derive a more or less customized strategy that permits the most potential with the least resistance to motivation.

In this case study, let us confine our view to the first two extremely similar theories, those of Maslow and Alderfer. Maslow's hierarchy idea emanates from the general belief that a person will work to attain a need (be it physiological, safety, belonging, self-esteem, or self-actualization). Clayton Alderfer's ERG theory is a revision of Maslow's theory. The acronym ERG stands for energy (physiological and safety), relatedness (social needs), and growth (need for self-esteem).

It is clear that both theories emphasize the belief that when a person has already attained what he needs, he is no longer motivated and will seek the second layer in the hierarchy. For example, if one already satisfied his physiological needs, he will transition to satisfying his safety needs, then his need to belong (Langton, 2013). Most experts point out that this transition comes in sequential stage. Others say that needs jump up, down, and around the scales for some.

As pointed out in Section 16.8 of this text, it is imperative that managers be very perceptive as to what their people need, as trying to motivate someone with something he is not particularly concerned about is a useless exercise.

16.7. Building More Effective Multicultural Teams

As mentioned in Section 16.5, there is no doubt that the key to good interpersonal relationship is cultural intelligence. One must remember however, that CQ is an individual thing. Although we consider an organization as a separate entity with its own personality, it does not have CQ.

The CQ of one leader in the organization among hundreds can sometime falsely reflect the culture of the whole organization. This is what Steve, and any leader has to watch for. A leader should be responsible enough to make an adaptive move to improve his CQ consciously.

Hiring new employees with more focus on attitudes might help. A new employee with a different cultural background challenges the company to build effective cultural teams. New people mean there are new personalities at play.

In spite of that negative perception, new employees present exciting opportunities that can accelerate quick integration into the company's values. The opportunity to work with a well-known business organization such as Lola

Ann can be quite useful for management.

The feeling of prestige, when reinforced, motivates a new employee to fly higher with spread wings. It is an opportunity for Lola Ann to demonstrate business perspectives that will stick. This is the employee's formative stage.

Steve should be sensitive to risks that can come in many forms. Threat brought about by a heated dispute with an employee is a good example. This is especially true when dealing with Latin American employees.

The close filial ties of employee means a manager will not only deal with the employee. He will bring about negative risks emanating from his relationship with the community, his friends, and families. If the relationship is good, it brings about positive risks.

Other source of threats and opportunities can come from the kind of relationship with other leaders, union, staffs, supervisors, contractors, and foremen on various subjects of interests such as compensation, benefits, implied promise, unspoken expectations, miscommunication, imaginary wrong-doing, and others.

A manager's run-in with an employee can be very sensitive, and has the potential to disrupt team progress, or even the operation of the company as a whole.

Schedule delay, economic downturn, changing requirements, political changes, labor unrest, influx of foreign workers, takeovers and acquisitions, and mergers are all valid concerns.

Advanced identification of such risks will help Steve manage his team.

Steve must develop the stakeholders register. This register should be included in the overall Lola Ann Courier Express communication plan. The register is a table containing stakeholder names, contact details, requirements, and classifications.

It is a living document, updated many times as stakeholder specific information changes. After identifying the stakeholders, Steve has to find out the individual expectations and make a strategy to manage those. All this information should be in the register.

Best practice recommends grouping stakeholders according to power, influence, and interest (TemplatesPMO, 2013). Figure 147 shows an example of this management grid.

By following this recommendation, Steve will have the register to guide him, with necessary information on how to manage expectations effectively. This will also facilitate risk management involving various stakeholders as a whole.

The rationale is this: if a room has 20 different stakeholders, it is wiser to deal with them according to their salience, power, and influence than to waste a lot of time and achieving nothing. We want to talk to the right person.

16.8.   Improving Employee Effectiveness and Commitment

How can Lola Ann Courier Express managers improve employee effectiveness and commitment to the organization? Lola Ann should find a way of working and thinking that makes the company an exciting workplace.

One of the largest oil and gas companies in Canada aptly worded it this way: "the powerful combination of culture, collaboration, discipline, integrity, and innovation that fuels our mission" (The Suncor Way, 2014). The statement is an inspiration to all its employees from bottom to the top.

TIP

Managers have to be very discerning. By simply knowing what interests his direct reports, managers will be more effective and have more than enough information available to motivate employees.

A manager who listens well will have the ability to discern what those interests are. You have likely read various theories on motivation, but I believe that one word sums up all of the psychological needs of a human being: interest.

The word "interest" is the feeling of a person whose attention, concern, or curiosity is particularly engaged in something. People might have great interest in achieving their sales target, or his interest in getting recognition, and promoted to the next level position in the organization (Dictionary.com, 2014).

It is almost like a bridge goal towards an ultimate goal.

If the manager, through active listening, learned that an employee longs for recognition, then his/her interest revolves around such needs. A challenging assignment might be in order, where recognition is at the end of the stick rather than monetary rewards.

If the employee leans more to pecuniary compensation, the manager can set up a reward system that meets his employee's interest.

Simply put, what interests a person shall govern his attitude, his behavior, and his personality. Providing the avenue for employees to achieve their interests makes them more likely to meet or exceed the employer's expectations.

The knowledgeable and adaptive manager produces relatively engaged, committed, and satisfied employees.

Maslow talks about the hierarchy of needs. Alderfer simplified Maslow's pyramid to come up with the ERG theory. Then, there was a further simplification made by Herzberg and McClelland (Langton, 2013) that meant practically the same thing.

It is good to know the framework of the motivation process, and knowing those motivation theories can be applied to a great degree of success, but honestly, it all comes down to identifying people's interests and their self-interest.

TIP Even the most charitable person, who someone might say, cares for others unselfishly and generously, cannot deny the fact that he does those things because it makes him happy. He feels fulfilled.

There is no shame in denying what is second nature. God, in His infinite wisdom, designed humans that way.

As such, the manager who understands the interests of his people holds the key to influencing them.

A word of caution: managers and employees must understand the boundaries, because there are rules regarding conflict of interest. If employees have interests, the company, as a distinct entity, has interests as well. The two interests must never collide.

Management should work hard to create an equitable workplace where all employees feel safe, valued, and respected. These workplace attributes inspire employees to be effective and committed. A good situational example that no company can escape from is change. As the saying goes, change is the only constant in this world. He who manages change effectively is the successful king.

An enterprise needs change to survive, yet people, managers, and employees alike most often than not, resist change. An awareness of what change is and what it entails, will improve performance and commitment.

Awareness must start from top management, to the managers and down to the ranks. Some insightful principles on the subject of change are in Section 16.8.

A manager should know how to make those critical connections with employees. Different work brings different scenarios, even with the same people involved.

Each work environment and sub-work environment is unique. Making the employee a part of the work that management is spearheading and asking for their input is an excellent start. This builds a foundation for collaboration and teamwork. Effective communication starts after establishing a connection, sustained by appreciation and recognition.

Sustainability is the key word. Timing and venue are risk factors.

Why timing? Recognition given at the wrong time holds no value. Recognition given in a wrong venue has no meaning. When that happens, motivation falters and performance becomes unsustainable.

Appreciation given in an inconspicuous place like inside a mall holds a different meaning from an appreciation in front of corporate leadership at the annual convention.

Recognition six months after an employee worked himself ragged to beat a deadline matters a lot less than recognition given within 24 or 48 hours of an exemplary performance.

Giving appreciation and recognition, much like giving discipline, has rules of thumb. They follow best practices that are almost like a code of ethics.

TIP If it is objectionable to give disciplinary action to an employee one year after the infraction, it is also objectionable to give recognition for an employee's exceptional job a year after.

Chapter 17

Risk-based Management Wisdom

17.1. Introduction to Risk-based Management Wisdom

In project settings or even in other endeavors, the manager has to contend with having too much information. Sorting through details takes time. Time is of the essence in making the most effective risk-based decisions. Time is limited in many instances, but decisions still have to be quick and dirty. In view of such limitations, people often rely on rules of thumb or "heuristics."

Talk with anyone you know and you will quickly pick up something that sounds like an example of heuristics applied to an ordinary life situation. Heuristics refer to typical experiences associated with risk taking, and risk-based management decisions that either worked or failed. Unfortunately, they might not give the best information, so it is always prudent to think of their applicability.

In the succeeding chapter sections, I have compiled some management heuristics. Let us call them, "The Old Man's Wisdom." The list barely scratch the surface of what a good risk-based manager needs to know but it is a start.

These project management rules of thumb are applicable to situations we face in our daily life. After all, our daily life proceedings are like a series of projects. Our very life span is a project where each year is a period in our project timeline, until we are hundred percent complete or terminated.

Travelling from Calgary to Phoenix is like a small project. Painting the fence to preserve the wood, replacing the water heater to address a low hot water supply, and watching a movie with friends to enjoy the evening are all risk-based projects. A singular activity is like a project. I want you to digest these heuristics carefully using the lens of a project manager, because they might become handy soon.

A project management professional who wants to be decisive and unfazed may find that heuristics can help him/her make the right call. It is sound, based on logic and on what works. It talks about key risk indicators, a good scale to measure decisions against. Heuristics are especially helpful in situations where information is unavailable. It is a good benchmark to have when assessing accuracy of data, and unsure if deliverables will come on time. It brings to surface discernable misalignment of supporting project elements.

For example, a project manager may have checked his engineering resources and noted that all the disciplines he needed for the project were registered. He asked the engineering manager for the summary of qualifications, but the summary table was not available.

The project manager reflected on the missing information and asked the engineering manager to pull together a summary table of experience within three days before he signed the engineering management plan on his table.

The result: forty percent of his engineering resources were juniors, 50% of which had less than one year of experience or were a fresh graduate. He also found out that they were assigned critical design roles. He asked the engineering manager to hire qualified resources to lead the juniors. He remembered what his mentor said: "The greatest asset an engineering manager has is not the quantity of his engineers, but the quality of his disciplines!" It is a valuable heuristic to analyze the quality of the project's resources.

Figure 148 - The Old Man's Wisdom

17.2. Project Plans Mean Little without Stakeholder's Buy-in

The wisdom residing in this quote points to the essential nature of an involved project team. It revolves around the mandatory requirement to undertake an interactive planning session to create and develop an execution plan, or to improve and finalize an existing plan, ending in declaring an agreed-to baseline. A successful interactive planning session is a hallmark of a well-developed project schedule.

For a project to proceed smoothly, without fear of major obstacles and contradictions, the stakeholders must be part of the planning process. They would like to be convinced that the plan is achievable, that the schedule derived from the plan is complete, and that the goals are attainable. This is what we are looking for when we require buy-in.

Stakeholders, especially the powerful and influential ones, should be a part of that participative planning discussion. This gives them a sense of ownership, and confidence that the execution plan will successfully work.

If this vital requirement is ignored, it will just be plain difficult, as the project will be going against the grain of it all. The resistance within could kill a project, or make it dismally unproductive.

17.3. Plan and Schedule According to the Right Level of Details

It is wise for the client organization to define the standard schedule level it is willing to use in each of the project phases. Considering the availability and maturity of information at each checkpoint, we can infer that the project will have to start with a high level schedule during the initiation and scoping stage (beginning stage), perhaps down to the area or phase level. Area includes the engineering plot layout and design subdivisions such as common areas (A1), utilities and off-sites (A2), infrastructure (A3), and so on. Examples of typical phases considered are engineering, procurement, construction, and commissioning. The work breakdown structure governs the level of detail.

Large organizations are bound to choose either level 2 or level 3 details for the control schedule detail (read Section 3.17 for related discussion). Let us say a level 2 schedule breaks down the activities to the discipline level, like electrical, mechanical, control system, civil, and structural. Level 3 on the other hand, breaks and groups the activities up by work package, such as module work package, engineering work package, construction work package, etc.

Planners and schedulers are an intelligent and creative bunch of professionals who sometimes, without a guiding PM strategist, can get lost in the details. Indications of too much detail start to become noticeable when the schedule starts showing hundreds of tasks that have very short durations, like a day or two.

When the client project manager starts seeing activity descriptions detailing the installation, such as receive and shake out materials, pre-tie re-bars, set form, pour concrete, cure, remove/strip form, etc., then the project might be wasting too much time tracking the details.

This kind of detailed schedule is the construction contractor's responsibility, and their schedule should be set up in a way that a convenient roll-up to the client's level 2 or level 3 is done during each reporting cycle, without too many complications.

TIP "Digging the best hole in the world is of little use if the hole is not needed (Lewis, 1997)."

The client's schedule is generally at a higher level, while main construction contractor at a lower field installation needs details to better manage their individual schedule. The sub-contractor, on the other hand, might find it more useful to further detail their schedule for better field control, but should roll up to the main/prime contractor's field installation work package (level 4) schedule, or perhaps even a level 5 schedule, assuming the sub-contractor is maintaining a nuts and bolts schedule.

TIP Rule of thumb: detail the project schedule down to the level where managing is more effective.

17.4. Project Control is Only Possible with a Baseline

The baseline plan is the formal instrument that a project needs to initiate project execution, monitoring, and control. Without this instrument, one does not even have as starting point for control.

It is difficult to know what to do next. It is a formulation of who, what, where, why, and how future activities will be executed to get all agreed-to end-results.

The plan is a necessary input into the scheduling process, an essential part of business decisions. It puts a crosshair on key organizational targets. It provides a handle in executing the risk-based project schedule. If you do not know where you are going, how will you know when you get there (Lewis, 1997)?

> "[Alice said] 'Would you tell me, please, which way I ought to go from here?"
>
> 'That depends a good deal on where you want to get to,' said the Cat.
>
> "I don't know where… " said Alice.
>
> "Then it doesn't matter which way you go," said the Cat (Carroll, Alice's Adventures in Wonderland).

New project management practitioners, however, must understand that planning is much more than just stating goals and objectives. It includes determining the most effective ways of reaching the end goals and in-between deliverables.

17.5. Planning and Scheduling are Inseparable

It is inconceivable that anyone can successfully divorce planning from scheduling. How can anyone begin to schedule anything if there is no plan?

Planning answers all the other questions like "who, what, where, why, and how." It also tries to provide limited answers to the question of when, by identifying key milestones and key target dates. Examples are first oil (first official volumetric production of oil), construction start, or mechanical completion. The schedule shows the entire menu, while the plan is a summarized, incomplete, and partial preview of the proposed schedule.

Scheduling pertains to the start and finish dates, aiming to answer the vital question of "when?" A schedule defines the project timeline and the activities that comprise it. A schedule is only a schedule if there is a beginning and an end that defines the entire integrated schedule, including all the activities that lie therein. A schedule is an output of the plan. Think about it and reflect.

It is amazing that some project managers fail to see the strong relationship between planning and scheduling, because it is common sense. The two processes are like husband and wife, bound together by marriage. Each one needs the other. One cannot effectively carry out the process without inputs from the other.

It is not that the schedule, although focused on the dates (time management), is only providing answers to the question of "when?" The schedule reflects the plan, including execution strategy, path of construction, scope, assumptions, constraints, key dates, resources, and other information. It has a bunch of embedded data and plenty of other useful derivative information.

The plan feeds the schedule, and the schedule feeds the plan. It is practically the plan-do-check-act (PDCA) collaborative cycle that makes the project successful. If this is the key to success, how can anyone expect to divorce planning from scheduling?

17.6. Plans and Schedules Works Best if Documented

In major projects, one important attribute of the plan and schedule is documentation. A plan is not a plan unless it is committed to paper. In today's technological world, it can be on whatever legal, acceptable medium or e-form of expression the project decides on. Of course, this is also true with the schedule. Baselines have to be established and committed on both.

An idea of a plan in the mind of a project manager does not qualify as a project plan.

It is not comparable to our daily life where one can say, "I should go to Vegas tomorrow" and in fact successfully goes the next day. This is something large, more complex, involving legalities, machinery, resources, risks, and other issues, with a longer timeline involved.

> "A goal without a written plan is just a wish (Exupery, A., disputed: 1900-1944)."

> "If it is not documented, it does not exist (Haughey, 2011)"

One cannot have a well-documented and successful plan with an imaginary schedule or vice-versa. The project will not have a workable, continuously elaborated plan without updating the schedule. An updated schedule is there to feed and perhaps adjust the plan. We all know there is no perfect plan. As soon as the project manager starts to say, "Our plan is perfect," things start to change.

17.7. Plan and Schedule Have One Overall Scope.

It is untrue that planning is looking at a much bigger scope than scheduling. Planning and scheduling are tightly connected. There is only one total scope in every project. The planned scope, baseline scope, or target scope are all expected to have the same scope as their schedule counterpart. Their scopes must be in alignment. The scope of one cannot be greater, and continuous collaboration shall see to it that it is that way throughout the project timeline.

Scope alignment should be part of the main review checklist for each gate, especially the gate leading to project execution.

Establishing the scope helps prevent uncontrolled growth in scope, also called scope creep. It prevents confusion, issues, risks, and additional cost resulting from activities that were not part of the plan. The plan cannot have a bigger scope than what is in the schedule. The work breakdown structure (WBS) set forth in the plan should be in the schedule to align the two.

You have probably seen it before, a schedule showing substantial work not actually part of the plan. On such occasions, the project manager should be notified promptly so that the work can be removed from the schedule, or be included in the plan. If the project carries on without managing change, the work becomes an unnecessary part of the critical path calculation. It will change the complexion of the project and its outcome. It will create risk by providing an output of wrong information to the decision-makers.

If the project carries out a work package that is out of scope, then we can bet our bottom dollar that some schedule deliverables will have issues. If the plan scope is greater than the scope reflected in the schedule, then it means the project will miss completing some work stated on the plan. The project is creating a big hole on the ground.

17.8. Execute Only Achievable Plans and Schedules

Avoid the classic problem of trying to put ten pounds of trash in a five-pound bag! It will not work (Project Planning, Scheduling & Control by Lewis 1997, p. 97). The amount of work and activities that can successfully be included in a project also has a certain limit. This constraint mainly dictates the capacity of the project to accommodate all works listed in the scope. If a specific timeline or delivery date drives the project schedule, we might ultimately find that resource allocation is the deciding factor as to whether the project is achievable or not.

Additional resources through crashing will not do. Forcing resources into an unwilling schedule scenario will only lead to failure. As the saying goes, we cannot put more riders on to a racehorse expecting that the horse will run faster (Project Planning, Scheduling and Control by Lewis 1991, p. 66).

Time management requires intelligence and good rationale. Time is the scarcest resource there is. Unless the assigned team managed their time properly, no one can deal or administer effectively with the other project elements

(Drucker, P., 1909-2005).

⚠ Unachievable schedule is a result of executing a poor quality schedule, a serious issue that generates variety of risks leading to project failure.

Aspects that touch schedule qualities are in Sections 4.5 to 4.23. The latter section includes more in-depth investigation of misaligned certainties as one of the major misalignment that makes a schedule unachievable. The lesson provided is that two or more independent variables connected to each other by a logical relationship can affect the dependent and overall result either positively or negatively. If the predecessor has a greater certainty than the successor, the unconstrained successors will improve their previous certainty value, keeping the same deterministic target.

It is wise to remind ourselves that as the present revolves, the future revolves with it. The way we execute the things we do today determines the shape of our results. The present and the future are always in motion. There is no perfect schedule, and the future is tough to predict, but knowing that our present touches what is to come gives a sensible risk-based manager some useful degree of confidence.

17.9. Do Not Ignore Project Charter

The charter is an important piece of the plan. I heard recently from one well-known project director in a recent symposium that the project charter is practically useless and is merely a cover page. He added that there is no need to update the document from the initial preparation and approval through to project completion. To this man, the charter is not a big deal; he almost declares it is something a project does not need.

A project charter is a formal authorization given to a project to start the effort. Given a project divided into four stages of initiating, planning, execution, and closeout, the charter first comes into view during the initiating phase so that planning can start. The sponsors provide the approval and mandate, thus giving the authority to commence acquiring resources.

The key target dates, project table of organization, regulatory consideration, technology, resources, issues, responsibilities, constraints, risk-based considerations, and other components use the charter as a launching pad. It becomes the base origin of all other project management plans.

I am not sure why there are project managers who ignore the importance of the charter. If one thinks about it, the managers are there because of the charter.

A project professional who discounts the importance of the charter while managing a project has to re-examine their thought process.

Such a frame of mind can easily turn a prospective success into abrupt failure.

The importance of the charter as a primary project document is undeniable. It is the only project document with a real direct connection to the main stakeholders, sponsors, and owners. It is important to update the charter such that it aligns well with the other execution document and output project information. The charter lines up with schedule, risk, cost, and scope and overall strategy.

Just imagine this: if the baseline execution information, such as key delivery dates, deviates greatly from what is in the charter, there is potential risk that some powerful and influential stakeholder can suddenly pull the plug.

For example: if the project has a first oil date of December 1, 2015 stated on the project charter, and the approved final project execution plan has March 31, 2016, then this is a grave misalignment. It is bad practice when a major sponsor expects the former but learn later that the charter was not updated, keeping him and all the other sponsors in the dark.

Although many contend that the project charter does not change through the project lifecycle, this does not make sense, because change is inevitable. Since project situation normally changes through time, it is unlikely that all the information in the charter will remain the same until closeout.

Data will change as the project approach the execution phase where a baseline is required. The charter has to line up with the latest project execution plan.

Expectations are managed effectively only by updating across-the-project information. Best practice says that the final update to the charter occurs when a baseline is established, that is before crossing the execution gate where the project gets full sanction.

17.10. Use an Integrated Approach

An integrated approach in risk-based management has a greater chance of success. An integrated plan deserves an integrated schedule. Poor integration results in counter-intuitive, disconnected, or disjointed plans and schedules. It will often translate to poor management of time, cost, and risk.

Other problems spawned by ignoring integration are flawed quantitative schedule risk assessment, faulty critical path calculation, miscommunication, negatively affected productivity, and decreased achievability. The project might fail meeting its most important objectives.

It is best to include the commissioning and start-up phase of a construction project (and projects of a similar nature) in the integrated schedule. A well-experienced project manager recognizes that the downstream requirements drive the front end.

It is for this reason that the commissioning window of activities should be part of the overall schedule, because it drives construction, while construction drives engineering, modularization, fabrication, and procurement. It is clear that operation effectively calls the shot affecting sequence to a larger degree than any other group. The downstream must drive the upstream. Farm out your plan and schedule sequence with the end in mind.

17.11. Schedule Resource Loading Should Align With Estimate

Schedule resource loading should align with the corresponding checkpoint estimate. An execution schedule corresponds to the execution estimate. Let no one forget that the schedule is an estimate. It is the time estimate of the project.

It is therefore logical to expect that the work hours reflected in the latest overall project estimate are the same as the one loaded in the schedule. Communicate any substantial variance against the frozen estimate to the project manager.

Let us look at an example. A large variance exists between construction work hours of the resource-loaded baseline schedule and the estimate. The variance is more than 850,000 hours. What runs through your mind as a project person upon learning this? Perhaps, it is an indication of missing scope or the other way around.

Variances such as this can become a threat to project objectives because it is bound to generate wrong projection on workforce requirements.

Wrong projection of workforce in turn results in wrong estimation of required logistical supports. Wrong quantities and derivative values can result in confusion, affecting plans and strategy due to incorrect expectations. Flawed resource distribution will affect labor density analysis, resulting in false risk or safety indicators.

Schedule achievability cannot be accurately quantified and properly assessed. Schedule resource leveling will be in error.

17.12. Schedule Sequence Should Match Path of Construction

The path of construction (POC) should match the schedule sequence. One major section of the overall plan is the construction execution plan. It contains the path of construction to follow. It outlines sequential work strategy across the geographical division of the project plot.

The schedule shall follow the plan. Project managers, planners, and schedulers should check and ensure the required alignments are correct. This is part of working the plan.

17.13. Create and Maintain Stakeholders Register

Many projects do not have a stakeholders register. Some projects have one but completely useless. Creating and maintaining stakeholders register requires serious thought, because it is there for some worthwhile objectives. This is usually a part of the execution plan, but can be a section of the overall communication plan. The register is a living document that contains specific names and contact information.

The tool helps effectively manage the project. It gives the necessary information to balance resources at its disposal, while respecting stakeholder expectations. The information available in the document helps optimize the project control effort.

The core data lies in a simple table with each stakeholder's name, contact details, and requirements. Update the register regularly as the changes occur, and as relevant information becomes available. Expectations are included in the register, including the strategy to manage them. The simple matrix shown on Figure 137 group stakeholders based on their power and interest rankings.

Having thirty stakeholders in the room, twenty-nine of whom have no say, no influence, and no power to decide or change anything, is useless. Just having the one who has power makes the most sense. Knowing how much power and influence a stakeholder has, give the project manager a good idea of how to handle him/her most effectively.

TIP "I do not exactly know the key to project success, but the key to failure is trying to involve everybody (Swope, H., 1882-1958)."

"Never allow anyone to tell you what needs not done who does not have the power to say yes (Roosevelt, E., 1884-1962)."

Chapter 18

What You Should Have Learned

This book is for everyone who wants to improve their knowledge and skills in understanding the risky world around them. The author uses a non-rigid, non-academic approach in the discussion of topics from the concepts and philosophies of risk, its management, and the various processes involved, to the common heuristics related thereto. The conversational approach hopes to provide the impetus of learning to those who are interested in risk-based management, regardless of whether they have just graduated from high school, or pursuing a college or university degree. Business owners, stock players, risk managers, engineers, and the common people leisurely passing the day have the opportunity to come up with an idea applicable to their current purpose and interest. It is not a forbidding knowledge area, where some sectors of the society are not welcome. This can add to your knowledge base and the learning is applicable to many of the things you do. This book will shore up existing understanding of risk among business owners and those who are already practicing risk-based management.

Chapter 1: Risk Concepts and Philosophies define the term risk and slice it into components. You become familiar with the introduction of common risk terminologies and business jargons. It discusses concepts, philosophies, methods, tools, and approaches in simple ways to encourage readers to relate. When a person starts to relate to the discussion, the learning curve starts to go up, accelerate and suddenly grasping knowledge becomes easier. Knowing that risk is an uncertain future event or condition that could have a positive or negative effect on objectives if it occurs sets the stage for the rest of the chapters. Understanding the two key components of risk, probability and impact, expands a person's horizon and appreciation of how risk control works. The importance of risk relativity, risk universe, and how risk revolves around objectives, including the usually controversial black swan events is undeniable.

In Chapter 2: Risk-based Management, the author shed lights on why risk-based management is the only thing we do for a living. He underscores the fact that, unconsciously or consciously, all of us practice the process. Appreciating that it is the main reason why your company or your client pays you for your expertise makes a good premise. The job title you have right now does not matter because when you look closer, managing risk is what you do and the reason why you go to work every day. Go back and review this chapter to dig a little deeper. Find out why you and I are all risk-based managers.

Processes such as risk-based planning, risk identification, risk analysis, risk response, and risk control, typical of project works, gives a bird's eye view of risk-based management. Other aspects of risk such as its duality (Section 1.3) are good additional knowledge. This chapter wants the reader to see the various categories of risk-based management as the same animal. The core process operating within each management type goes beyond purpose, function, and objectives. All aspects of management identify risk management as the core value of the management function.

Chapter 3: Risk-based Planning opens up the fundamental essence of the planning process and later on explains how a schedule becomes a planning output. The relationship between planning and scheduling became a collaborative focal point of interest throughout the succeeding sections. There is a strong emphasis on the 4Cs of planning, schedule development, monitoring, and control. Sections 3.12 to 3.16 enumerate the top most concerning pitfalls in planning and scheduling. The latter part of this chapter reminds all that there are pertinent connections between proper planning and scheduling, and safety (see Section 3.9). We introduce the word "schedule risk" and "schedule-driven project" (section 3.19) in this chapter, highlight the significance of the basis of schedule, explain the levels of schedule, and put into perspective the categories of project capitalization.

Chapter 4: How to Prepare for SQRA itemizes the work instruction on how to carry out a good and proper schedule quantitative risk analysis. This is a very nice section for beginners because it is simple and easy to understand. The guideline offers the most practical approach to quantification. As a risk practitioner, one must know how to undertake the risk analysis session and who should be involved. Some of the most important information in this book is in this section, i.e. a brief but substantial discussion on the idea of organization having a minimum schedule quality (see Section 4.5) requirement. The rationale of the quality attributes is clear. Readers learn to relate the importance of quality assurance in the development of a schedule baseline. A good schedule is a mandatory requirement in risk modeling and the subsequent risk analysis process. The list of consequences resulting from a poor quality schedule ends the chapter (Section 4.23).

Chapter 5: Schedule Quantitative Risk Analysis embarks into more details in explaining what quantitative risk is about, applied to the project schedule. Schedule quantitative risk analysis quantifies the overall probability or chance of completing a project on time and on budget. The author explains the various distribution profiles in quantification, the danger of double dipping, approaches to duration ranging, issues with scheduling calendars, and all related matters as lightly as possible. In this chapter, several risk modeling point of thinking are revisited. Other areas of learning include three-point estimating or traditional method of duration ranging, and the use of medium and very high summary level risk modeling. The book's strategy takes you on a knowledge progression that allows you to learn more.

Chapter 6: Importing Schedule to OPRA directly refers to a schedule and cost risk analytic tool called OPRA. This chapter hopes to address the persistent issues encountered by many risk analysts after import, which is the unexplained large discrepancy between the risk plan file and the original multi-calendar. Failing to properly address or reference, the original deterministic dates of affected activities will stay misaligned, producing erroneous results. This chapter provides the key to how to avoid such misalignment. A guide to the correct methods of importing or converting Primavera project files to Oracle Primavera Risk Analysis (OPRA) capped this chapter. By the time you complete the chapter, you have learned a valuable method, a solution that saves time, and improves analytic results.

Chapter 7: RBM and Natural Disasters explore the challenge posed by the constant presence of natural disasters in the Philippines. Discussion revolves around what can be possibly be done by the government in response. The discussion takes the reader amidst the center of devastation brought by super typhoon Yolanda (International Code name Haiyan) in December of 2013. On that date, tens of thousands of people died or injured, while thousands more are missing. Since natural disasters are not preventable, one of the questions we want to answer is how to reduce their impacts. This chapter examines the unique geographical location of a country so prone to the primary risks of damaging natural forces that the probability of a typhoon or earthquake hitting the Philippines in any twelve-month period is 100% certain. As such, the author asks the readers to think deeply on the premise that, if an event is no longer a risk due to certainty, "how should a responsible technocrat handle the fact?" An explanation of the differences between risks, issues, problems, and facts makes the last few sections of this chapter's learning quite entertaining.

Chapter 8: Managing Cultural Diversity brings us to the core of people management and the risk it faces daily. Regardless of whether you are an internationally trained professional working in the Canadian workplace, a Canadian working overseas, or whatever locality you work in, you will appreciate this chapter. When communication becomes a challenge, it does not always mean one cannot speak the language. There are other reasons that prevent a message from getting there exactly as intended. If you find your actions and your words always get misinterpreted, this is a good starting point to discovering why. Understanding that mixing cultures introduces both threats and opportunities is the start of awareness. From awareness, one can cultivate knowledge and appreciation. Two cases illustrate the struggles that one might face. One key idea presents a solution to avoid and mitigate negative risks due to wrong perception. Another key idea offers a perspective governing human relationships.

Chapter 9: Project Integration tackles the question of whether to integrate or not to integrate, especially when it comes to very large projects or mega-projects. The causes of project failure are scrutinized (Section 9.2) and examples given. The chapter introduces project cost and project schedule management plans. Part of the message imparted is making sure that the schedule aligns with the project execution plan and strategy. To integrate the project, all stakeholders should contribute and work the plan. The section on the integrative planning and scheduling process describes that pulling the project portfolio together has pre-requisites in order to achieve full integration. One of them is making sure that the sub-elements are they themselves complete. The temptation of going ahead with the project despite a deficient plan, an incomplete scope, engineering holds, and high uncertainty is highly discouraged. This chapter shall attempt to share some stories that can reinforce that integrative project management concept, while demonstrating the importance of a good quality plan in pursuit of an effective risk-based project execution.

Chapter 10: Key Risk Indicator (KRI) delivers a practical message to the risk practitioners: Always look for gaps between actuals and benchmark values, because the variances are most likely your key risk indicators. In this chapter, the gap becomes the reference point, which in turn becomes the benchmark for comparison. Major differences between KRI and KPI are noted. Section 10.4 lists simple examples of KRI to ensure better understanding of the concept.

Chapter 11: P50 Risk-based Baseline Schedule underscores the importance of time as a commodity. Project managers receive a reminder of how valuable it is, so it is only proper to treat it with respect. Since the schedule is an important leg of management, a good schedule quality (Section 11.2) will result in a successful outcome. The quality of the schedule translates easily to the end quality and cost of the project. A project manager is foolish to expect a timely delivery of a bad schedule. Section 11.13 writes about enhancing success by creating a P50 Risk-based Baseline schedule. Section 11.8 deciphered the explanation why competing probabilities have big influence to the overall outcome of a schedule. Analysis of a bias, called planning fallacy, in Section 11.7 is quite informative. The details on how to generate the P50 Risk-based Baseline using Oracle Primavera Risk Analysis tool is described here in this chapter.

Chapter 12: Mega-projects Schedule Integration looks closely at the daunting challenge of schedule integration and offers a solution using the Primavera Project Management tool. Full integration using hard linking between areas is always the main issue. Everyone knows that without inter-project links (IPL) in a portfolio, an accurate critical path calculation is very difficult, if not impossible. The reader will understand that there exists a workable alternative to the common KIM schedule management method, where critical path calculation and identification is preserved. Sections 12.5 to 12.9 demonstrate details of simplifying the management of the overall schedule without losing essential inter-project relationships. It is doable regardless of the project portfolio's sheer size.

Chapter 13: Risk Assessments and Treatments takes into its view a school district operation case (Section 13.2). Looking through the eyes of various stakeholders, the readers will feel that they represent the business. Topics touch risk identification, assessment, and control techniques like avoidance, modification of likelihood or consequence, risk transfer, and retention (Sections 13.3 to 13.8).

Chapter 14: Root Cause Analysis (RCA) is easy to understand. Young readers who are fresh from high school will have no difficulty grasping the idea that RCA is an approach, a process, and a methodology. The analysis to determine the root causes and effects examines the driving relationships leading to the main issue. This offers an interesting subject to someone with an investigative spirit. Section 14.2 sets the stage of learning on a make-believe accident involving a taxi rollover. We applied Fault Tree Analysis (FTA) and Failure Mode and Effects Analysis (FMEA) approaches to a transport business called WOW Taxi.

Chapter 15: Road to Operational Excellence (OE) makes the readers aware that although OE is simply a business state of continuously achieving top business objectives, it takes real effort and commitment to be successful. It can be a five-point or ten-point high-level objective, yet it covers everything that the company values. Operational excellence is doing the right thing, the right way, at the right time, always. The subject tackles another make-believe case study about an enterprise called the SFF Group (Section 15.2). You will learn about the group's desire to revive leadership and stimulate organizational quality onwards to operational excellence. This involves strategic planning at various levels, motivating and empowering employees (Section 15.6), communicating effectively (Section 15.7), resolving conflicts, preventing abuse of power (Section 15.8), increasing engagement (Section 15.9), encouraging innovation, supporting creativity (Section 15.10), and changing organizational culture (Section 15.11). The question of how to bring that desire to fruition to the complete satisfaction of their clients is the secret sauce described in this chapter. The case study inspects, assess, and address the group's current issues and potential risks. The result of this case study gives SFF Group the roadmap to organizational and operational excellence (OE).

Chapter 16: Keys to Organizational Success is a supplementing, as well as complimenting, follow-up to Chapter 15. Using the company Lola Ann Courier Express as a case study, the reader gets into the company's struggle to improve relationships between management and its mostly South American workforce. The cultural makeup between two individuals drives the kind of relationship they will have. Developing empathy is the central skill elaborated on in Section 16.3. It is laughable for an individual to say he has a good relationship with himself and that is all that matters. We need at least two people to create a relationship. Motivation drives satisfaction and performance. Putting diversity in the mix makes the situation more interesting. The company uses CPP to augment the stimulus process of making employees feel they belong to one family, where the leaderships understand their needs (Section 16.6 and Section 16.8).

Chapter 17: Risk-based Management Wisdom brings the reader to the expert's realm where rule of thumb resides. When project managers have too much information to contend with, making a decision through details takes time. Since time is of the essence in many critical decisions, the most effective risk-based decisions uses time-tested heuristics or rules of thumb. Each section in this chapter offers one heuristic, its rationale, and its possible practical applications.

ABBREVIATION and ACRONYMS

AACE   Association for the Advancement of Cost Engineering

ALAP   As Late As Possible

BL   Baseline

BOS   Basis of Schedule

CLT   Central Limit Theorem

CMP   Continuity Management Plan

CP   Critical path

CPP   Community Practicum Program

CPM   Critical path method

CQ   Cultural IQ

DBM   Design Based Memorandum

DD   Data Date

EDS   Engineering Design Specification

EPC   Engineering, Procurement, and Construction

EPC/S   Engineering, Procurement, Construction, and Start-up

ERM   Enterprise Risk Management

FF   Finish to Finish

FMCSA   Federal Motor Carrier Safety Administration

FMEA   Failure Mode and Effect Analysis

FS   Finish to Start

FTA	Fault Tree Analysis
GIGO	Garbage in, Garbage out
IAP	Interactive Planning
ICSQRA	Integrated Cost and Schedule Quantitative Risk Analysis
IPL	Inter-project Links
ISO	International Organization for Standardization
KIM	Key Interface Milestones
KPI	Key performance indicator
KRI	Key risk indicator
LH	Latin Hypercube
LOE	Level of Effort
MAX	Maximum or Pessimistic
MIN	Minimum or Optimistic
ML	Most Likely
MLS	Medium Level Summary
MS	Milestones
MSP	Microsoft Projects
MSQ	Minimum Schedule Quality
OE	Operational Excellence
OPRA	Oracle Primavera Risk Analysis (previously Pertmaster)
PDCA	Plan-Do-Check-Act
PM	Project Management
PMBOK	Project Management Body of Knowledge
PMI	Project Management Institute

PPM	Project Portfolio Management
PRM	Project Risk Management
QRA	Quantitative Risk Analysis
RBM	Risk-based Management
RCA	Root Cause Analysis
RD	Remaining Duration
RFSQRA-C	Ready for SQRA-Criteria
RMP	Risk Management Professional
RRT	Risk Relativity Theory
SF	Start to Finish
SMART	Specific, Measurable, Achievable, Results-oriented, and Time-bound
SME	Subject Matter Expert
SQRA	Schedule Quantitative Risk Analysis
SRP	Strategic Redeployment Plan
SS	Start to Start
SWOT	Strength, Weakness, Opportunity, and Threat
TF	Total Float
VHLS	Very High Level Summary
WBS	Work Breakdown Structure
ZFF	Zero Free Float

BIBLIOGRAPHY

AACE. (2013). AACE 14R-90 Responsibility and Required Skilld for Project Planning.

Althouse, N. et al. (2013). The Future of Business, 4th Edition. In e. a. Althouse, *Creative Thinking Case-Potash Corp- Diversity & Safety* (p. 270). Ontario, Canada: Nelson Education Ltd. Retrieved from The Future of Business 4th Edition.

AMA. (2011, February). AMA Foundation for Traffic Safety-Hand outs.

Australia, G. o. (2011, October). *Construction Procurement Policy\Project Implementation Process*. Government of SouthAustralia, ISBN 978-0-7590-0181-7. Retrieved from www.bpims.sa.gov.au: Government of South Australia Copyright

Bacani, C. a. (1979). *Business and Statistics-Revised Edition*. Manila: GIC Enterprises & Co., Inc., Philippines.

Baird, J. e. (2010, October 28). In e. a. J. Baird, *Happiness Genes: Unlock the Positive Potential Hidden in Your DNA*. New Page Books, ISBN 978-1-60163-105-3. Retrieved from Planning\Bright Hub-Project Management: http://www.brighthubpm.com/project-planning/93262-stakeholders-in-project-management/

BBCNews. (2013, November 15). *Typhoon Haiyan: Plight of survivors 'bleak' despite aid effort*. Retrieved from http://www.bbc.co.uk: http://www.bbc.co.uk/news/world-asia-24950905

Bloch, B. (2013). *Black Swan Events and Investment.Retrieved from* . Retrieved from http://www.investopedia.com: http://www.investopedia.com/articles/trading/11/black-swan-events-investing.asp

Bonner, T. (2010, October 28). *Stakeholders in Project Management*. Retrieved from Planning\Bright Hub-Project Management: http://www.brighthubpm.com/project-planning/93262-stakeholders-in-project-management/

Boundless. (2013). *Business Stakeholders*. Retrieved from Boundless: https://www.boundless.com/management/ethics-in-business/business-stakeholders/internal-stakeholders/

Brooks, K. (2005). *Risk Assessment Contract Bus*. Retrieved from www.leics.gov.uk: http://www.leics.gov.uk/sample_generic_risk_assessment_for_transport.do c

CalgaryHerald. (2007). *Huge Cost Overruns*. Retrieved from http://www.canada.com: http://www.canada.com/story.html?id=afeb07dc-a5ff-4608-a9f7-450367ff99ef

Canada, G. o. (2014). *A Guide to Copyright*. Retrieved from www.cipo.ic.gc.ca: http://www.cipo.ic.gc.ca/eic/site/cipointernet-internetopic.nsf/eng/h_wr02281.html

Carroll, L. (1993). *Alice in Wonderland.* NY, USA: Dover Publication ISBN-13: 978-0-486-27543-7.

Carroll, L. (n.d.). *Alice's Adventures in Wonderland.*

Crowley, J. (2013). *Stop Catastrophizing Relief Efforts in the Philippines.Time Ideas.* Retrieved from http://ideas.time.com: http://ideas.time.com/2013/11/14/stop-catastrophizing-relief-efforts-in-the-philippines/

Dictionary.com. (2014). *Interest.* Retrieved from Dictionary.com: http://dictionary.reference.com/browse/interest

Discussion Thread Started & Facilitated by Rufran C. Frago, P. E.-R. (2009, August 28). *Schedule Risk Analysis (Methods and Concept).* Retrieved from AACEi: http://www.aacei.org/cgi-bin/forums/board-auth.cgi?file=/245/11264.html

Discussion thread started & facilitated by Rufran C. Frago, P. P.-R. (2009, August 28). *Risk Analysis (Interpreting Results and Indicators).* Retrieved from AACEi: http://www.aacei.org/cgi-bin/forums/board-auth.cgi?file=/245/11259.html

Duncan, J., & Duncan, L. (1993). Culture. In J. Duncan, & L. Duncan, *Place/Culture/Representation* (pp. P205-206). ISBN 0-415-09451-8.

E.Scarlat, N. (2012). *Indicators and Metrics Uses in ERM.* Retrieved from http://www.ecocyb.ase.ro: http://www.ecocyb.ase.ro/20124pdf/Emil%20Scarlat%20(T).pdf

Ehrenfreund, M. (2013, 11 11). *Evacuees in shelters were not safe as Haiyan ravaged Tacloban, the Philippines.* Retrieved from www.washingtonpost.com: http://www.washingtonpost.com/world/evacuees-in-shelters-were-not-safe-as-haiyan-ravaged-tacloban-the-philippines/2013/11/11/30fb51f2-4aec-11e3-ac54-aa84301ced81_story.html

Elliott, M. (2012). *Risk Assessment and Treatment.* PA, USA: The Institutes.

Elliott, M. (2012). *Risk Assessment and Treatment.* Malvern, Pennnsylvania: The Institutes.

Emil Scarlat, N. C. (2012). *INDICATORS AND METRICS USED IN THE ENTERPRISE RISK MANAGEMENT (ERM).* Retrieved from www.ecocyb.ase.ro: http://www.ecocyb.ase.ro/20124pdf/Emil%20Scarlat%20(T).pdf

Ferguson, R. (2014, February 19). *Ferguson, R. (2014).The Science of Managing Black Swans.Big Idea\Data Anlytic blog.Retrieved from.* Retrieved from http://sloanreview.mit.edu: http://sloanreview.mit.edu/article/the-science-of-managing-black-swans/

Few, S. (2007). *The Three Blind Men and an Elephant: The Power of Faceted Analytical Display.* Retrieved from Perceptual Edge.com: http://www.perceptualedge.com/articles/Whitepapers/Three_Blind_Men.pdf

Frago, R. (2008). *Project ABC Construction Schedule Analysis\E-mail flag.* Calgary.

Frago, R. (2012). MP Planning & Scheduling Awareness Course-Lev1.

Frago, R. (2013, October 30). *Case Study: Potash Corporation.* Retrieved from Slideshare: http://www.slideshare.net/rfrago/103013-case-study-potash-corporation

Frago, R. (2013, July). *How to Prepare for Schedule Quantitative Risk Assessment*. Retrieved from Slideshare.com: http://www.slideshare.net/rfrago/071513-how-to-prepare-for-sqra-by-rcf

Frago, R. (2013). *How to Prepare for SQRA.Slideshare*. Retrieved from http://www.slideshare.net: http://www.slideshare.net/rfrago/071513-how-to-prepare-for-sqra-by-rcf

Frago, R. (2013). *Mega-project Schedule Integration and Management*. Retrieved from Slideshare: http://www.slidesharenet.org/rfrago/080613-mega-project-schedule-integration-management

Frago, R. (2013, August 06). *Mega-project Schedule Integration and Management*. Retrieved from Slideshare.com: http://www.slidesharenet.org/rfrago/080613-mega-project-schedule-integration-management

Frago, R. (2013, November 12). *Preliminary Project Execution Plan (Schedule & Cost)*. Retrieved from Slideshare: https://www.slideshare.net/secret/17BHyTp4nV5dtA

Frago, R. (2013). *Risk Concepts, Philosophies, Methods and Approaches*. Retrieved from http://www.slideshare.net: http://www.slideshare.net/rfrago/082213-risk-concepts-philosophies-methods-and-approaches

Frago, R. (2013, July). *Schedule Quantitative Risk Assessment (SQRA) Fundamentals: Using Three Point Estimate*. Retrieved from Slideshare.com: http://www.slideshare.net/rfrago/071613-introduction-to-sqra-traditional-method

Frago, R. (2014, October 29). *Risk Assessment and Treatment*. Retrieved from www.slideshare.net: http://www.slideshare.net/rfrago/110314-risk-assessment-treatment-school-district-bussing

Frago, R. (2015, April 18). *DBM Schedule Development Workshop*. Retrieved from www.slideshare.com: http://www.slideshare.net/rfrago/032815-dbm-schedule-development-workshop-46694734

Frago, R. (July 2001). *NPA Rebel-Bus Burning Incident Report (JGSPC)*. Simlong, Batangas City, Philippines.

Frago, R. (July 2010). *Schedule Risk Analysis Report (Final) of XYZ Upgrader Project*. Calgary, Alberta, Canada.

Frago, R. *Planning and Scheduling Quandry*. Calgary.

Frago, R. *The Second Seal - Revelation 6:3-6*. Lipa City, Philippines.

Gardenswartz, L., & Rowe, A. (2003). The Four Layers of Diversity. In L. Gardenswartz, & A. Rowe, *The Effective Management of Cultural Diversity* (p. P37). Retrieved from http://www.sagepub.com: http://www.sagepub.com/upm-data/26078_pt2.pdf

Gilbeaux, K. (2013). *Philippines - Super Typhoon Yolanda (Haiyan) Information*. Retrieved from www.globalresiliencesystem: http://www.us.resiliencesystem.org/category/general-topic-tags/extreme-weather

GMANews. (2013, 12 11). *NDRRMC: Yolanda death toll climbs to 5,959; damage at P35.5B*. Retrieved from www.gmanetwork.com: http://www.gmanetwork.com/news/story/339269/news/nation/ndrrmc-yolanda-death-toll-climbs-to-5-959-damage-at-p35-5b

Goldratt, E. (1997). Critical Chain. The North River Press. ISBN 0-88427-153-6. Retrieved from (1997). Critical Chain. The North River Press. p. 246. ISBN 0-88427-153-6.

GovernmentofSouthAustralia. (2011, October). *Construction Procurement Policy\Project Implementation Process*. Retrieved from www.bpims.sa.gov.au: www.bpims.sa.gov.au/bpims/library/downloadResource.do?id=1027

Grey, S. (2007). *Tutorial\Project Range Analysis*. Retrieved from Broadleaf.com: http://broadleaf.com.au/old/pdfs/trng_tuts/Tut_Project_Range_Analysis. pdf

Grey, S., & company. (2007). *Tutorial\Project Range Analysis*. Retrieved from Broadleaf.com: http://broadleaf.com.au/old/pdfs/trng_tuts/Tut_Project_Range_Analysis. pdf

Guzman, S. d. (2013, 08 05). *The pork barrel scam a perfect model of corruption*. Retrieved from www.philstar.com: http://www.philstar.com/opinion/2013/08/05/1053441/pork-barrel-scam-perfect-model-corruption

Harris, P. (2013). *Project Planning and Control Using Primavera P6*. Retrieved from http://books.google.ca/books?id=ep50AO-B06oC&pg=SA11-PA2&lpg=SA11-PA2&dq=Primavera+As+late+as+possible+constraint&source=bl&ots=k1798rx5V9&sig=zommYX_5Jdwcab-VEVbieXDpplw&hl=en&sa=X&ei=IGRwUeaHC-mUiAL0uIDoBA&ved=0CDQQ6AEwAQ#v=onepage&q=Primavera%20As%20la

Haughey, D. (2011). *http://www.compensationanalytics.com/_resources/pmquotes.pdf*. Retrieved from http://www.compensationanalytics.com: http://www.compensationanalytics.com/_resources/pmquotes.pdf

Hildebrandt, A. (2013, November 20). *Mass burials may complicate Philippines Typhoon Haiyan*. Retrieved from CBC News/World: http://www.cbc.ca/news/world/mass-burials-may-complicate-philippines-typhoon-haiyan-recovery-1.2430868

Hofstede, G. (2015, 06 01). *National Culture*. Retrieved from http://geert-hofstede.com: http://geert-hofstede.com/national-culture.html

Hohberger, C. (1971). Introduction to Boolean Algebra. In *Number Systems and Logic Part 2* (p. 9). Scranton, PA, USA: Intext, Inc.

Hudson, B. (2012). *Blurred Boundaries between public service and private interest*. Retrieved from http://www.theguardian.com: http://www.theguardian.com/healthcare-network/2012/oct/22/public-service-private-blurred-boundaries

IbTimes. (2013). *Tacloban1*. Retrieved from google.ca: https://www.google.ca/search?q=haiyan's+dead&source=lnms&tbm=isch&sa=X&ei=N1CGUpXNGqKsjAKRsYCACw&ved=0CAcQ_AUoAQ&biw=1272&bih=791

Insight-WFP. (2014). *Workface Planning*. Retrieved from http://www.insight-wfp.com: http://www.insight-wfp.com/learn_about_workface_planning.php

Intaver. (2006). *Psychological Issues in Identification of Uncertainties*. Retrieved from http://www.intaver.com:

http://www.intaver.com/Articles/RP_Art_MindManagerRiskAnalysis1.htm
l

IPA. (2010). *IPA Finds That Most Site-Based Projects Fail to Meet Business Objectives.* Retrieved from https://ipaglobal.com/News-Room/Press-Releases: https://ipaglobal.com/News-Room/Press-Releases/IPA-Finds-That-Most-Site-Based-Projects-Fail-to-Me

IT-Cortex. (2013). *Failure Causes.* Retrieved from http://www.it-cortex.com: http://www.it-cortex.com/Stat_Failure_Cause.htm

Jeges, F. f. (2013, April). *ISO 31000 Risk Management Standard\Can there be risk without an objective?* Retrieved from Linkedin\ISO 31000 Group: http://www.linkedin.com/groups/Can-there-be-risk-without-1834592.S.228645871?trk=group_search_item_list-0-b-cmr&goback=%2Egna_1834592

Jeston, J. (2013). *7FE Project Framework.* Retrieved from http://www.managementbyprocess.com: http://www.managementbyprocess.com/joomla/index.php?option=com_c ontent&task=view&id=16

Jill Butler, W. L. (2010). Garbage in-Garbage out. In W. L. Jill Butler, *Universal Principles of Design 2nd Edition* (p. 112). Gloucester, MA: Rockport Publishers, ISBN 1-59253-587-9.

Jones, B. (2012, June). *Legal Privilege.* Retrieved from www.bennettjones.com: http://www.bennettjones.com/uploadedFiles/Publications/Guides/Privile ge_June2012-web.pdf

JournalofCommerce. (2008). *Cost overruns delay production at Long Lake Oilsands project.* Retrieved from http://www.journalofcommerce.com: http://www.journalofcommerce.com/article/id31166

Katz, A. (2013, November 15). *Filipino Official Fired for Inflated Estimate of Typhoon Deaths.Time World.* Retrieved from http://world.time.com: http://world.time.com/2013/11/14/filipino-official-fired-for-inflated-estimate-of-typhoon-deaths/?iid=obnetwork

Kobayashi, A. (1993). Multiculturalism:Representing a Canadian Institution. In A. Kobayashi, *Multiculturalism and Making a Difference* (pp. P205-31). London.

Koplowitz, H. (2012). *Mega Millions Jackpot: Is Winning The Lottery A Curse? Two Tales Of Misfortune.* Retrieved from http://www.ibtimes.com: http://www.ibtimes.com/mega-millions-jackpot-winning-lottery-curse-two-tales-misfortune-432274

Langton, N. R. (2013). *Organizational Behaviour - 6th Edition.* Toronto, ON: Pearson Education.

Laroche, L. (2003). *Managing Cultural Diversity in Technical Professions .* Burlington, MA: Butterworth-Heinemann.

LCE. (2013). *Risk-based Asset Management.* Retrieved from http://www.lce.com: http://www.lce.com/RiskBased_Asset_Management_209.html

Leach, P. (2005). *http://www.aertia.com.* Retrieved from Modeling uncertainty in Project scheduling: http://www.aertia.com/docs/crystalball/cbuc05-leach.pdf

Leach, P. (2005). *Modeling Uncertainty in Project Scheduling.* Retrieved from http://www.aertia.com: http://www.aertia.com/docs/crystalball/cbuc05-leach.pdf

Lewis. (1997). In Lewis, *Project Planning, Scheduling & Control* (pp. 25, 53, 66, 97, 117, 167).

Linkedin, R. C. (2012, May 22). *OPRA (Pertmaster) Linkedin*. Retrieved from Linkedin: http://www.linkedin.com/groupItem?view=&gid=2006047&type=member &item=117620856&qid=f7d4f093-498d-4fb1-ac94- 332812d7cafd&trk=group_search_item_list-0-b-ttl

Livelux. (2012, December 20). *New British Airways Dreamliner-Luxury Aircraft Seating and Cabin design*. Retrieved from Thelifeofluxury.com: http://www.thelifeofluxury.com/new-british-airways-dreamliner-luxury-aircraft-seating-cabin-design/

LloydRegisterConsulting. (2013). *Risk based Management*. Retrieved from http://www.scandpower.com: http://www.scandpower.com/services/business-solutions/

Lorenz, E. (1972). *Butterfly Effect*. Retrieved from http://en.wikipedia.org: http://en.wikipedia.org/wiki/Butterfly_effect

Lorenz, E. (2013). *Wiki\The Butterfly Effect*. Retrieved from Wikipedia.com: http://en.wikipedia.org/wiki/Butterfly_effect

LSE/NCVO/ESRC. (2009). *Blurring of Boundaries Seminar Series*. Retrieved from http://www.lse.ac.uk: http://www.lse.ac.uk/internationalDevelopment/research/NGPA/publicat ions/Blurring%20boundaries%20NCVONGPA%203%20final%20version. pdf

Mangini, F. (2007). *Risks or Problems-What's the Difference?.svprojectmanagement.com*. Retrieved from http://svprojectmanagement.com: http://svprojectmanagement.com/risks-or-problems-whats-the-difference

Measham, F. (2013). *Typhoon Haiyan: Disasters on this scale are never entirely an 'act of God*. Retrieved from The Guardian.com: http://www.theguardian.com/commentisfree/2013/nov/14/typhoon-haiyan-philippines-disasters-act-of-god

Menevse, A. (2012). *LinkedinISO31000 Standard Group\Origin of Risk discussion*. Retrieved from http://www.linkedin.com: http://www.linkedin.com/groups/Origin-Risk-Do-we-know-1834592.S.95193215?trk=groups_search_item_list-0-b-ttl&goback=.gna_3813796.gmp_3813796.anb_3813799_*2_*1

MindTools. (2013). *Hofstede's Cultural Dimensions\Understanding Workplace Values Around the World*. Retrieved from mindtools.com: http://www.mindtools.com/pages/article/newLDR_66.htm

Minitab. (2015). *Repeatability and reproducibility in measurement systems.Retrieved from*. Retrieved from www.minitab.com: http://support.minitab.com/en-us/minitab/17/topic-library/quality-tools/measurement-system-analysis/gage-r-r-analyses/repeatability-and-reproducibility/

Morris, P. (2013). *Managing Project Interfaces* . Retrieved from http://gspa.grade.nida.ac.th: http://gspa.grade.nida.ac.th/pdf/PA%20780%20(Pakorn)/18.Managing%2 0Project%20Interfaces-key%20Points%20for%20Project%20Succes.pdf

Mulcahy, R. (2003). Qualitative Risk Analysis. In R. Mulcahy, *Risk Management-Tricks of the Trade for Project Managers* (p. 119). RMC Publications ISBN 0-9711647-9-7, USA.

Mulcahy, R. (2005). Common Errors and Pitfalls even of an Experienced Project Managers. In R. Mulcahy, *PMP Exam Prep 5th Ed (For PMBOK Guide - Third Ed)* (p. 20). USA: RMC Publication.

Mulcahy, R. (2005). Time Management. In R. Mulcahy, *PMP Exam Prep* (p. 179). RMC Publications, USA, ISBN 1-932735-00-3.

Mulcahy, R. (2013). *Risk Management Tricks of the Trade for Project Managers.*

Mungin, L. (2013). *More than 100 dead after earthquake hits the Philippines.* Retrieved from http://www.cnn.com:
    http://www.cnn.com/2013/10/16/world/asia/philippines-earthquake/

Mustafa Malik, T. (2004). 4Cs of Planning, RCF's Lecture Notes-Administrative Control System, Keyano University. (R. Frago, Interviewer)

NASA. (2013). *Images\NASA-Typhoon Haiyan.* Retrieved from earthobservatory.com:
    http://earthobservatory.nasa.gov/NaturalHazards/view.php?id=82348

Nordquist, R. (2013). *Pragmatic Competence.* Retrieved from grammar.about.com:
    http://grammar.about.com/od/pq/g/pragmaticcompetenceterm.htm

NRDC. (2001). *What Parents Need to Know About Diesel School Buses.* Retrieved from www.nrdc.org: http://www.nrdc.org/air/transportation/qbus.asp

O.Renn, A. a. (2002). Risk-based, Precaution-based, Discourse-based. Risk Analysis. In A. a. O.Renn, *A New Approach to Risk Evaluation and Management* (p. Volume 22).

O'Donnell, H. K. (1976). *Management, Systems and Contingency Analysis of Managerial Functions-Student Edition.* McGraw-Hill, Kogakusha Ltd.

O'Malley, W. J. (1999, February 21). *Teaching Empathy.* America 180 (12): 22–26. Retrieved from Leading Answers:
    http://leadinganswers.typepad.com/leading_answers/2008/02/pmbok-4-this-ti.html

OnlineEtymologyDictionary. (2013). *Online Etymology Dictionary\Risk.* Retrieved from http://www.etymonline.com:
    http://www.etymonline.com/index.php?term=risk

OracleUniversity. (2011). *Managing Risk in Oracle Primavera Risk Analysis.Versions 6.0/6.1 Course Manual.* Retrieved from 20) Oracle University (2011).Managing Risk in Oracle Primavera Risk Analysis.Versions 6.0/6.1 Course Manual

Osborne, H. (2013). *WHO:Removing Bodies Not a Priority.* Retrieved from http://www.ibtimes.co.uk:
    http://www.ibtimes.co.uk/articles/521600/20131112/typhoon-haiyan-world-health-organisation-removing-dead.htm

Osgood, C. (2009). *Quote/Unquote: Charles Osgood on Responsibility.Minding Gaps.* Retrieved from http://rainbows.typepad.com:
    http://rainbows.typepad.com/blog/2009/10/quote-unquote-charles-osgood-on-responsibility.html

Palisade. (2014). *Palisade.* Retrieved from Risk Analysis:
    http://www.palisade.com/risk/risk_analysis.asp

Palisade. (2014). *Risk Analysis.* Retrieved from www.palisade.com:
    http://www.palisade.com/risk/risk_analysis.asp

Palomino, J. (2013, January 22). *The Actionable SWOT Analysis.* Retrieved from ValueProp Interactive: http://www.valueprop.com/blog/2013/01/the-actionable-swot-analysis/

Patterson, D. (2010). 5-step Intelligent Optimization. *Acumen Integrated Cost/Schedule Risk Analysis.*

Payne, M. (2006). *Olympic Turnaround,page 9.*

Phelm, J. (2013). *What is the difference between an Issue and a Problem.* Retrieved from www.wikianswers.com: http://wiki.answers.com/Q/What_is_the_difference_between_an_issue_an d_a_problem#slide=15&article=What_is_the_difference_between_an_issu e_and_a_proble

Planck, M. (1858-1947). *Quantum Theory.* Retrieved from WikiQuote: http://en.wikiquote.org/wiki/Max_Planck

Plotnick, F. (2004, 02 28). Review of 14R-90 (Rev. 11/190) e-mail to Vera Lovejoy. Retrieved from A) Plotnick, Fredric L., Review Comments for 14R-90 (Rev. 11/1990), E-mail to Vera Lovejoy, February 28, 2004.

PMBOK. (2013). *Project Management Body of Knowledge 5th Edition.* PMi.

PMI. (2009). *Project Management Book of Knowledge, 4th Edition.* Pennsylvania, USA: Project Management Institute.

PMI. (2009). Project Risk Management Definition/Principles and Concepts. In PMIGlobalStandard, *Practice Standard for Project Risk Management* (pp. 4, 9). USA: PMi Book Center.

PMI. (2009). Project Risk Management Definition/Principles and Concepts. In PMiGlobalStandard, *Practice Standard for Project Risk Management* (pp. 4, 9). USA: PMi Book Center.

PMI. (2013). Project Risk Management. In PMI, *A guide to the Project Management Body of Knowledge (PMBOK Guide) - 5th Edition* (pp. 40,50,61,310). Newtown Square, PA, USA: Project Management Institute.

PMI. (2013). Project Risk Management. In P. M. Institute, *A guide to the Project Management Body of Knowledge (PMBOK Guide) - 5th Edition* (pp. 40,50,61,310). Newtown Square, PA, USA: Project Management Institute.

PMI. (2013). Project Risk Management Overview. In PMI, *A Guide To the Project Management Body of Knowledge (PMBOK Guide)-Fifth Edition* (p. 310). PA, USA: Project Management Institute.

PMI. (2013). Reserve Analysis. In PMI, *A Guide to the Project Management Body of Knowledge 5th Edition* (p. Section 6.5.2.6). PMi.

PMI. (2013). Reserve Analysis. In PMI, *A Guide to the Project Management Body of Knowledge 5th Edition* (p. Section 6.5.2.6). PMi.

PMI. (2013). Schedule Development Overview. In PMI, *A Guide to the PMBOK, 5th Edition, e-file, Version 1.3* (pp. 172, 173 Section 6.6, Figure 6-16). Newtown Square, PA, USA: PMi, ISBN: 978-1-935589-67-9.

PMI. (2013). Schedule Development Overview. In PMI, *A Guide to the PMBOK, 5th Edition, e-file, Version 1.3* (pp. 172, 173 Section 6.6, Figure 6-16). Newtown Square, PA, USA: PMi, ISBN: 978-1-935589-67-9.

PMI. (2014). Critical Path Method. In PMi, *PMBOK Edition 2013* (p. 145).

PMI. (2014). Critical Path Method. In PMI, *PMBOK Edition 2013* (p. 145).

Polen, T. (2012, November 2). *Deltek/Acumen-Guide to Acumen Fuse Scoring.* Retrieved from Deltek/Acumen: http://www.projectacumen.com/resource/scoring-in-acumen-fuse/

PRCSoftware. (2013). *Primavera Risk: Step 2 – Pertmaster Import Check*. Retrieved from PRC Software: http://www.prcsoftware.com/product-primavera-risk-pertmaster-training/41-pertmaster-step-2-import-validation.html

Ranf, D. E. (2010). *Cultural Differences in Project Management*. Retrieved from http://econpapers.repec.org: http://econpapers.repec.org/article/alujournl/v_3a2_3ay_3a2010_3ai_3a12_3ap_3a18.htm

Rappler. (2015, March 27). *MAP: Strongest earthquakes in the Philippines*. Retrieved from www.rappler.com: http://www.rappler.com/science-nature/33807-map-strongest-earthquakes-in-ph

Read, T. s. (2010, March 23). *Decision and Risk Management\Optimum Risk Schedule Size (AACEi Forum)*. Retrieved from AACEI Forum: http://www.aacei.org/cgi-bin/forums/board-auth.cgi?file=/245/17136.html

Reuters. (2011). *Update Aecon sees $56M to $59M hit*. Retrieved from http://www.reuters.com: http://www.reuters.com/article/2011/02/04/aecongroup-idUSSGE71307O20110204

Rice, J. (1995). *Mathematical Statistics and Data Analysis (Second Edition)*. Duxbury Press, ISBN 0-534-20934-3.

RiskTec. (2013). *RiskWorld, 2005\Risk-based Decision Making*. Retrieved from http://www.risktec.co.uk: http://www.risktec.co.uk/knowledge-bank/technical-articles/risk-based-decision-making.aspx#!

Robert V. Wendling, a. R. (1999). Basic Techniques for Analyzing and Presenting Schedule Risk Analysis. *RISK.08, 1999 AACE international Transactions*.

Roger Buehler, D. G. (1994). Exploring the Planning Fallacy. *Journal of Personality and Social Psychology, Volume 67, No. 3*, 366-381.

Rufran C. Frago, P. E.-R. (2013, July 22). *Understanding Acumen Fuse Score (Slideshare)*. Retrieved from Slideshare: http://www.slideshare.net/rfrago/072213-understanding-acumen-fuse-score-use-this

Rufran C. Frago, P. P.-R. (2013, July 15). *How to Prepare for Schedule Quantitative Risk Analysis (SQRA)*. Retrieved from Slideshare: http://www.slideshare.net/rfrago/071513-how-to-prepare-for-sqra-by-rcf

Rufran C. Frago, P. P.-R. (2013, April 18). *Slideshare*. Retrieved from www.slideshare.net: http://www.slideshare.net/rfrago/041813-understanding-alap

Rush, J. (2011). *Intercultural Business Strategies News & Views\52 Activities of Improving Cross-Cultural Communication*. Retrieved from www.crossculturalstrategies.com: http://www.crossculturalstrategies.com/2011/01/27/52-activities-for-improving-cross-cultural-communication/

Russell, D. (2014, November 14). *The Mean, the Median, and the Mode*. Retrieved from MathAbout.com: http://math.about.com/od/statistics/a/MeanMedian.htm

Safran. (2014). *Managing Uncertainty in Project Schedules*. Retrieved from www.safran.com: http://www.safran.com/uploads/documents/Safran-whitepaper-SRA.pdf

Samenow, J. (2013). *Super typhoon Haiyan: One of world's most powerful storms in history from space*. Retrieved from WashingtonPost.com: http://www.washingtonpost.com/blogs/capital-weather-gang/wp/2013/11/08/super-typhoon-haiyan-one-of-worlds-most-powerful-stor

Schacter, D. (2011). *Psychology-2nd Edition*. Worth Publishers.ISBN 978-1-4292-3719-2. Retrieved from Templates PMO: http://www.templatespmo.com/identify_stakeholders.html

Schacter, D. e. (2009, 2011). *Psychology-2nd Edition*. Worth Publishers.ISBN 978-1-4292-3719-2. Retrieved from Templates PMO: http://www.templatespmo.com/identify_stakeholders.html

Sexton, C. A. (2006). Philippines in Pictures. In C. A. Sexton, *Philippines in Pictures*. Twenty-First Century Books. ISBN 978-0-8225-2677-3. Retrieved from Colleen A. Sexton (2006). Philippines in Pictures. Twenty-First Century Books. ISBN 978-0-8225-2677-3. Retrieved 2008-11-01.

Six, T. (2012). *http://www.tensixconsulting.com*. Retrieved from Schedule Risk Analysis:What is it and why do it?: http://www.tensixconsulting.com/2012/02/schedule-risk-analysis-what-is-it-and-why-do-it/

Six, T. (2012). *Schedule Risk Analysis:What is it and why do it?* Retrieved from http://www.tensixconsulting.com: http://www.tensixconsulting.com/2012/02/schedule-risk-analysis-what-is-it-and-why-do-it/

Skjong, R. (2005, February 25). *Etymology of Risk*. Retrieved from http://research.dnv.com: http://research.dnv.com/skj/Papers/ETYMOLOGY-OF-RISK.pdf

Smith, J. (2012). *Creamer Media-Engineering News\Risk-based Approach, the best way to avoid project failure*. Retrieved from http://www.engineeringnews.co.za: http://www.engineeringnews.co.za/article/risk-based-approach-best-way-to-avoid-project-failure-2012-08-31

Smith, J. (2012, September 07). *Risk-based approach best way to avoid project failure*. Retrieved from www.engineeringnews.co.za: http://www.engineeringnews.co.za/print-version/risk-based-approach-best-way-to-avoid-project-failure-2012-08-31

Stratos-IndustryCanada. (2013). *Suncor–Sustainability Integration Case Study*. Retrieved from http://www.stratos-sts.com: http://www.stratos-sts.com/wp-content/uploads/2013/04/2007_07_Case-Study-Suncor.pdf

Stringer, D., & Cassiday, P. (2013). *52 Activities for Improving Cross-Cultural Communication*. Retrieved from www.amazon.com: http://www.amazon.com/gp/product/193193083X?ie=UTF8&tag=enabled4succe-20&linkCode=as2&camp=1789&creative=390957&creativeASIN=193193083X#reader_193193083X

SuncorProjectManagement. (2013). *Suncor Project Implementation Model (SPIM) Framework*. Calgary: Suncor.

Symonds, M. (2011, June 13). *15 Causes of Project Failure*. Retrieved from ProjectSmart.co.uk: http://www.projectsmart.co.uk/15-causes-of-project-failure.html

Taleb, N. (2010). *The Black Swan: the impact of the highly improbable-2nd Edition*. London, UK: Penguin, ISBN 978-0-14103459-1.

TemplatesPMO. (2013). *Identify Stakeholders Templates*. Retrieved from Templates PMO: http://www.templatespmo.com/identify_stakeholders.html

The Phrase Finder. (2015, 05 28). Retrieved from http://www.phrases.org.uk: http://www.phrases.org.uk/meanings/beauty-is-in-the-eye-of-the-beholder.html

TheHofstedeCentre. (2014). *What about Canada?* Retrieved from geert-hofstede.com: http://geert-hofstede.com/canada.html

ThePhraseFinder. (2014). *Beauty is in the eyes of the Beholder*. Retrieved from http://www.phrases.org.uk: http://www.phrases.org.uk/meanings/beauty-is-in-the-eye-of-the-beholder.html

Topinka, U. W. (1997). *Cascades Volcano Observatory*. Retrieved from vulcan.wr.usgs.gov: http://vulcan.wr.usgs.gov/Glossary/PlateTectonics/Maps/map_plate_tectonics_world.html

UnknownAuthor. (2013). *Stories\Friendship Stories\Story Of A Mouse And A Mousetrap*. Retrieved from SmilePls.com: http://smilepls.com/stories/friendship-stories/story-of-a-mouse-and-a-mousetrap.html

UnknownPhotographer. (2009, September 30). *Typhoon Ketsana (Ondoy)*. Retrieved from boston.com: http://www.boston.com/bigpicture/2009/09/typhoon_ketsana_ondoy.html

UrbanDictionary. (2006). *Layman's terms*. Retrieved from http://www.urbandictionary.com: http://www.urbandictionary.com/define.php?term=layman's%20terms

USGS. (2012, February 7). *Phivolcs: Maps are incomplete due to lack of geologists*. Retrieved from www.gmanetwork.co: http://www.gmanetwork.com/news/story/247144/scitech/science/phivolcs-maps-are-incomplete-due-to-lack-of-geologists

VariousAuthors. (2009, October). *AAcei Forums\DARM\General\Monte Carlo vs Latin Hypercube*. Retrieved from AACEi.org: http://www.aacei.org/cgi-bin/forums/board-auth.cgi?file=/245/12133.html

WebMD. (2014). *Child Safety: School Bus Still Best*. Retrieved from www.webmd.com: http://www.webmd.com/parenting/features/child-safety-school-bus-still-best?page=4

WebMod. (2009, September). *Images from Typhoon Ondoy Onslaught*. Retrieved from typhoonondoy.org: http://www.typhoonondoy.org/category/pictures/

Wendling, R. (1999). Basic Techniques for Analyzing and Presenting Schedule Risk Analysis. *RISK.08, 1999 AACE international Transactions (Co-authored with Randal Lorance)*.

Whitchurch, C. (2009). *Shifting Roles and Blurring Boundaries:Reconstructing Professional Identities in Higher Education*. Retrieved from Escalate.ac.uk.JOE London Presentation: http://www.google.ca/url?sa=t&rct=j&q=&esrc=s&frm=1&source=web&cd=4&cad=rja&ved=

Wicklund, A. (2013, September). *Primavera Risk (Pertmaster) - Step 1 - P6 Database Import*. Retrieved from Youtube.com: http://www.youtube.com/watch?v=jIq1xjZ6_io

Wicklund, A. (2013, September). *Primavera Risk (Pertmaster) - Step 2 - Import Check Tab*. Retrieved from Youtube.com: http://www.youtube.com/watch?v=jIq1xjZ6_io

Wikipedia. (2013). *Cost Overrun*. Retrieved from http://en.wikipedia.org: http://en.wikipedia.org/wiki/Cost_overrun

Wikipedia. (2013). *Cultural Pluralism*. Retrieved from Wikipedia.com: http://en.wikipedia.org/wiki/Cultural_pluralism

Wikipedia. (2013). *Cultural Pluralism*. Retrieved from Wikipedia.com\Cultural Pluralism: http://en.wikipedia.org/wiki/Cultural_pluralism

Wikipedia. (2013). *Garbage in, Garbage Out*. Retrieved from Wikipedia The Free Encyclopedia: http://en.wikipedia.org/wiki/Garbage_in,_garbage_out

Wikipedia. (2013). *List of Earthquakes in the Philippines*. Retrieved from Wikipedia.com: http://en.wikipedia.org/wiki/List_of_earthquakes_in_the_Philippines

Wikipedia. (2013). *Olympic Stadium (Montreal)*. Retrieved from http://en.wikipedia.org: http://en.wikipedia.org/wiki/Montreal_Olympic_Stadium

Wikipedia. (2013). *Project Management Iron Triangle*.

Wikipedia. (2013). *Project Management Triangle*. Retrieved from http://en.wikipedia.org: http://en.wikipedia.org/wiki/Project_management_triangle

Wikipedia. (2013). *Wikipedia\Desiderata*. Retrieved from Wikipedia: http://en.wikipedia.org/wiki/Desiderata

Wikipedia. (2013). *Wikipedia-SWOT Analysis*. Retrieved from Wikepedia Free Encyclopedia: http://en.wikipedia.org/wiki/SWOT_analysis

Wikipedia. (2014). *Empathy*. Retrieved from Wikipedia: http://en.wikipedia.org/wiki/

Wikipedia. (2014). *Key Risk Indicators*. Retrieved from http://en.wikipedia.org: http://en.wikipedia.org/wiki/Key_Risk_Indicator

Wikipedia. (2014). *Learning*. Retrieved from Wikipedia: http://en.wikipedia.org/wiki/Learning

Wikipedia. (2014). *Student Syndrome*. Retrieved from Wikipedia: http://en.wikipedia.org/wiki/Student_syndrome#cite_note-1

Wikipedia. (2014). *Wiki\Planning*. Retrieved from http://en.wikipedia.org: http://en.wikipedia.org/wiki/Planning

Wikipedia, T. F. (2013). *Garbage in, Garbage Out*.

Wikipedia\Aesops. (2015, May 2). *Wikipedia*. Retrieved from www.wikipedia.com: http://en.wikipedia.org/wiki/Aesop's_Fables

Wikipedia\StudentSyndrome. (2014). *Student Syndrome*. Retrieved from Wikipedia: http://en.wikipedia.org/wiki/Student_syndrome#cite_note-1

Wladawsky-Berger, I. (2013). *Spotting Black Swans with Data Science.Retrieved from* . Retrieved from http://blogs.wsj.com: http://blogs.wsj.com/cio/2013/05/17/spotting-black-swans-with-data-science/

Yew, M. A. (2014, December 8). *TSX has biggest one-day drop in 18 months* . Retrieved from www.thestar.com: http://www.thestar.com/business/2014/12/08/tsx_plunges_292_points_as_oil_prices_retreat.html

INDEX

About the Author

Rufran C. Frago is a Filipino born Canadian. Rufran C. Frago is a Filipino born Canadian. He is practicing Professional Engineer (APEGA), a PMP (PMI), a CCP (AACE) and a RMP (PMI).

He studied at Batangas State University (previously Pablo Borbon Memorial Institute of Technology) and University of Batangas (formerly Western Philippine College) graduating with a Diploma in Petroleum Refinery Maintenance Technician (1979), Bachelor of Science in Mechanical Engineering (1984), and Bachelor of Science in Management Engineering in 1987 respectively. He was in his senior year taking up Bachelor of Science in Electrical Engineering, needing only one semester to complete, when he took a break to concentrate on married life.

Rufran has never stopped academic learning after getting his degrees in the University. He continues his education by taking up some MBA courses under the University of the Philippines-PBMIT Consortium (1987-1988). He completed Computer Technician Program at International Correspondence School, Pennsylvania, USA in 1994, Applied Project Management Certificate program at Southern Alberta Institute of Technology in 2009, and Professional Management Certificate program specializing in Construction Management in 2014. He is now completing the Professional Management Certificate program specializing in Risk Management.

He was a recipient of the Gerry Roxas Leadership Award (1976) and the American Field Service (AFS) Scholarship in 1976-77, studying in America for a year. Upon his return in 1977, California-Texas Philippines (Caltex Philippines Inc.), one of Asia's biggest oil and gas refineries at the time, awards him with a two-year national college scholarship, specializing in Petroleum Refinery Maintenance. He went on extensive training in various maintenance disciplines for the next two years. Upon his graduation in 1979, Caltex hired him to work in Caltex Operation Department's Oil Movement Group.

He has now spent more than 38 years of his life working in the following industries: Oil & Gas, Petrochemicals, Oleo-chemicals, Sugar Refining/Manufacturing, Consultancy, High School and University Education (Location: Asia, Middle East, Canada, and North Africa). Rufran has worked with Caltex, Uniman, Unichem (now Cocochem), ARAMCO-KSA, Central Azucarera de Tarlac, Arabian Gulf Oil Company-Libya, Batangas State University, St. Bridget's College, JG Summit Petrochemicals, Halliburton-Kellogg, Brown and Root, and OPTI Canada. He now works with Suncor

Energy Inc.

He has wide range of expertise that includes problem solving, project management, training and mentoring, programs and projects planning and scheduling, cost management, risk-based management, construction management, project review and auditing, estimating, engineering and design, fabrication and module management, maintenance, operation, material selection, warehousing, EH&S and reliability engineering (predictive and preventive maintenance). He has worked as a plant maintenance technician, plant operator, staff engineer, university teacher, safety manager, head of planning, senior mechanical engineer, maintenance planner, vibration (NDT) analyst, planning supervisor, senior project controls specialist, risk analyst, and many other related roles.

Rufran loves writing poems, short stories, lessons learn, and short articles because it is his passion. He shoots camera, photo and video edits, paints, draws, illustrates, and sculpts.

He wants to share his knowledge and leave behind some form of legacy to all readers, most especially to his wife, children and grandchildren.

Contact information: rcfrago@gmail.com

Personal Websites:

https://www.amazon.com/author/rufrancfrago

http://ca.linkedin.com/in/rufranfrago

http://www.facebook.com/RCFrago.RiskBasedManagement

Announcement

Go to Linkedin and join the Risk-based Management Group (RBM) so we can continue collaborating. The group provides a professional environment dedicated to all risk-based management interactions. Also, look for the book **How to Create a Good Quality P50 Risk-based Baseline Schedule**. It will be available soon in Amazon Kindle e-shelf and print on demand.

If you are looking for a good method of baselining the project schedule, this is what you are looking for. **Check it out!**

Made in the USA
Charleston, SC
25 September 2016